# Understanding
# Supreme Court
# Opinions

# WHY DO YOU NEED THE NEW EDITION OF THIS BOOK?

Here are five reasons why the Sixth Edition of *Understanding Supreme Court Opinions* will help you succeed in your course.

- **The most current discussion of Supreme Court opinions.** Recent Supreme Court opinions have taken on such issues as the president's war powers, the authority of school districts to regulate student speech or of the police to search one's home, and the constitutionality of the death penalty. In this new edition, you will find the latest analysis of these important opinions that are actively shaping our political and social environment.

- **New analysis of the legal materials Supreme Court justices use to build opinions.** With new examination in Chapter 4 on judicial activism, conservativism, and liberalism, as well as discussion of the controversial issue of Supreme Court justices engaging in "interpreting" the Constitution, this new edition will prepare you to debate and discuss the constitutional issues that play a decisive role in every Court decision.

- **New chapter providing a detailed briefing of a recent Supreme Court case.** *Parents Involved in Community Schools v. Seattle School District No. 1,* in which the Court barred two school districts from using race as a criterion in admitting students to schools. The detailed commentary will help you understand the process of briefing a case, and critical analysis will provide you with the tools and methods you need to undertake an in-depth analysis of a Supreme Court opinion.

- **Enhanced discussions of Constitutional precedents and legal reasoning.** Reorganization in Chapter 6, which clarifies the important doctrine of precedent and the principle of *stare decisis,* and significant revisions in Chapter 8, which better demonstrate how in-depth legal analysis should be undertaken, give you a superior understanding of the legal reasoning behind the judicial opinions and decisions that directly impact your life.

- **Updated and expanded resources for comprehension and study.** New and revised "Practice Pointers" at the end of each chapter clarify legal terminology, highlight Court techniques, provide resources and guidance in analyzing opinions, and help you learn how to use constitutional materials to make strong legal arguments.

Learn more about Longman Political Science at www.pearsonhighered.com/polisci.

# Understanding Supreme Court Opinions

---

SIXTH EDITION

## T. R. van Geel

*Professor Emeritus, University of Rochester*

PEARSON

Longman

New York   San Francisco   Boston
London   Toronto   Sydney   Tokyo   Singapore   Madrid
Mexico City   Munich   Paris   Cape Town   Hong Kong   Montreal

*For my colleagues and friends at the
University of Rochester.*

Editor-in-Chief: Eric Stano
Executive Marketing Manager: Ann Stypuloski
Production Manager: Denise Phillip
Project Coordination, Text Design, and Electronic Page Makeup: TexTech International
Cover Design Manager: Wendy Ann Fredericks
Cover Designer: Bernadette Skok
Cover Photo: © Matthew Cavanaugh/epa/Corbis
Senior Manufacturing Buyer: Dennis J. Para
Printer and Binder: R. R. Donnelley & Sons/Crawfordsville
Cover Printer: R. R. Donnelley & Sons/Crawfordsville

**Library of Congress Cataloging-in-Publication Data**

Van Geel, Tyll.
    Understanding Supreme Court opinions / T. R. van Geel.—6th ed.
        p.    cm.
    Includes index.
        ISBN-13: 978-0-205-62161-3
        ISBN-10:    0-205-62161-9
    1. United States. Supreme Court.    2. Judicial process—United States.    3. Judicial
opinions—United States.    4. Constitutional law—United States.    I. Title.
        KF8742.V36 2009
        347.73' 26—dc22                                2008003522

Please visit us at www.ablongman.com

ISBN 13: 978-0-205-62161-3
ISBN 10:    0-205-62161-9

1 2 3 4 5 6 7 8 9 10—DOC—11 10 09 08

# Contents

## CHAPTER 3   Opinion Writing in the Supreme Court   41

## PART 2                                                                53

## CHAPTER 4   The Legal Materials Used in Building a Constitutional Opinion   55

## CHAPTER 5   Tests or Standards of Review   75

## CHAPTER 6   Precedent   89

# Preface

This book provides an introduction to the legal reasoning and the modes of persuasion and justification used by Supreme Court justices, as well as others engaged in constitutional adjudication. It attempts to provide a new perspective on the workings of the Supreme Court, and also seeks to shed new light on the workings of our constitutional system and to enrich our understanding of the notion of the rule of law.

The book is intended to be used in several ways. It is designed to be used as a supplement to a constitutional law casebook, as well as in combination with materials written from the perspective of the political scientist.

*Understanding Supreme Court Opinions*, Sixth Edition, incorporates materials on opinions issued by the Supreme Court since the Fifth Edition was published. These recent opinions address such issues as the authority of the police to engage in searches of one's home, the authority of school districts to regulate student speech, the president's power as it relates to the war on terror, the constitutionality of executing a delusionary felon, and the constitutionality of school district efforts to correct racial imbalance in their schools by integration plans that rely on a racial criterion.

In addition, important changes have been made in central chapters of the book to clarify the material and to assist students. Chapter 4 begins with a new subsection addressing the question of whether the justices of the Supreme Court ought to engage in the practice of "interpreting" the Constitution. In addition, the chapter significantly reorganizes and shortens the discussions of originalism and nonoriginalism with a view to making these materials clearer and more accessible for students. The chapter also includes a substantially revised discussion of the notion of judicial activism and judicial conservativism and liberalism. Reorganization in Chapters 6 and 8 help to communicate more clearly the key points of the chapters and help to preserve the original length of the volume.

Finally, a new Chapter 9 illustrates and discusses in great depth the briefing and analysis of a recent Supreme Court case, *Parents Involved in Community Schools v. Seattle School District No. 1*. In this case, the Supreme Court barred two school districts from using race as a criterion in admitting students to schools the students had selected under a freedom of choice plan. The detailed commentary is included to help students understand the process of briefing a case, and the accompanying follow-up analysis provides them with an illustrative example of how to undertake an in-depth constitutional analysis of a opinion.

The development of this Sixth Edition was enhanced by the insightful comments by several reviewers:

Philip Dynia, Loyola University
Ray Kessler, Sul Ross State University
Chris Bonneau, University of Pittsburgh

I also want to thank Jason Blokhuis for his able assistance in reviewing and editing.

T. R. van Geel

# Introduction

Some years ago, when I was in college and about to go on to law school, I had a conversation with a lawyer in my hometown. He told me that I would enjoy law school if I enjoyed reading lots of "little stories." Well, in law school I did read lots of little stories, but it was also clear that what that lawyer had told me was misleading. It was true that the judicial opinions I read were stories with considerable human conflict, drama, and passion. But by calling these accounts "little stories" he had intimated that these stories were not complex and intricate. He seemed to suggest that they were no more than a series of interesting anecdotes. In reality, each was more like a Shakespearian play with multiple characters, a complex structure, densely packed language, and several layers of meaning. These were not mere tabloid accounts of human conflict, but rich pieces of writing that even with multiple readings yielded new insights.

The reading and understanding of law is often compared to the reading and understanding of literature, but let me suggest a different comparison. You are a historian of ancient Rome, and you are working with the speeches of a famous Roman senator delivered in the Roman senate. In trying to understand the meaning and significance of these speeches you will be asking yourself these and other questions:

- What social function did the giving of speeches serve? Why did this senator and other senators give speeches? What role did the Roman senate have in the system of government?
- On what occasion was this speech given? Who was the audience?
- Under what constraints did a senator operate when delivering a speech?
- Were there things that Roman senators could not say or were expected to say?

- What was the logical argument of the speech? What point was it making and how did it justify that point?
- What materials did the speech rely on to make its point?
- Were the assumptions and premises of the speech plausible at that historical moment in time? Are they still plausible today?
- How does this speech compare with previous speeches given by the same senator? other senators? Are there different styles of speeches?
- What underlying values and beliefs were embodied in the speech?
- What were the political, economic, and social effects of this speech?

The questions you may wish to ask about the speeches of the Roman senate are in many respects the same questions you should be asking about the opinions of the U.S. Supreme Court. As was true of the speeches of the Roman senators, the opinions of Supreme Court justices are written within a particular institutional setting and are designed to serve certain social, political, and, of course, legal functions. A judicial opinion must be understood in light of the institutional setting in which it was written. Not the least of these functions is that these opinions are intended to be persuasive arguments. The opinion is designed to convince the reader that the judgment reached in the case—the bottom line—was correct.

You need to understand all this as well as why this particular opinion was being delivered at this time. How did it come to be that the Supreme Court rendered this opinion at this point?

To understand the opinion one needs to realize that the justices operate under a variety of legal, political, and social constraints and expectations. These limitations force the opinion writer to write in a certain style, to use only certain kinds of materials to support his or her arguments. These constraints and expectations have an important effect on the tone, the voice, and the style of the opinion. It is these constraints and expectations that force the opinion to sound and look like a legal opinion and not just, for example, the expression of a political opinion.

Beyond trying to understand the social and political function of opinions in general, one must also get into the content of the opinion. What was its point? What were the arguments made in support of that point? Were the premises of those arguments well supported? What are its unspoken values, assumptions, and principles? And what was the political, economic, and social effect of the opinion?

Clearly, reading and understanding Supreme Court opinions involves something more than reading little stories. And this book is designed to help in the learning of the skills needed to come to a full understanding of these documents that have such a special place in our legal and political system. To that end, Chapter 1 provides background information essential to understanding these opinions. This chapter briefly discusses the Constitution itself and the Supreme Court's role in interpreting and enforcing the United States Constitution. The chapter also examines how cases or problems get to the Supreme Court, and how it comes to be that the Court issues its opinions.

Chapter 2 provides a brief but more extensive introduction to the Constitution itself. In Chapter 3 we turn to the writing of a Supreme Court opinion as seen from the perspective of a justice. Thus Chapter 3 discusses the constraints and expectations a justice faces in writing an opinion. I believe that one can become a better reader or consumer of Supreme Court opinions if one can appreciate the writing of those opinions from the perspective of a justice.

Part 2 of the book comprises four chapters that provide a more detailed introduction to the task of writing a constitutional opinion, and, for that matter, other constitutional arguments. Chapter 4 introduces the general range of legal materials out of which judicial opinions are built; it pays special attention to the debate regarding the use of the "intent of the framers" to come to an understanding of the Constitution. Chapter 5 turns to a common element found in the opinions of the court—the constitutional test, or standard of review. Chapter 6 addresses the Court's use of precedent and the formulation of the *ratio decidendi* of a prior opinion. The concluding chapter of this part, Chapter 7, introduces the concept of a strategy of justification. A strategy of justification is the general approach an opinion can take to accomplish its task of persuading a reader of the correctness of the Court's judgment. To take one example, the opinion may use the strategy of justification called the analogy: (1) This case is like previous case A. (2) Like cases ought to be treated alike. (3) In the previous case we did X. (4) Therefore, in this case we shall also do X. This, and the other strategies of justification, are the blueprints used to assemble the legal materials discussed in Chapters 4 through 6.

Part 3 consists of Chapters 8 and 9. These concluding chapters bring the materials of the previous chapters together by providing a detailed analysis of a Supreme Court opinion. Just one caution: Each Supreme Court opinion is in important respects a unique document, different from other opinions. Thus, the kind of analysis you may undertake of one opinion will differ in some respects from the analysis of other opinions. But Chapter 8 should help you get started in the interpretation and analysis of other opinions. A sample brief is included to introduce the craft of writing briefs. Chapter 9 includes a brief with commentary of a significant case along with an extended illustrative analysis of the case.

To summarize, an opinion is not a self-report of the internal decision-making processes of the Court itself or the internal mental deliberations of the individual justice who wrote the opinion. Opinions are documents designed to persuade, to convince the reader that the judgment the opinion reached was correct. That is to say, opinions are documents designed to serve legal, political, and social functions. And when a justice approaches the writing of an opinion, he or she, typically, has several ways available in which justification of the judgment can be written. The opinion writer thus can choose among different options in crafting the justification for the decision reached. Crafting the argument in such a way that it has the appearance of there having been no other way the opinion could have been written, and is so convincing that it appears that no other decision could have been reached, is a high art form.

Viewing Supreme Court opinion writing as a high rhetorical form can make one cynical about the Supreme Court, the justices, lawyers, and law school training. Are

judges and lawyers merely people with great rhetorical skills that they can use to justify any position they want to justify? Are law schools and courses in law vehicles for
preparing people to be skilled rhetoricians? I believe the answer to these questions is
in part yes. But this is only a fraction of the story. It is also important that courts and
judges reach wise decisions, sound decisions. It is important that lawyers consider
seriously the cases they take, the kinds of clients they represent, and the positions
they advocate.

Thus it is important, vitally important, for the future of law and our society that
law schools and undergraduate courses in law be concerned not merely with preparing people to be rhetorically skilled. I believe teachers of law should wrestle in their
courses with questions of right and justice. Students of the law should be concerned
not only with developing analytical and rhetorical skills but also with formulating
their own values and beliefs, their own views of right and justice. The following
story illustrates my concern:

> DEVIL SPEAKING TO AN ATTORNEY: I can give you riches beyond your
> wildest dreams. I can make you the most famous lawyer in all the land. You will
> win every case you undertake. The world will beat a path to your door. And in
> exchange for all this I will merely take your soul, the soul of your spouse, and the
> souls of your children.
>
> ATTORNEY: That's great! But what's the hitch?

## ABOUT THE AUTHOR

T. R. van Geel is a professor emeritus of political science and held the Earl B. Taylor
Chair in the Margaret Warner Graduate School of Education and Human Development at the University of Rochester. He is the author of numerous law review articles
and books, which include *The Courts and American Education Law; Education Law*,
Third Edition; and *A Teacher's Guide to Education Law*, Third Edition (the latter two
titles coauthored with Michael Imber). Professor van Geel is the recipient of a John
Simon Guggenheim Fellowship, a Fulbright Fellowship, and a Spencer Fellowship.

PART _____ 1

The complete understanding of a Supreme Court opinion requires both a grasp of a certain body of background information and certain techniques of analysis. The three chapters that compose this part of the book provide essential background information regarding the Supreme Court, as an institution, and the Constitution. Chapter 1 simultaneously introduces constitutional conflicts and the role the Supreme Court plays in resolving those conflicts. Chapter 2 carries the discussion begun in Chapter 1 of the Constitution's content a step further by examining in more detail five of the most important areas of the Constitution and constitutional law. Chapter 3 also extends a point raised in Chapter 1—the topic of judicial opinion writing. Though you are not reading this book in order to prepare to be a justice of the Supreme Court, it is useful to look at the writing of opinions from the perspective of a justice in order to become a better reader of them.

*Chapter*

1

# The Supreme Court: Policy Maker and Teacher

The United States Constitution is the supreme law of the land. Federal, state, and local governments; their legislative, judicial, and administrative branches; as well as all federal and state officials and employees must conform their actions, policies, and laws to constitutional requirements (see the Addendum to Chapter 2). Sometimes this task is easily accomplished because the constitutional text is precise. Few would debate whether each state is to be represented by two senators. But other phrases and words of the Constitution are not so clear. For example, Article 2, Section 1, states that no person except a "natural born" citizen is eligible to become president. Presumably this requirement means the president must have been born on American soil and not have obtained citizenship through naturalization procedures. But what of the person born on an American ship sailing in international waters? Less seriously, does the phrase "natural born" exclude from the presidency men and women born by means of cesarean section? These "silly" questions have not yet been officially answered, and the very fact we can ask them suggests that the constitutional text is not always clear.

A vague or ambiguous constitutional text, conflicts between different parts of the Constitution, and omissions are obvious invitations to disputes over its meaning. In fact, disputes regularly arise between different branches of the federal government, between the federal government and the states, and between federal or state government and individuals. Therefore a need exists for having some way to resolve disputes and for providing authoritative interpretations. Since 1803 the Supreme Court has played this role. In *Marbury v. Madison* (1803) the Court declared that the Constitution authorized it to determine when the challenged law or policy was inconsistent with the Constitution.[1]

In deciding a question of this sort the Court plays three roles. First, it is a court of law that settles the legal dispute between the parties. Its ruling is binding on the

---

[1] In addition to cases in which the Supreme Court reviews the constitutionality of a policy, it also decides cases that solely involve a conflict regarding how a federal statute should be interpreted. These statutory interpretation cases are not the focus of this book.

parties before it and settles the rights and duties that are to shape the legal relationship of the parties. In addition, the Court's ruling in the case establishes law and doctrine that is binding on the lower courts, which must now follow the Court's ruling when confronted with cases like that in which the Court ruled. Lawyers use this same precedent when they advise their clients (which include governmental officials) regarding what they now believe is constitutionally permitted and what is constitutionally prohibited. (Whether the precedent established in the Supreme Court controls the case before the lower court, or whether the precedent with which the lawyer is dealing applies to the problem the client has brought to the lawyer is often a matter of dispute, as we shall discuss. See Chapter 6.)

A second role the Court plays is that of policy maker. By ruling on what is constitutionally permissible and impermissible the Court affects the direction of public policy. (It is widely assumed that the other parts of the government are obligated to follow the rulings of the Supreme Court.) Goals that the legislature may have wanted to pursue may now be seen to be permissible or impermissible. Methods of achieving permissible goals may now be declared to be permissible or impermissible.

Third, the Court often acts as teacher to the nation. Because we as a people expect the Supreme Court to justify its exercise of this politically, economically, and socially important power of judicial review, the Court at the conclusion of many of its cases writes an opinion explaining and justifying the decision it reached. The opinions serve to educate the general public, especially in our age when far-reaching media extensively report on the Court's rulings. Sometimes the Court educates like an Old Testament prophet announcing to the nation that a course of conduct is constitutionally unacceptable. At other times the Court is cast more in the role of a teacher like Socrates who is engaged in a protracted "dialogue" with the other branches of government. In these situations the policy-making branch speaks first, and the Court responds in an opinion saying, "No, that is not permissible." Then the other branch responds by adopting a modified policy, saying in effect, "Well, how about this?" The Court then may respond, "Yes, but only if modified in this way."

In carrying out these functions some justices believe it is the role of the Court to "keep the Constitution up to date," whereas other justices believe changes in the Constitution must be the result of the formal amendment process. This crucial dispute derives from two different conceptions of the Constitution itself—is it a document of binding law that enshrines fixed fundamental values, or is it a document that speaks to our aspirations and puts into place new principles that had not been sufficiently recognized in the past?

## CONSTITUTIONAL CONFLICTS

Constitutional conflicts involve fundamental issues of right and wrong; principles of social justice, power, and authority; oppression and liberty; economic development; and even war and security. But the language of right and wrong, liberty and justice, is not the language in which the Supreme Court discusses these disputes. Take, for example, the issue of the minimum wage. In the legislature the question of whether a law should be passed requiring employers to pay a minimum wage may be debated in terms of the free market versus the welfare state, or the protection of the working poor versus the loss of jobs. Once a minimum wage law has been passed it may be subjected to several different constitutional challenges; for example, it may be challenged as beyond the power delegated to Congress in Article 1 of the U.S. Constitution and, or alternatively, it may be challenged as a violation of the Fourteenth Amendment's prohibition against the deprivation of life, liberty, or property without due process of law.

The difference between policy-making language and constitutional language can be illustrated in a different way. Of central importance to American policy makers is the problem of how to honor the principle of tolerance of antithetical political and cultural differences without going so far as to flirt with social disunity. The Supreme Court has played an important "navigator's" role in steering the ship of state on this course. But it has done so using language and concepts derived from the constitutional text. Thus the Court's opinions touching upon these issues have spoken in terms of concepts such as equal protection and the free exercise of religion.

It is important to realize that the language of the law is not merely a verbatim "translation" of the language of policy making or the language of morality. Take for example the phrase "equal protection of the laws" from the Fourteenth Amendment. You cannot assume that this phrase means precisely the same thing as what, for example, your favorite moral philosopher means when he or she speaks of equality.

Thus because Supreme Court opinions speak about fundamental issues of social policy in the language of the Constitution, it is important to move toward an understanding of these opinions by looking at the Constitution itself.

## AN OVERVIEW OF THE CONSTITUTION

The Constitution includes these five fundamental features:

- Provisions that touch upon such matters as the relationship between Congress, the president, and the Supreme Court, their respective powers, and how the officers of these three branches are elected or appointed
- Provisions that regulate the relationship between the federal government and the states
- Provisions designed to protect individuals against governmental invasions of their liberty, privacy, and other rights
- Provisions that guarantee persons the equal protection of the laws or otherwise prohibit invidious discrimination
- The two clauses of the First Amendment regulating the relationship between government and religion

There are, of course, other provisions of the Constitution of great importance (e.g., Article 4, Section 3, which governs the admission of new states to the Union;

Article 5, which establishes the procedures for amending the Constitution; and Article 6, which declares the Constitution the supreme law of the land). Although these other provisions of the Constitution exist, one can nevertheless obtain a general understanding of the constitutional framework and the interpretative role that the Supreme Court has played by addressing only the five features listed above.

In most situations no one would have difficulty deciding whether the offending party was a governmental entity (federal, state, local) or a governmental official or a private actor. But there are "gray" areas that have led to litigation to decide this question. As a consequence, the Supreme Court has developed various tests for resolving the question of whether or not the offending actor is the "state" or a private actor, and hence whether the Constitution may be used in a suit against the offending party. The typical gray area is one in which a private entity is somehow involved with the government—the nature and degree of that involvement is what the Court examines to determine whether the otherwise private entity should be considered for these purposes as a "governmental" actor. The mere fact that a private entity, for example, a private university, receives governmental assistance or has its charter from the state government does not turn it into a "governmental" actor. The "entwining" of the private entity and the government must be, according to the cases, qualitatively and quantitatively different. These are decisions made by the Court on a case-by-case basis. Thus the Court has concluded that the National Collegiate Athletic Association (despite the fact that many of its members are public colleges and universities) was not a government actor, but that the Tennessee Secondary School Athletic Association was a "state actor" (*National Collegiate Athletic Association v. Tarkanian* [1988]; *Brentwood Academy v. Tennessee Secondary School Athletic Ass'n* [2001]).

Whether or not the offending party is seen as a "state actor" is a threshold issue in constitutional litigation. A finding that the offending party is not a "state actor" means that the case cannot proceed as a constitutional case. The suit, if it is to proceed, must rely on nonconstitutional theory, such as a breach of a statute, a breach of contract, or it may proceed as a tort suit claiming personal injury of some kind.

This reality of constitutional law leads to some perhaps surprising conclusions. Take the case of the father who had been beating his infant son for two years. Local officials were aware of the problem but took no steps to remove the boy from the father's care until after the child was brain damaged. Does this raise a constitutional issue? "No," said the Supreme Court. First, the father's abuse was the abuse by one private individual of another. The Constitution does not itself regulate this behavior (state criminal law does). Second, the failure of the local social services agency to act also was not a constitutional violation because the Constitution does not require government to protect the life, liberty, and property of its citizens. "The [Constitution] is phrased as a limitation on the State's power to act, not as a guarantee of certain minimum levels of safety and security" (*DeShaney v. Winnebago County Department of Social Services* [1989]). In fact, the police do not have a constitutionally based duty to respond to even repeated calls for assistance (*Castle Rock v. Gonzales* [2005]).

# GETTING THE SUPREME COURT TO PLAY ITS ROLE

The Supreme Court has played the role of educator and policy maker in each of the five basic areas listed above. Now it is time to look at the mechanics and procedures by which the Court is brought into the policy-making process.

The Supreme Court, in sharp contrast to the other branches of the federal government, may not on its own initiative thrust itself into a policy arena and start issuing opinions announcing that this policy is constitutionally permissible but that policy is not. The Court may act only when a suit is initiated by someone else and brought to the Court for resolution. To see how these cases get into the Supreme Court we need to take a quick look at the federal judicial system.

## A Snapshot of the Federal Judicial System

The federal judicial system consists of four basic types of courts: a small number of specialized federal courts that deal with specific matters such as customs and patent appeals, federal district courts found in the states and U.S. territories, U.S. courts of appeal, and the U.S. Supreme Court. Our discussion will omit any further description of the specialized courts. (For more information about the federal judicial system and the Supreme Court go to www.uscourts.gov/ and www.fjc.gov/ and www. Supremecourtus.gov/.)

The **federal district courts** are the trial courts of the federal system (i.e., the courts where legal action originates, where evidence is received, witnesses are questioned, and the first legal judgment in the case is reached). There are today 94 federal district courts in the states and U.S. territories staffed by 679 judges. States with more than one federal district court are divided into separate parts, so that one court might be the U.S. District Court for Western New York and another the federal district court for the southern district. These courts have both criminal and civil (i.e., noncriminal) jurisdiction. Thus though these courts try a variety of cases, for our purposes we need note only that the federal district courts will try civil suits involving a "federal question," a federal constitutional issue, or one arising under a federal statute, as well as federal criminal cases. Federal courts do not take cases that raise an issue of state law exclusively. Pure state law cases must originate in a state court and will not be reviewed by the U.S. Supreme Court.

A constitutional law case touching on a matter of civil law typically is begun in the federal district courts when a complaint is filed alleging that some law, policy, or action of a branch of the federal, state, or local government is unconstitutional. Constitutional issues arise in different ways in the criminal context. In these cases the whole conflict may get under way when the federal or state government charges and prosecutes someone for a crime. At this point the criminally accused may raise a constitutional challenge to the criminal law he or she is accused of having violated. Frequently, the accused claims that the police acted illegally and violated his or her rights under the Fourth or Fifth Amendments. For example, the accused may say he or she was improperly questioned without a lawyer present, or evidence was illegally seized. A constitutional issue also arises when the accused says that the trial itself was conducted in violation of a constitutional provision (e.g., he or she was not provided an attorney at state expense).

However the constitutional issue is first raised, it is the resolution of that issue by the trial court that may then be appealed to the second tier of the federal system with general jurisdiction, the **U.S. courts of appeal.** The 13 U.S. courts of appeal are the intermediate appellate courts between the federal district courts and the highest appellate court, the Supreme Court. Congress has divided the country geographically into 12 circuits, including the District of Columbia, with each state assigned to a circuit. (The Thirteenth Circuit, the Federal Circuit, consists of three specialized federal courts.) There are approximately 180 appeals court judges assigned in varying numbers to the different circuits: the Ninth Circuit has 28 judgeships whereas the First Circuit has six. Appeals are normally heard by groups of three judges, but cases are also heard *en banc*, meaning all the judges assigned to the circuit hear the case (up to a limit of, say, nine judges).

Generally speaking, the losing party in a federal district court has the right to appeal to the appropriate U.S. court of appeals. The appeal must be to the court of appeals with jurisdiction over the particular federal district court that had original jurisdiction. Thus a decision by the Southern District of New York must be appealed to the Second Circuit. These appeals courts also hear appeals of decisions from federal administrative agencies, such as the Federal Communications Commission. One may not appeal simply because one is unhappy with the result; the appeal must raise a claim of a legal error committed by the lower tribunal. Appellate courts do not retry the case, collect new evidence, or reexamine the witnesses; they only review the printed transcript of the proceedings in the federal district court and look at the evidence already presented in that proceeding to determine whether the federal district court made any errors of law (e.g., misinterpreted precedent, a statute, or the Constitution itself).

Before we turn to the Supreme Court, you should be aware of the fact that states have their own multitiered judicial systems, systems that comprise specialized courts, trial courts, and several levels of appellate courts, including usually a single highest state court. (Texas is an exception with two highest courts, one for civil and one for criminal cases.) Issues of federal law and the constitutionality of federal and state laws under the U.S. Constitution may be raised in the state courts. (One may not challenge a federal law on the grounds that it violates the state constitution, since federal law is supreme pursuant to the U.S. Constitution.) The Supreme Court may review state court decisions dealing with the constitutionality of federal and state laws under the U.S. Constitution.

## The Jurisdiction of the Supreme Court

The Supreme Court's jurisdiction is of two sorts. Article 3, Section 2, of the Constitution gives the Court **original jurisdiction** in certain cases. (Original jurisdiction extends to cases affecting ambassadors, ministers, consuls, and cases in which a state is a party, i.e., disputes between states, disputes between a state and the federal government, and certain other cases brought by a state. In these kinds of cases the Supreme Court may take the case at its inception, try it, and pass judgment as opposed to acting only as an appellate court.) Only some 200 cases have arisen in the Court's original jurisdiction. Nothing more will be said about original jurisdiction.

Constitutional law deals primarily with cases arising under the Court's **appellate jurisdiction** (i.e., those cases in which the Supreme Court is asked to review the decisions of inferior courts for errors of law). Article 3, Section 2, grants the Court appellate jurisdiction subject to "such Exceptions, and under such Regulations, as Congress shall make." Pursuant to its appellate jurisdiction, the Supreme Court reviews constitutional issues raised in both the federal and state court systems.

There are a number of ways a case may find its way to the Supreme Court. Arguably the two most important are by means of the **writ of habeas corpus** ("produce the body") and the **writ of certiorari**. The writ of habeas corpus is filed by prisoners who claim that their incarceration was premised on a violation of their constitutional rights. Thus, for example, prisoners on death row may seek a review of their death penalty using this writ. But most cases are brought to the Court by the petitioner filing a writ of certiorari, which is merely a request made to the Court that it exercise its discretion to hear the case. A writ of certiorari can be filed to seek review of the following types of decisions (28 U.S.C. §§1254, 1257):

- All cases decided by *federal* courts of appeal
- A case decided by the highest *state* court in which the validity of a treaty or statute of the United States is drawn into question on grounds of its being repugnant to the Constitution, treaties, or law of the United States
- Decisions of special three-judge federal district courts (mandatory)

Review on the first two bases is not a matter of right and will be granted only if four justices agree that the controversy is of sufficient importance for the Court to review the case.[2] The Court denies most petitions for certiorari. As many as 7000 cases are filed in the Court, but the Court accepts only a small number; in recent years as few as 80–90 cases have been dealt with in full opinions. The task of reviewing the writs of certiorari falls to the clerks. Clerks of each justice used to review all the writs. Today

---

[2] In addition to the requirements just noted, the Court will not review a case, and will not permit the lower federal courts to take a case, that does not meet other requirements. The suit must involve a real dispute between genuinely adverse parties, one of which has been injured or one of which faces an immediate threat of injury to a legal right. This statement roughly summarizes a body of constitutional law touching on the question of whether a litigant has "standing" to invoke the authority of a federal court. Note that besides this "standing" requirement the cause must meet certain other requirements. It must not be "moot"; it must be "ripe"; it must involve a genuine "case" or "controversy;" must not involve a "political question," and must satisfy other jurisdictional requirements. Other criteria the Court takes into account are the presence in the case of an important legal question in the case, conflict between a lower court and the Supreme Court's prior decisions, and a departure from the accepted and usual course of judicial proceedings. Justices also decide what to hear based on their own policy preferences; that is, a justice may vote to hear a case because it provides an opportunity to advance that justice's policy goals.

most justices participate in the "cert pool." Under this arrangement certiorari petitions are divided among the clerks of the justices who participate in the pool and the cert memos prepared by the clerks are circulated to the participating justices.

Despite the efforts of many scholars we do not have a complete understanding of the "politics" involved in the decision whether to grant certiorari. We do know that justices will seek to avoid review of cases when they predict that the outcome upon review would be a defeat for their views. Thus the justices engage in what is called the "defensive denial" of certiorari.

Denial of the writ of certiorari means that the decision of the lower court stands. But it is important to note that denial of a writ of certiorari is not a decision "on the merits." That is, it does not necessarily mean the Court approves of the correctness of the decision in the case being appealed. Technical considerations having nothing to do with the merits of the case may be the basis of the denial (*Maryland v. Baltimore Radio Show* [1950]).

Incidentally, until 1988 one set of cases followed the "appeal" basis for review, and for these cases review was mandatory by the Supreme Court. When a case came to the Supreme Court under its "mandatory appellate" jurisdiction, the party appealing was called the **appellant**, and the other party, the **appellee**. All other cases had to follow the certiorari route. If a case came to the Court via a writ of certiorari, then the party seeking reversal was the **petitioner**, and the other was the **respondent**. In 1988 Congress eliminated the mandatory appellate jurisdiction of the Supreme Court in order to let the Court decide for itself just which cases it would and would not hear.

Having been accepted for review, the case proceeds as follows: Appellant/petitioner and appellee/respondent file briefs (written legal arguments that must follow a prescribed format), and the two sides then present their positions orally before the entire nine-member Supreme Court (each side is usually allotted only one-half hour to speak). At the conclusion of the oral argument the case is ready for a decision by the Supreme Court.

Today in important cases the Court releases audio tapes of the oral argument. It is also possible to obtain copies of the briefs from certain libraries, and occasionally in important cases they are made available on the World Wide Web through organizations such as the law school libraries of Stanford University and the University of Michigan.

## The Supreme Court's Processes of Decision Making and Justification

In a book entitled *The Judicial Decision* (1961) Richard Wasserstrom draws a distinction between "the process of discovery" and "the process of justification."[3] Processes of discovery are those processes involved in arriving at the judgment, for example, the petitioner should win. Processes of justification are processes used for publicly giving reasons to support the judgment. In a cynical view of the relationship between the two processes, the process of justification merely involves a rationalization of

---

[3] Richard A. Wasserstrom, *The Judicial Decision* (Stanford, Calif.: Stanford University Press, 1961), p. 27.

a decision that may have been reached for entirely different and undisclosed reasons; the reasons publicly given for the decision need not, and probably did not, affect, determine, or cause the decision reached. A less cynical view holds that a judge begins with a vaguely formed conclusion, tries to find premises and arguments to support it, and if the judge cannot find sound arguments, he or she may reject the conclusion and seek another. If one accepts this view, then the reasons for the decision may have a bearing on the judgment. Thus, there are important reasons for being concerned about the kinds of justifications used and the criteria of an adequate justification. Not the least of these reasons is the fact that these opinions are binding precedent for the lower federal courts and state courts.

After reading the briefs and hearing the oral arguments, the Supreme Court justices discuss and vote on the case at a conference. The chief justice opens the conference by making a brief statement regarding what the case is about. Discussion and voting take place in descending order of seniority. The discussion of the justices focuses not just on the basic merits of the case, but also on such "threshold" questions as whether the Court should avoid reaching a decision on the merits because, for example, the case is moot, or the Court lacks jurisdiction. Regarding the merits, the justices may even disagree over which provision of the Constitution is relevant for deciding the case as well as over whether a particular provision means the law is unconstitutional.

It takes at least five of the nine justices voting on behalf of a result in the case to reach a definitive outcome regarding which party wins or loses. A proposition of law announced by the Court is binding on the lower courts only when backed by a minimum of five justices. The chief justice has only one vote and in that sense is no more powerful than any other justice.

What leads an individual justice to vote a certain way on a particular case is part of the process of discovery. Once the vote is taken, the justices have entered into the process of justification. Who has the responsibility of writing this public justification, the opinion? If the chief justice votes with the majority (five or more of the nine justices), it is his or her prerogative to assign the task of drafting the majority opinion. The chief justice may assign the task to herself or to another justice in the majority. If the chief justice votes with the minority, the most senior justice in the majority has this prerogative. The privilege of controlling who writes the opinion is an important source of influence over the ultimate rationale provided for the judgment in the opinion.

In fact, this voting process and the switching of votes that can take place after the conference may produce a number of different kinds of voting patterns and, accordingly, opinions. The vote may be unanimous and result in a single opinion signed by all nine members. The Court may also be split into a majority (five or more members) and a minority. When this occurs, several different types of opinion may be written:

- There may be a single **majority opinion** (signed by all the justices in the majority) and one or more **dissenting opinions**. Dissenting opinions have no formal legal weight.
- A split Court may issue one or more special **concurring** opinions. In this situation the writer of the concurring opinion may agree with the majority on the judgment,

but not on the majority's reasoning. For example, the majority opinion in *Lawrence v. Texas* (2003) struck down a sodomy law on the grounds that it violated liberty, but the concurring opinion found the law unconstitutional because it denied equal protection of the laws. A concurring opinion may have some legal weight if that concurrence was necessary to form a five-vote majority for the judgment.

Occasionally the Court is so badly split that there is no majority opinion. In these situations there may be only a majority that agrees in the judgment alone (e.g., petitioner wins, but there is no majority in support of a set of reasons for this outcome). In this case, the justices who compose the majority supporting the judgment only may split themselves up in such a way that there is a **plurality opinion** signed by, say, three justices, and one or more concurring opinions agreeing in the judgment, but for different reasons. (Sometimes the "opinion of the Court" has sections that are joined in by a majority of the Court and other sections supported only by a plurality of the Court.) Of course, in this situation there may still be one or more dissenting opinions. Without a majority agreeing upon a set of reasons for the judgment, the results have less value as a precedent. Deciding what constitutes authoritatively established doctrine in this situation requires careful interpretation of the plurality and other concurring opinions.

There are occasions in which only eight members participate in deciding a case. For example, one justice may recuse him- or herself from the case for a number of possible reasons, or the Court may temporarily be staffed with only eight justices because of the death or retirement of a justice. In these circumstances the possibility exists that the Court may split 4 to 4, in which circumstance the decision of the lower court stands.

How complex matters can become is illustrated by *Regents of University of California v. Bakke* (1978). Justice Powell wrote "the Court's" opinion, but he was the only justice who fully agreed with everything in that opinion. Roughly speaking, one group of four other justices agreed with part of what he had to say (but for different reasons), making a majority of five on part of what the opinion announced. These same justices disagreed with other parts of the opinion. But a different set of justices agreed with another part of Powell's judgment, but, again, for different reasons. Thus another block of five, including Powell, supported part of what Justice Powell wrote and dissented as to part. As this case shows, justices can write opinions that concur in the judgment in part and yet also dissent. In another race case, *Parents Involved in Community Schools v. Seattle School District No. 1* (2007) there was an "opinion of the Court" but selected parts of that opinion were supported by only four justices and other parts by a majority of five. There were then two concurring opinions that supported the basic judgment in the case but for different reasons. (See Chapter 9.)

Mention should also be made of the **per curiam** (for the Court) opinion, which announces the judgment of the majority in a brief, unsigned opinion. This opinion may be accompanied by nine separate concurring and dissenting opinions for a total of ten, the maximum number of opinions possible in a single case (*New York Times Co. v. United States* [1971]).

The processes of opinion drafting are, as one might expect, both complex and fluid. The justice assigned to write the majority opinion drafts an opinion with the assistance of three to four law clerks. These clerks are recent law school graduates with extraordinary law school records. Although each justice uses his or her clerks differently, it is common for the clerks to assist a justice by summarizing the thousands of petitions for review, reviewing and commenting on the writs of habeas corpus, doing legal research, writing legal memoranda, and even writing drafts of the opinions ultimately issued in the justice's name.

Once the majority opinion has been drafted, the justice responsible for it then circulates it for review and comment by the other justices in the majority. The dissenters also begin drafting their opinion(s). These initial drafts may go through many revisions as the justices negotiate over the wording of their opinions and take into account the arguments made in either the majority or dissenting opinions. In the course of the process, the justices may switch their votes. One study found that 10 percent of the justices shifted sides between the conference and the announcement of the decision.[4] Coalitions may form and disintegrate, and new coalitions may form. What started out as the majority opinion may have to be converted to a dissenting opinion.

Most of the time these vote changes increase the size of the majority, but the study just noted found that, about 9 percent of the time, an initial minority became a majority because of the vote shifting. These changes in position occur largely without the justices interacting personally; exchanges of opinion for the most part occur through the exchange of written work. Face-to-face interaction among the justices tends to be limited to the conferences and the courtroom. But it has been reported that conferences themselves involve little more than a presentation by the justices of their own positions as opposed to a true consultation with a view to reaching an agreement.

Vote switching is not the only change that may occur between the conference and the announcement of the decision. In writing an opinion a justice may begin justifying the decision in one way, only to end up writing a different justification. Severe and angry conflict may arise outside the conferences as the justices in the majority seek to construct a single umbrella under which they can all live comfortably. Justice Holmes said of the process that "the boys generally cut one of the genitals" out of his opinions.[5] However difficult the process of opinion writing, evidence of the justices' struggle usually does not appear in the opinion. In fact, the late Justice Black advised Justice Blackmun as follows: "Harry, never display agony in public in an opinion. Always write it as though it's clear as crystal."[6]

Thus, interpretation of the Constitution is a political process in several respects. First, it involves bargaining over the shape of the opinions to be issued. Second, to interpret the Constitution and act on that interpretation has direct consequences in

[4] Saul Brenner, "Fluidity on the Supreme Court: 1956–67," *American Journal of Political Science* 26 (May 1982): 388–390.

[5] Quoted in Walter F. Murphy, James E. Fleming, Esq., and William F. Harris II, *American Constitutional Interpretation* (Mineola, N.Y.: Foundation Press, 1986), p. 60.

[6] Quoted in Howard Ball, *Courts and Politics* (Englewood Cliffs, N.J.: Prentice-Hall, 1987), p. 277.

the world on real people and real institutions and affects who gets what, when, and how. Life and death, wealth and fortune, war and peace, dignity and respect, and freedom and liberty are among the matters at stake in constitutional disputes. The justices understand and perceive that the significance of their decisions extends beyond the parties before them to additional untold millions of people now and in the future; it can affect the institutions of government, the Court itself, and the nation as a whole.

Furthermore, the act of interpretation itself is one that unavoidably entails applying theories of law—a theoretical conception of what a constitution is; a theory of democracy and a theory about the underlying principles of our Constitution; theories of constitutional interpretation, justice, morality, and politics to specific problems and choices. Beyond this, the act of interpretation involves calling upon a general understanding of the world, human beings, the workings and sociology of the society, historical perspectives, and tradition. Take one example: To decide whether the Constitution's proscriptions against "cruel and unusual punishment" should be read to prohibit capital punishment requires a justice to develop (albeit sometimes subconsciously) a theory of constitutional interpretation that itself entails a philosophy of law and language. The justice must also develop an understanding of theories of punishment and insight into the actual effects and sociological consequences of capital punishment as carried out by the modern-day criminal justice system against a background of social, economic, and racial inequalities.

One might ask, as political scientists have, whether the justices base their decisions on reasoned judgment arrived at through a process of mutual deliberation or whether the decisions of the justices depend essentially on their fixed political ideologies. There is considerable research supporting the conclusion that ideology and attitudes are the best explanation for the positions the individual justices take and that the official opinions are "mere rationalizations." Yet as is true with regard to all research these findings need to be questioned on a variety of grounds.[7] We know, for example, that the men and women who serve on the Court may, as they go through this deliberative process, end up taking positions on the issues before them different than the positions they took as public officials prior to becoming a justice. In adopting a different position on reapportionment than he had when he was governor of California, Chief Justice Warren said to his law clerk that "I was just wrong as Governor."[8]

More controversial is the question of whether the justices do act for partisan political reasons. In the aftermath of the Court's controversial decision in 2000 that led to the election of the Republican candidate, George W. Bush, as president, accusations were raised that the justices appointed by prior Republican presidents acted for partisan reasons. Those suspicions remain, despite the claim of Justice Thomas that the Court was not influenced by partisan or political considerations.[9]

---

[7] Frank B. Cross, "Political Science and the New Legal Realism: A Case of Unfortunate Interdisciplinary Ignorance," 92 *Northwestern University Law Review* 251 (Fall 1997).

[8] Quoted in Bernard Schwartz, *Decision* (New York: Oxford University Press, 1996), p. 105.

[9] Jack M. Balkin, "Bush v. Gore and the Boundary Between Law and Politics," *Yale Law Review* 110 (June 2001): 1407–1458.

## Judicial Sovereignty

A charge occasionally lobbed at the Court is that it has been seeking "judicial sovereignty" and no longer accepts the other branches of government as having equal standing to interpret the Constitution. One version of this charge is that the Court has simply issued rulings that disagree with what, say, Congress or the president took to be constitutionally permissible. But any decision that finds a policy unconstitutional can be attacked as an exercise in "judicial sovereignty." "Virtually every time the Court strikes down a statute, the justices assert the supremacy of their own constitutional judgment, with the implicit corollary that the other 'branches do not have equal standing to interpret the text.'"[10]

Another version of the judicial sovereignty charge actually does raise a profound question: In what sense should the Court's interpretations of the Constitution be the supreme law of the land? One answer that everybody would agree with is that a ruling of the Court is binding on the parties to the case with regard to that case. A party to the case who flouted the Court's ruling would be acting in contempt of Court. Everyone would also agree that the Court's rulings are binding precedent on the lower courts and should be honored by the Supreme Court itself in keeping with the principle of *stare decisis*. (See Chapter 6.) Similarly, everybody would agree that even if the Supreme Court were to say that XYZ is constitutionally permissible, neither Congress nor the president need follow this ruling (e.g., the president is free to veto legislation on the grounds that in his view it is unconstitutional even if the Court, if asked, would say it was permissible). Most people would also agree that public officials remain free to criticize the Court's ruling and even to attempt to have the ruling overturned by amendment to the Constitution or by seeking to place people on the Court who eventually will overrule the decision. And no one would disagree that the other branch of government may proceed to enact a policy or statute that was distinguishable in a material way from the policy or statute that the Court struck down. For example, in *Texas v. Johnson* (1989) the Court struck down a Texas statute that prohibited flag burning "in a way that the actor knows will seriously offend" people likely to observe the act. Congress then passed a statute that prohibited flag mutilation, period. The argument that this new law did not target "expressive conduct on the basis of the content of its message" made the new law constitutionally permissible. The Court, nevertheless, disagreed, striking down the law (*United States v. Eichman* [1990]). Yet the congressional effort to attempt to draft a law that protected the flag was itself a legitimate, albeit, unsuccessful, attempt. It is also widely conceded that legislators may reasonably believe that, because of a changeover in the composition of the Court, it would now overrule a prior decision if the case again went before the Court. Hence despite the prior ruling a new law might be passed to test these judicial waters. This happened in the decision in which the Court upheld a ban on partial birth abortion after previously prohibiting such a ban (*Gonzales v. Carhart* [2007]).

---

[10] Jed Rubenfeld, *Revolution by Judiciary* (Cambridge, Mass: Harvard University Press, 2005), p. 159.

Here are two additional scenarios in which a claim of judicial supremacy is controversial. Suppose the Court struck down the ABC law as beyond the Article I power of Congress. Is Congress now *legally* obligated not to readopt the identical law knowing that it would probably get struck down again if the challenge were brought? Or take the situation in which the Court has declared the forced separation of the races in public schools is unconstitutional (*Brown v. Board of Education* [1954]). In *Cooper v. Aaron* (1958), in the wake of chaos caused by the intervention of the segregationist governor, the Little Rock school district filed a petition in federal district court seeking postponement of an integration plan the district had *voluntarily*—in the absence of a judicial order—undertaken in order to comply with the decision in *Brown*. The Supreme Court ruled that the local officials were not free to postpone their desegregation effort especially in light of the fact that it was the intermeddling by state officials who had made their task so difficult. Hence there was a clear implication in *Cooper* that local officials were required to desegregate, to follow *Brown*, even though they had not been directly ordered to do so by a Court. Further, the Court went on to address the premise of the action of the governor (and state legislature) that they were not bound by the *Brown* decision, not having been parties to *Brown*. In response the Court said in dictum that no state executive or state legislator can "war against the Constitution" as the Supreme Court has interpreted it. It was the providence and duty of the Court to say what the law is. Further, "the federal judiciary is supreme in the exposition of the law of the Constitution." *Brown* was the supreme law of the land; and Article VI of the Constitution makes it of binding effect on the states, "any thing in the Constitution or Laws of any State to the Contrary notwithstanding."

Public officials also need to be aware that by reason of a federal statute they have a legal obligation not to violate the clearly established federal rights that they reasonably should have been aware of (*Harlow v. Fitzgerald* [1982]). Violation of such clearly established rights opens the officials to a suit for damages under the statute.

## BASIC FEATURES OF A SUPREME COURT OPINION

This chapter concludes with a review of the standard elements common to the Court's opinions. First is the **title**. The name of the opinion is based on the names of the parties to the controversy. The party listed first is the one who seeks reversal of the lower court decision, whereas the second-named party seeks to have that decision affirmed. Recall that the parties seeking reversal and affirmance may be called appellant and appellee, or petitioner and respondent, respectively.

A useful tip: At this point look for an indication in the opinion as to whether the lower court's decision was affirmed or reversed, whether the appellant/petitioner won, or whether the appellee/respondent won. Knowing this helps make more sense of the opinion.

The next major element is the recitation of the **facts of the case:** who did what to whom, when, how, and why. These are the facts actually adjudicated in the case, the **adjudicated facts** that had to be decided upon by the trial judge or jury, and that are particular to the dispute, for example, what did the Ku Klux Klan members actually say when they burned the cross (*Virginia v. Black* [2003]). Note that the justices may disagree in their characterization and interpretation of the facts of a case. In the cross-burning case the majority said cross-burning could be a way to express a shared ideology, whereas dissenting Justice Thomas saw cross-burning as merely a conduct designed to intimidate. The opinion will also specify the relevant statutes, regulations, or policies involved in the dispute.

Be sure to get a fix on the **procedural history** of the case. The opinion will describe who complained and what the result was in the trial court, who appealed to an intermediate appeals court, and what the result was there. The opinion will also make clear who is now appealing or petitioning to the Supreme Court. Understanding this sequence of events will help in understanding the remaining parts of the opinion. Especially important is who seeks review in the Supreme Court.

Next, look for the **legal claims** or legal arguments made in the case. What did the plaintiff claim and how did the defendant respond? What are the claims on appeal of the appellant/petitioner and the response of the appellee/respondent? Look for the specific section of the Constitution said to have been violated and why the appellant/petitioner thinks it has been violated. Also be aware of the response of the appellee/respondent. Be careful to note that the appellant/petitioner may have raised several constitutional claims involving different parts of the Constitution, for each of which there may be alternative arguments supporting the claim.

You are now in a position to look for the **issues** in the case. The issues are those *questions* that the party seeking reversal would answer differently from the party seeking to affirm the decision. Answer the question(s) one way, and the appellant/petitioner wins; answer another way, the appellee/respondent wins. But be careful. Sometimes the opinion itself expressly states the issues ("The issue in this case is . . ."); sometimes not. You may have to figure out the issues yourself. Sometimes the majority, concurring, and/or dissenting justices disagree over the phrasing of the crucial issue. For example, one justice may say the crucial issue in the case is whether the **plaintiff** has shown that government's differential treatment of men and women, in requiring draft registration of men but not women, does not serve an important purpose. Another justice may say the issue is whether the **defendant** government has shown that including women in the registration program would impede its purposes in having a draft registration program (*Rostker v. Goldberg* [1981]).

We come now to the main body of the opinion, which deploys the chosen "strategy of justification" (Chapter 7). These sections of the opinion announce the Court's decision and outline the remedy (if any). In these sections the Court justifies the decision and remedy by providing its answers to the issues. The Court may comment upon, analyze, and react to the arguments of the parties to the case. The opinion may accept, reject, modify, or ignore these arguments. In addition, the justices in the majority may criticize the argument of the dissenters and vice versa. These disputes have from time to time become very bitter. (See Chapter 9.)

As part of this justificatory effort you will find the justices using rules, principles, doctrines, tests, and standards of review rooted in their interpretation of the original meaning of the Constitution and precedent. (These concepts will be discussed further in Chapters 5 and 6.) In addition the justices will often rely on other historical and empirical facts, **background facts**, that were not decided upon by trial judge or jury, for example, "the character of a juvenile is not as well formed as that of an adult" (*Roper v. Simmons* [2005]).

Law students are frequently encouraged, if not required, to **"brief"** the cases they are assigned to read. A brief is nothing but a short summary of a judicial opinion, a way to take notes on a case. These briefs can be organized in different ways, but one form a brief can take is as follows:

- Name and date of case
- Facts (adjudicated facts) of the case (who did what to whom, when, why, how, etc. The specific law, policy, or action being challenged as unconstitutional and the claims as to why the law, policy, or action is unconstitutional should be mentioned in the description of the facts)
- The vote (number of justices in the majority, number concurring, number dissenting; author of the majority opinion, authors of the other opinions)
- Procedural history of the case (decision in federal district court, decision in court of appeals, who is appealing to the Supreme Court)
- Issues or questions
- The answers to the questions given by the majority (**holdings** or rulings)
- Summary of the majority opinion's reasoning (see strategy of justification, Chapter 7)
- The *ratio decidendi* of the majority opinion (see Chapter 6)
- Summaries of significant other opinions (concurring, dissenting)

Briefing serves an important purpose besides providing a handy synopsis of an opinion. The very effort put into briefing a case helps to focus the mind on what is truly important in the opinion. Briefing is, thus, a useful form of self-discipline for the inexperienced legal researcher. The more experienced researcher recognizes that briefing holds important traps for the unwary. This is so because the attempt to reduce a complex opinion from 30 pages to one or two unavoidably means that much important material never finds its way into the brief. Although the brief serves as a handy reminder of the content of an opinion, it cannot substitute for a more extended description and analysis.

## Practice Pointers

1. The Constitution is only relevant in suits involving the government, which is broadly defined to include individuals, agencies, and organizations that carry out governmental functions. In legal disputes involving defendants other than the government, you must rely on law other than the Constitution (e.g., a federal or state statute, or the common law).

2. When dealing with a dispute or conflict that you think should be taken to the Supreme Court, first determine whether it is the kind of dispute over which the Supreme Court has jurisdiction.

3. The total cost of arguing a case in the Supreme Court is considerable. Your decision to appeal to the Supreme Court must take into account: (a) the likelihood that the Court will hear the case; (b) the chances of winning the appeal; (c) the cost of arguing the case, if leave to appeal is granted; and (d) the costs associated with an unsatisfactory lower court decision, should it stand.

4. Lawyers who seek leave to appeal their case to the Supreme Court, or who have succeeded in getting the Court to hear their case, must adhere to certain rules of the Court. These rules can be found at: http://www.supremecourtus.gov/ctrules/rulesofthecourt.pdf.

5. When preparing to argue a case, bear in mind that all lawyers arguing before the Supreme Court will be intimately familiar with all the precedent relevant to the issues involved in their case. An attorney must be able to recite from memory all the details of all opinions relevant to his or her case, whether favorable or unfavorable to the client.

6. An interesting site to learn more about the Court and the justices is: http://www.oyez.org.

# Chapter

# 2

# The Constitution
# in a Nutshell

Chapter 1 provided a five-point outline of the main features of the Constitution (see p. 5). This chapter elaborates upon those five points in order to provide a thumbnail sketch of the role the Supreme Court has played in developing the meaning of these five features.

## THE COURT AS SUPERVISOR OF THE BOUNDARIES OF EXECUTIVE, LEGISLATIVE, AND JUDICIAL AUTHORITY (THE FIRST FEATURE)

### Judicial Power

The Constitution establishes the three branches of the federal government and defines their respective powers. Because the grants of power to the three branches are phrased in general terms, disputes regularly arise regarding the scope of these grants. Take for example the problem of **judicial power**. Article 3 of the Constitution gives the Supreme Court "judicial power." This general grant of power does not explicitly empower the Supreme Court to review the constitutionality of the statutes adopted by Congress and signed by the president. Thus one must turn to other materials to answer the question of whether the notion of "judicial power" includes the power of **judicial review**, the power to strike down as unconstitutional the acts of the other branches of government. The Supreme Court addressed this question in one of its earliest cases.

In *Marbury v. Madison* (1803), Chief Justice John Marshall wrote that the Supreme Court did have the power, even the duty, to review the constitutionality of the acts of Congress. The chief justice offered several justifications for the Court's exercise of this power, including the following:

1. The Constitution is a form of law. In fact, it is the supreme law of the land.
2. As the supreme law it also binds the Supreme Court.
3. When a federal statute conflicts with the Constitution, the statute is void.

4. When confronted with a case that involves a federal statute in conflict with the Constitution, the Court must determine which of these two laws is to be used in resolving the case before the Court—statute or Constitution.
5. Since the Constitution is superior to any ordinary law, the Court is duty bound to give force to the Constitution; to do otherwise would subvert the principle of a written constitution.

(Scholars have criticized this justification on the grounds that it begs the question of who is to determine what the Constitution means. Although Marshall may be correct that the Court is duty bound to enforce the Constitution, that still does not answer the question of whether the Court may willy-nilly adopt an interpretation of the Constitution different from that relied upon by the legislature.)

Having taken for itself the power of judicial review, the Court set itself up as an important arbiter of disputes regarding the scope of the authority of the president and Congress. Specifically in the *Marbury* case, the Court decided the question of whether Congress constitutionally could expand the Supreme Court's "original" jurisdiction. The Constitution gives the Supreme Court two forms of jurisdiction, original and appellate. (Original jurisdiction exists when a court takes a case at its inception, tries it, and passes judgment. Appellate jurisdiction is the authority to take and review a case after it has been decided by a court with original jurisdiction.) As noted earlier, the Supreme Court's original jurisdiction is limited to a narrow class of cases, namely, cases affecting ambassadors, other public ministers, and consuls and those in which a state is a party. One issue in the *Marbury* case was whether Congress had the authority to expand the Court's original jurisdiction to include a much broader class of cases. The Court said no and, using the power of judicial review, declared a federal statute that expanded the Court's own original jurisdiction to be unconstitutional.

### Legislative Power

Article 1 of the Constitution vests a list of specific and general legislative powers in Congress. One of the most famous examples of the Supreme Court's defining these powers came in *McCulloch v. Maryland* (1819). In that case the Court was asked to decide whether Congress had the authority to charter a national bank. Article 1's listing of the powers of Congress makes no express mention of such a power; thus the Court was forced to ask whether bank chartering was an implied or inherent authority.

To begin answering this question, Chief Justice Marshall started by reviewing other provisions of the constitutional text. He took note that Article 1, Section 8, of the Constitution empowered Congress to "make all Laws which shall be necessary and proper for carrying into Execution" both the specific powers granted to Congress and "all other Powers vested by this Constitution in the Government of the United States, or in any Department or Officer thereof." He also noted that the Constitution expressly granted Congress authority to impose taxes, to borrow money, to regulate commerce, to declare and conduct war, and to raise armies and navies. He next suggested that it was in the interest of the nation to facilitate the execution of these powers, and that we must presume that the framers intended to give to Congress the appropriate means to carry out these powers. The Constitution, he said, should not be read as a "splendid bauble." Thus, he argued, the "necessary and proper" clause authorized Congress to use any means calculated to produce the end. And, since chartering a bank is an appropriate means to the ends specifically mentioned in the Constitution, bank chartering was a power incidental to those powers that are expressly listed in the text.

Historically the Court has also played an important role in defining congressional power to regulate interstate commerce. To understand these disputes, let's draw a distinction between two types of challenges. Constitutional challenges that claim (for example) that the term "legislative power" does not include the power to charter a bank, raise an "internal" question of power (i.e., a question of the definition of the term "legislative power"). Now assume Congress has the legislative power to carry out a specific act, given the definition of the term "legislative power," but the exercise of this power may, nevertheless, transgress an "external" check on the power. Such an external check might be a constitutional right of an individual, the authority of another branch of the federal government to deal with the matter, or the sovereignty of a state.

Article 1 expressly authorizes Congress to regulate "interstate commerce," but serious questions exist regarding the scope of that power and, especially, whether "external" limits are imposed upon that authority by the separate existence and sovereignty of the states. Consider, for example, the following issues with which the Court had to deal: May Congress prohibit the transportation across state lines of lottery tickets? (Yes.) May Congress regulate labor practices in the steel industry on the grounds that intrastate labor disputes affect interstate commerce? (Yes.) May Congress control the amount of wheat a farmer grows solely for his family's private consumption, that is, wheat that will not enter the flow of interstate commerce? (Yes.) May Congress, pursuant to its power to regulate interstate commerce, prohibit a small family-owned barbecue, serving a local clientele, from refusing to serve customers on the basis of race? (Yes, again.) May Congress make it a crime to possess a firearm in a school zone? (No.) May Congress, under the power to regulate commerce, create a civil remedy for victims of gender-motivated violence? (No.) May Congress prohibit the purely local cultivation and local use (as prescribed by a physician in conformity with California state law) of medical marijuana? (Yes.)

The Court has also examined the scope of Congress's authority to tax and spend (Article 1, Section 8). Again the express words of the text do not provide a definitive answer to the question of whether Congress may "coerce" states or individuals to take certain actions, or adopt certain policies, by using federal funds as a carrot. For example, the issue arose whether Congress may withhold federal highway funds from those states that permit individuals under 21 to purchase or possess in public an alcoholic beverage. (The answer is yes [*South Dakota v. Dole* (1987)].) In justifying its answer the Court made reference to the text of the Constitution, the debate between James Madison and Alexander Hamilton over the meaning of the general welfare clause, the definition of the concept of "coercion," and the principle of federalism.

Congress also has been granted power under the Thirteenth, Fourteenth, and Fifteenth Amendments to "enforce" those provisions. In defining the scope of that power the Court read the enforcement clause of the Fourteenth Amendment as giving Congress the *remedial* power to eliminate English literacy tests as a requirement to vote (*Katzenbach v. Morgan* [1966]). Thirty years later the Court sharply limited this power. The Court has said in *City of Boerne v. Flores* (1997) this power is strictly "remedial," meaning Congress may only use the power to enforce rights that the Court itself has defined. Congress may not expand upon or add new constitutional rights. "Congress does not enforce a constitutional right by changing what the right is. It has been given the power 'to enforce,' not the power to determine what constitutes a constitutional violation." The line between a law that enforces and one that creates a new right is to be determined by a test: "There must be a congruence and proportionality between the injury to be prevented or remedied and the means adopted to that end." The Court further cut back Congress's power to enforce the Fourteenth Amendment when it said that the power could only be used if Congress could prove the exercise was warranted by the failure of the state to protect the Court-defined rights with sufficient vigor, hence making remedial action necessary (*Florida Prepaid Postsecondary Education Expense Board v. College Savings Bank* [1999]). In *United States v. Morrison* (2000), the Court blocked a portion of the Violence Against Women Act of 1994 that gave a victim of sexual violence a right to sue the perpetrator. In another case the Court said Congress lacked the power to require the University of Alabama to make special accommodations for a disabled employee (*Board of Trustees of the University of Alabama v. Garrett* [2001]). Yet in a different case the Court reached a markedly different conclusion. Relying on the "congruence and proportionality" test it ruled that Congress could allow a paraplegic to sue, under a federal statute, the state for money damages for failing to provide an elevator in a courthouse with the consequence he had to crawl up two flights of stairs to appear in court to answer a set of criminal charges (*Tennessee v. Lane* [2004]). And as noted below the Court has also used the Eleventh Amendment to strike down federal legislation said to impinge upon state sovereignty. All these cases under the commerce clause, the Fourteenth Amendment and the Eleventh Amendment, represent a significant redefinition of the relationship between the federal and state governments.

The authority of Congress extends beyond purely domestic policy into the areas of declaring war; suspending the writ of habeas corpus in cases of rebellion, or invasion; raising and supporting armies; and regulating immigration, aliens, the naturalization of citizens, and even the divesting of citizens of citizenship. In many of these areas the Court has adopted a deferential posture vis-à-vis Congress. As to the divesting of citizenship and denying resident aliens of procedural due process rights, however, the Court has checked the power of Congress.

## Presidential Power

Article II of the Constitution vests in the president an undefined "executive power"; makes the president "Commander in Chief of the Army and Navy of the United States, and of the Militia of the several States, when called into actual Service of the

United States"; empowers the president to grant pardons, and to make appointments to the Supreme Court with the consent of the Senate (as well as other appointments); and is charged with faithfully executing the laws.

Just as the Court has demarked the boundaries of congressional authority, it has also done important work in defining the power of the president. One famous occasion of the Court's exercise of this responsibility arose when President Truman directed the secretary of commerce to seize the operation of the nation's steel mills during wartime. The president issued this directive in the face of a strike by steelworkers that threatened to interrupt the flow of steel necessary for the war effort. Significant to the case was the fact that the president acted without any authorization from Congress; he simply relied on the Constitution's general grant of executive authority (*Youngstown Sheet & Tube Co. v. Sawyer* [1952]). To answer the question of whether the president had the authority to commandeer the steel mills, the justices asked (1) whether the power had been expressly granted by the Constitution, (2) whether the power may be implied from the constitutional text, and (3) whether the power was an inherent power of the president.

The Court began its analysis by turning to the constitutional text itself, but it found no express authorization for such an order. The justices next examined the concept of "executive power" and the role of the president in our constitutional scheme of government in an attempt to answer questions 2 and 3. Even assuming the justices had concluded that the president had the authority to issue such an order (they, in fact, did not so conclude), they would still have had to ask whether the president's authority was limited by considerations "external" to the grant of power to him. These "external" checks on the president's power include (1) a constitutional grant of authority over the same topic to Congress (e.g., Congress's authority to declare and make war); and (2) the separate existence and "sovereignty" of the states. That is to say, the scope of presidential power must be reconciled with the grants of authority to Congress and to the states—grants that may authorize them to deal with the same subject matter.

Although the majority opinion in *Youngstown* settled the case, it is Justice Jackson's concurring opinion that has emerged as perhaps the most famous opinion dealing with presidential power. His opinion outlined three categories of presidential authority.

1. When the President acts pursuant to an express or implied authority granted by Congress his authority is at its maximum.
2. When the President acts in the absence of either a Congressional grant or denial of authority, he relies only upon his own independent powers and there is a "zone of twilight" in which the President and Congress may have concurrent authority, or "in which its distribution is uncertain."
3. When the President "takes measures incompatible with the expressed or implied will of Congress, his power is at its lowest ebb."

In several cases the Supreme Court concluded that president's actions fell into the first category having been implicitly authorized by Congress. (*Ex Parte Qurin* [1942]; *Dames & Moore v. Regan* [1981]; *Hamdi v. Rumsfeld* [2004]). These are the least deeply fundamental cases for the Supreme Court as the issue is one of statutory interpretation and not directly one of constitutional interpretation. Of course, these statutory cases still may address important issues such as whether Congress gave the president authority to incarcerate indefinitely without trial a legal alien arrested on U.S. soil (*Al-Marri v. Wright* [2007]).

But the fact that the president may have congressional authorization does not, and did not, eliminate the possibility that the action violates the Constitution by violating an individual right. This was the conclusion of the Court in the *Hamdi* case, in which the Court ruled that an American citizen captured in a foreign country and detained as an "enemy combatant" constitutionally must "receive notice of the factual basis for his classification, and a fair opportunity to rebut the Government's factual assertions before a neutral decisionmaker."

In *Hamdan v. Rumsfeld* (2005) the Court, dealing with a case that fell into Justice Jackson's third category, ruled that President Bush had contravened the will of Congress when he authorized trying those being held in Guantanamo in military commissions, which violated the Uniform Code of Military Justice and Third Geneva Convention, concerning prisoners of war. The Court refused to reach the question whether the president had independent power absent congressional authorization to convene military commissions.

The problems falling into Justice Jackson's second zone remain unexplored territory by the judiciary. Also not yet the subject to a ruling by the Supreme Court are such questions as: whether the president has inherent authority as commander in chief that Congress may not constrain by statute; whether he has inherent authority as commander in chief to suspend the writ of habeas corpus and to imprison without trial (assuming there is no statute constraining the president) as enemy combatants citizens and legal aliens caught on U.S. soil; and whether he has inherent authority to engage in activities (e.g., domestic spying) that violate individual constitutional rights in the absence of either statutory authorization or statutory constraint. Issues such as these have been the subject of much scholarly discussion, especially in the face of the necessity to deal with both state-sponsored and privately instigated terrorism. Over the years individual justices have offered their views on the scope of the president's authority. Thus in *Hamdi* Justice O'Connor wrote, "We have long since made clear that a state of war is not a blank check for the President when it comes to the rights of the Nation's citizens." In that same case Justice Thomas, dissenting, wrote "it is crucial to recognize that judicial interference in these domains destroys the purpose of vesting primary responsibility in a unitary Executive."

## Separation of Powers

A brief glance at the Constitution reveals that the *legislative* branch has been given neither "judicial" nor "executive" power, that the *judicial* branch enjoys neither legislative nor executive power, and that the *executive* branch has neither legislative nor judicial power. Yet, at the same time, the Constitution often requires the cooperation of two branches of government (e.g., Congress has the power to declare war, but the president is the commander in chief; enacting a law requires involvement of both the Congress and president).

The complexity of this arrangement, the interdependence of the branches, has led to continuing competition and conflict among the federal branches—conflict that can threaten their independence and integrity. Thus it often falls to the Court to umpire among the three branches, even when its own integrity is at stake. Consider, for example, the case of *United States v. Nixon* (1974).

In that case, several former aides and advisers to President Nixon were under criminal indictment, and the court in which they were being tried issued a subpoena to President Nixon ordering him to produce certain tape recordings and documents concerning his conversations with his aides and advisers. The president claimed that the principle of "executive privilege"—the notion that the president may withhold information from the other branches of government—justified his request to quash the subpoena. The lower court refused to quash the subpoena, and the president appealed to the Supreme Court. The principle of separation of powers figured into the question of (1) whether the Supreme Court could review the president's claim of the privilege; (2) whether there was an absolute and unqualified executive privilege; and (3) if there were only a qualified executive privilege, when that claim might be overridden.

The Supreme Court in *United States v. Nixon* concluded there was only a "qualified privilege," and that in this instance the privilege could not be invoked (the Court refused to quash the subpoena). The Court concluded that there was a "qualified privilege" despite the fact that the notion of executive privilege was not expressly mentioned in the Constitution itself.

The Court justified its conclusion that there was a qualified privilege by arguing that it was implied by a tacit principle embedded in the constitutional structure—the principle of the separation of powers. The integrity of the presidency, said the Court, required the existence of such a privilege. But the Court also concluded that the integrity of the judicial branch, the need for a fair criminal trial, required that the qualified privilege be denied in this case. To justify this conclusion, the Court's opinion mounted a pragmatic argument: To allow the privilege in this instance would do more harm to the judiciary than good to the presidency; the harm done to the presidency by not recognizing the claim to executive privilege in this case was offset by the benefits of protecting the integrity of the judicial system and the public's belief in the possibility of obtaining a fair trial in the nation's judicial system.

The *Nixon* case represents only one way in which the separation of powers principle comes into play. Perhaps more typical are the disputes that arise when Congress attempts to carry out a social policy by setting up institutional structures that comingle the functions of the branches of the federal government. For example, the delegation by Congress to an officer in the executive branch or to a judge in the judicial branch of certain "legislative" powers raises the issue of the separation of powers (*Mistretta v. United States* [1989]; *Bowsher v. Synar* [1986]). Similarly the Court struck down the grant of the line-item veto to the president on the grounds that it gave the president authority to change the text of a duly enacted statute: to unilaterally change the policy rather than merely to execute that policy (*Clinton v. New York* [1998]).

## THE COURT AS UMPIRE OF FEDERAL–STATE RELATIONS (THE SECOND FEATURE)

### Federalism and the Federal Government's Control of the States

The Supreme Court has been called upon not only to resolve disputes among the three branches of the federal government but also to supervise the relationship between each of those three branches, on the one hand, and the states, on the other. This role has led the Court to consider questions of federal power touching upon the following:

- Direct federal regulation of the operations of state and local government
- Federal taxation of state and local activities
- Federal regulation of an activity that preempts state efforts to regulate that same activity

Behind each of these problems lies the general question of whether Congress may regulate the states themselves as states. Relevant to answering this question is the principle of federalism, acknowledging that the states have separate and independent existences that are to be preserved as a check against excessive centralized power.

Let us look at two related examples of the Court's work in this area. In *National League of Cities v. Usery* (1976) the Court concluded that Congress improperly invaded the sovereign and independent status of the states when it undertook to prescribe a minimum wage for state and local public employees. A minimum wage law imposed on state and local operations, said the Court, impaired an indisputable attribute of state sovereignty and a function that traditionally had been exercised by state and local government. Only nine years later, in *Garcia v. San Antonio Metropolitan Transit Authority* (1985), the Court reconsidered this conclusion and ruled that Congress did have this authority. The Court stated that its experience with the rule from *Usery* showed that it was unworkable. Over the years the Court had been unable to define in a consistent way which local functions were protected from congressional control and which were not. And the Court relied on its newer understanding of the intent of the framers. In *Garcia* the majority said that the framers intended to have the sovereignty of the states protected through the political process rather than by the Court. That is to say, because states as states had representation in the Senate, those representatives could themselves guard against overreaching by the federal government.

In recent years the Court has once again stepped in to protect state sovereignty. The Court, for example, struck down a federal law on the grounds it violated state sovereignty—a law that required state and local law enforcement officers to conduct background checks on prospective handgun purchasers (*Printz v. United States* [1997]). In another series of cases the Court ruled that the Eleventh Amendment was a check on Article 1 authority of Congress. Based on that assumption the Court struck down federal laws that permit individuals to sue an unconsenting state for damages for violations of various federal antidiscrimination and other federal laws

(*Board of Trustees of Univ. of Alabama v. Garrett* [2001]; *Kimel v. Florida Board of Regents* [2000]; *Alden v. Maine* [1999]; *Seminole Tribe of Florida v. Florida* [1996]).

## Federalism and State Control of Federal Operations

Not only has the Court been asked to supervise federal control of the states, it has also been called upon to examine the scope of state authority involving such issues as:

- State imposition of term limits on candidates for Congress
- State taxation of the operations of the federal government
- State regulation and taxation of interstate commerce, which the federal government is expressly authorized to regulate
- State discrimination—barriers and obstacles against goods and services coming from other states intended to protect local industries

If left unchecked these state activities could arguably lead to "a patchwork of state qualifications" for congressional office, severe frustration of the federal government, and the balkanization and weakening of the national economy. Thus, over the years the Court has played the important role of defining and limiting state power to prevent these arguably damaging consequences.

Take, for example, state regulation of interstate transportation. The Court's opinions typically begin by noting that Congress has been expressly granted authority to regulate interstate commerce. The Court interprets this grant of authority to Congress as an external limitation on the concurrent power of the states to regulate interstate commerce. That is, the Court has said that the grant of authority to Congress to regulate interstate commerce, even if the Congress has not used its power and it lies dormant, is relevant to understanding the scope of the states' authority to regulate interstate commerce.

Using this approach, the Court has fashioned over the years different ways for gauging the legitimate scope of state authority. At one point in the Court's history it said that state authority to regulate depended on whether the impact of the state's regulation on interstate commerce was "direct" or "indirect." Today the Court justifies its conclusions in terms of balancing several considerations:

> Where the statute regulates evenhandedly to effectuate a legitimate local public interest, and its effects on interstate commerce are only incidental, it will be upheld unless the burden imposed on such commerce is clearly excessive in relation to the putative local benefits. If a legitimate local purpose is found, then the question becomes one of degree. And the extent of the burden that will be tolerated will of course depend on the nature of the local interest involved, and on whether it could be promoted as well with a lesser impact on interstate activities. (*Pike v. Bruce Church, Inc.* [1970])

Thus an opinion involving the "dormant commerce clause" will set forth and then "apply" this test to the facts of the case. The discussion applying the test will constitute a major portion of the opinion leading up to the conclusion. And the judgment regarding the constitutionality of the state policy will be justified in terms of whether the state regulation satisfied or failed this "test."

State laws also violate the Commerce Clause if they mandate "differential treatment of in-state and out-of-state economic interests that benefits the former and burdens the latter" (*Oregon Waste Systems, Inc., v. Department of Environmental Quality of Ore.* [1994]).

Not all the justices agree with these restrictions on the states. Justice Scalia, for one, rejects the *Pike v. Bruce Church* test, and rejects the position that the Commerce Clause contains a negative component that operates to limit that state's regulation of commerce (*Tyler Pipe Industries, Inc., v. Washington State Department of Revenue* [1987]). And four of the nine justices dissented in the congressional term limits case, arguing the states did have the constitutional authority to limit candidates to three terms in the House and two terms in the Senate (*U.S. Term Limits, Inc., v. Thornton* [1995]).

# THE COURT AS SUPERVISOR OF GOVERNMENT'S RELATIONSHIP TO THE INDIVIDUAL (THE THIRD FEATURE)

One of the Court's most visible activities is its role in supervising the relationship between government (all federal, state, and local branches) and the individual. It carries out this function by discovering, recognizing, defining, and protecting the constitutional rights of individuals. The rights protected by the Constitution include freedom of speech and religion, protection against bills of attainder and ex post facto lawmaking, protection against coerced confessions and cruel and unusual punishments, protection against unreasonable searches and seizures, protection of property rights and contractual rights, and protection of liberty.

The significance of these rights is that they operate as an external restraint on the power of all levels of government. Generally speaking, the individual rights protected by the Constitution are of the so-called negative variety—rights that impose a duty on government not to do something. Except, arguably, in the criminal area where government must, among other things, provide a fair trial, these rights do not impose a duty on government to take affirmative steps to do something such as to guarantee the poor a minimum level of income or even minimum levels of safety and security. Welfare programs may voluntarily be undertaken by government, and having undertaken such a program, the government is under the negative duty not to operate the program in, for example, a racially discriminatory manner. But the Constitution today is not understood to require government to establish a social safety net.

Some constitutional rights are treated as if they were absolute (e.g., the right of a criminal defendant to a lawyer). This means that if the right exists, a violation of it cannot be justified, or excused, by a claimed overriding public interest. The right operates as a kind of trump card that overrides any governmental claims.

Outside the criminal field, people talk about rights differently. Although rights tend to be broadly defined (e.g., the right to freedom of speech), they are not treated as absolute. Instead their violation may be justified in certain instances when government may have sufficient reason to infringe them. For example, you may have a general right of freedom of speech, but the governmental interest in preventing panic in theaters is so strong that if you were falsely to yell "fire" in the theater, the government could punish you for doing so.

Before examining some generic features of cases claiming unjustified invasions of individual rights, it is important to take note of who enjoys these constitutional protections. For example, do children and students enjoy the protection of the rights mentioned in the Constitution? The Court has said yes even though the degree to which those rights are protected is somewhat less than the protection afforded adults. And in the context of deportation hearings, resident aliens have been extended some procedural due process rights. But it is unclear whether an alien may be deported for engaging in activities that a citizen would have a First Amendment right to engage in.[1] The Court has also ruled that it will not apply the Fourth Amendment exclusionary rule to deportation hearings; hence aliens may not exclude evidence from deportation hearings that was seized in violation of the Fourth Amendment.[2] However, resident aliens outside of the context of deportation proceedings do enjoy constitutional protections.[3] And aliens also enjoy, again outside of the context of deportation hearings, the protections of the equal protection clause.[4] In fact, even illegal alien children were extended protection under the equal protection clause.[5] American citizens who are detained as "enemy combatants" are protected by the Fourteenth Amendment and must be provided a "meaningful opportunity to contest the factual basis for that detention before a neutral decisionmaker."[6] The Court said that under federal statutes noncitizens held as enemy combatants at Guantanamo Bay, Cuba, may file habeas corpus petitions in federal court in order to argue they are being held unlawfully.[7] Subsequently Congress passed the Military Commissions Act of 2006, which prohibits any court from considering a writ of habeas corpus filed by a person held as an enemy combatant. The constitutionality of this provision will be decided by the Court in 2008 (*Boumedjeme v. Bush* [2007]).

Let's turn now to the generic issues typically addressed in cases claiming individual constitutional rights have been violated. The first three steps listed below are

---

[1] Cf. *Reno v. American-Arab Anti-Discrimination Committee*, 525 U.S. 471 (1999).

[2] *I.N.S. v. Lopez-Mendoza*, 468 U.S. 1032 (1984).

[3] *Bridges v. Wixon*, 326 U.S. 135 (1945).

[4] *Hampton v. Mow Sun Wong*, 426 U.S. 88 (1976).

[5] *Plyler v. Doe*, 457 U.S. 202 (1982).

[6] *Hamdi v. Rumsfeld*, 542 U.S. 507 (2004).

[7] *Rasul v. Bush*, 542 U.S. 466 (2004).

involved in all individual rights cases. Steps 3 to 5 arise only in nonabsolute right opinions.

1. Does the Constitution recognize the claimed right? Is it a right expressly mentioned in the Constitution or a right implied by the text? What is the scope of the right?
2. Did the government's policy or practice infringe upon or impact on the right? Was the impact minimal or more than minimal? (Only the nonabsolute right opinions move on to deal with points 3 to 5.)
3. What justification does the government offer for adoption of its policy, and how important are the interests the government seeks to promote?
4. How important or fundamental is the individual right at stake in the case?
5. What strategy of justification, tests, precedent, and other materials should be used in crafting the opinion? (See Chapters 4, 5, 6, and 7.)

*Problem 1.*    The very existence of a right is, of course, not disputed when the text of the Constitution itself gives it express recognition. For example, given the text of the First Amendment, no one doubts the existence of a right to freedom of speech. There is similarly no doubt that individuals and businesses have a right to their private property, which, according to the Fifth Amendment, may only be taken "for public use" and only if "just compensation" is provided. Yet even when the right is expressly provided for in the Constitution, there will be disputes over the scope of the right. People do have the right to free speech, but does this include the right to sell obscenity? The Fourth Amendment generally requires the police to obtain a warrant before engaging in a search, but this is true only if the person has a reasonable expectation of privacy. Hence many cases must resolve whether the individual did have a reasonable expectation of privacy.

But when a claimed right is not even mentioned in the constitutional text, then its very existence, as well as its scope, is in doubt. Take the famous example of a right to use contraception. The word "contraception" does not appear in the Constitution; hence the claim that married and/or single couples have a constitutional right not to be subjected to state criminal penalties for using contraception forces us to engage in constitutional interpretation. One easy solution would be to say that failure of the text to mention the right means there is no such constitutional right. A majority of the Supreme Court took an equally controversial but different approach. As one example of how an inferred right can be justified using only "legal" materials, look at Justice Douglas's opinion in *Griswold v. Connecticut* (1965) discussed in Chapter 8. Stated briefly, Justice Douglas inferred the existence of a right of privacy from amendments that did not specifically mention the word "privacy." And when you look at that opinion, note that the scope of the right of privacy was not fully worked out by the Court. Left for determination at a later time were such questions as whether the right to privacy included a right on the part of a woman to terminate her pregnancy with an abortion, or whether it included a right of gays and lesbians to engage in sodomy. Subsequent decisions have made clear that government may not make it a crime to obtain an abortion or to engage in gay sex. Yet to be determined is whether states may refuse to acknowledge marriage between two people of the same gender.

*Problem 2.*    Surprising as it may seem, it is sometimes not clear whether a governmental policy actually infringed a constitutional right. For example, the Court had to decide whether the right to use contraception had been infringed by a New York state law that permitted only licensed pharmacists to sell contraception (*Carey v. Population Services International* [1977]). The Court concluded that limiting the distribution of nonprescription contraceptives to licensed pharmacists did impose a severe burden on the right to use contraceptives.

It may be asked whether the right(s) protected by the Constitution are "absolute," hence may never be infringed no matter how strong the government's reasons for doing so, or whether the right(s) may be "balanced away," that is, infringement is permissible because the government had strong enough reasons to infringe the right. This is a question that has arisen regarding freedom of speech, the impairment of contracts, and other rights. As a general matter the Court has tended to embrace the nonabsolute interpretation of many rights, for example, freedom of speech, and privacy. But the Fifth Amendment requires just compensation for *all* "takings" of property unless the taking was not "for public use." If the property was not taken "for public use" the taking is simply forbidden and the question of just compensation is moot.

*Problem 3.*    After concluding that there is a right at stake, that it is a nonabsolute right, and that it was invaded, the Court must then turn to an examination of government's reasons for its actions (i.e., the governmental interests at stake). This step involves the Court in several "suboperations," including the task of discovering what in fact are government's interests at stake. Typically the government's attorney supplies the answer to this question in his or her presentation of the government's case to the Court. For example, in the contraception case Connecticut's attorney said the anticontraception policy, among other things, served government's interest in prohibiting illicit sexual activities. It is a separate question whether this was the real reason for the anticontraception law, and whether the proffered reason is a sufficient reason to invade the privacy right of married couples (see problem 5).

*Problem 4.*    At some point in the opinion the Court will assess the interests of the individual in the constitutional right at stake. The Court's opinions address this topic by drawing a distinction between ordinary constitutional rights and those rights considered to be "fundamental." If the Court terms a right "fundamental," it is less tolerant of governmental infringement of the right. That is, when an opinion declares the right involved to be fundamental, the opinion writer will concur in its infringement only if the writer concludes that government's policy is backed by interests that are extraordinarily important. On the other hand, the less weighty the right, the less difficult it will be for the opinion writer to find that government's invasion of the right was constitutionally permissible. (See Chapter 5.)

In the contraception case the Court concluded that the right of privacy, and the included right of married couples to use contraceptives, was a right of significant importance. This conclusion led the Court to the next step of its opinion, the selection and application of the appropriate test.

*Problem 5.*　The opinion writer now must choose among several justificatory strategies, discussed more fully in Chapter 7. For example, one available alternative is to proceed by balancing the interests of state and individual, and justifying the conclusion by announcing that one set of interests outweighed the other. This was not the approach adopted in the contraception case. In that opinion Justice Douglas declared that because the right of privacy was fundamental, Connecticut could not pursue the objectives of its policy (reducing illicit sex) by means that swept unnecessarily broadly (i.e., by means that unnecessarily invaded the right to privacy). That is to say, the opinion announced a test or standard of review that the state law had to meet. This test held that a law that infringes fundamental rights will be upheld only if it pursues its goals by means that are the least restrictive of the rights of the individual.

The opinion then went on to "apply" the test to Connecticut's law. The Court's conclusion was that this law deeply invaded the rights of married couples, and as the concurring opinions noted, Connecticut had available other, less intrusive means to deal with illicit sexual activities. Those other means included simply making adultery and fornication crimes. (These opinions assumed that adultery and fornication could constitutionally be made crimes. This raises a separate problem that must await a decision in another case.) In other words, after finding the right had been **infringed,** the Court concluded the infringement was not justified; hence there was a constitutional **violation.** There are of course many cases in which the Court finds that there was an **infringement,** but that the infringement was justified; hence the infringement was **permissible,** that is, the Constitution was **not violated** (*Kelo v. City of New London* [2005]; *Home Building & Loan Ass'n v. Blaisdell* [1934]). Thus it is the unjustified or inadequately justified infringement of a right that amounts to a violation of the Constitution.


# THE COURT AS ENFORCER OF GOVERNMENT EVENHANDEDNESS: EQUAL PROTECTION (THE FOURTH FEATURE)

Since the beginning of the second half of the twentieth century, the Court has played a significant role in policing governmental policies to assure that they do not, without sufficient justification, group people into separate classifications for differential treatment. The Court is given this role most significantly by the Fourteenth Amendment, which specifically provides that the *states* shall not deny any person the equal protection of laws. (The Supreme Court interprets the Fifth Amendment's due process clause to impose the same equal protection prohibition on the federal government. And Article 4, Section 2, says that the citizens of each state shall be entitled to all privileges and immunities of citizens in the several states; this provision operates as a kind of equal protection clause to prevent states from arbitrarily denying to non-residents certain rights and privileges they extend to their own residents.)

The Court's role in enforcing these provisions has not been one of requiring government always to treat everybody the same way. Government could not operate if everybody had to be treated identically.[8] The blind, for example, should not be licensed to drive, and government should be free to provide price supports for farmers but not for automobile companies. Hence the real problem for the Court has been whether government's treating one group of people differently from another has an adequate justification. Put differently, because discrimination is not always unconstitutional, the problem for the Court is to sort out which discriminations may continue and which are unconstitutional.

Again it is possible to characterize the Court's execution of this role as following a series of steps. How these steps relate to each other and build toward a resolution of the case will become clear in a moment.

1. Determination of the criterion used by government to classify people into different groups for differential treatment
2. Determination of the purpose or goal served by government's policy of dividing people into different groups for differential treatment
3. Determination and assessment of the effect of the differential treatment on the complaining party
4. Selection of a test or standard of review that is to be used in assessing government's policy
5. Application of that test or standard of review and statement of a conclusion

*Problem 1.*   Sometimes it is obvious what criterion government has used to classify people for differential treatment. For example, no one would deny that a distinction based on age has been used when the policy expressly states that those over the age of 50 must retire from the police force. Nor is there any doubt that gender is the criterion when the law says that women between the ages of 18 and 21 may purchase 3.2 beers, but men of the same age may not. But what if all you know is that an official who is operating under a law that on its face does not require discrimination on the basis of race, that is, is neutral on its face, in fact hands out licenses in such a way that all 80 of the non-Chinese applicants get the license, but none of the 200 Chinese applicants do? What was the criterion used here? Was it race? Or consider this example. The Bureau of Corrections requires all applicants for the position of prison guard to be able to lift 150 pounds. Almost all the women who apply for the position fail the test. Is this a case of discrimination on the basis of gender? What if people who are pregnant are treated differently from those who are not? Is this "gender"

---

[8] The equal protection clause may be interpreted to require that government treat everybody with equal dignity and respect. But fulfilling this requirement does not mean that after full and fair and unprejudiced consideration a policy may not end up granting different benefits to people, or imposing different burdens.

discrimination? Or suppose a school board assigns pupils to the school nearest their home. Because blacks and whites live in different sections of the town, this policy has the predictable, the foreseeable, effect of segregating the schools: Some schools are virtually all black, others all white. Did the school board foresee the results of its neighborhood policy and really assign students on the basis of their race?

When it is not clear what criterion government actually intended to use, the Court must first try to figure this out. To make this determination, the justices have resorted to a variety of special tests and rules of thumb. In rough terms, when the Court sees that a policy has had an adverse effect upon, say, the Chinese, women, or blacks, it asks (1) whether those adverse effects were foreseeable at the time of the adoption of the policy; and (2) whether government adopted the policy because of, not in spite of, those effects. These are not easy judgments for the Court to make. But at some point in working through the case the Court must decide what exactly it believes was the real criterion used by government for distributing its benefits or burdens.

*Problem 2.*   As the Court moves toward its final determination regarding the constitutionality of the policy, it must also determine the policy's purpose or goal. Again, sometimes the answer is easily determined. The government's attorney honestly explains, for example, that imposing the mandatory retirement requirement was designed to help assure that all police are physically up to their demanding jobs. But let us look at the weight-lifting requirement. If the Court concludes that the weight requirement was in fact a gender criterion, it must still examine the question of why government wanted to exclude women from the job of prison guard. Perhaps the answer is easy: male prejudice against women. But perhaps the answer is a set of complex concerns about the effects the presence of women would have in an all-male penal institution. In any event, the Court will determine, for good or ill, the goal(s) of government's policy.

*Problem 3.*   Assessing the impact of differential treatment upon the complaining party is also sometimes easy (e.g., the complainant loses or fails to get a job). But sometimes the effects are more complex, subtle, and arguably even more far-reaching. Take the example of racial segregation in the public schools. Excluding black students from attending school with white students certainly has the effect of limiting the range of schools both black and white can consider attending. But, in addition, this forced separation of the races may very well have deep and damaging (albeit different) psychological effects on black and white pupils (*Brown v. Board of Education* [1954]).

*Problem 4.*   Having determined the criterion used by government, government's purpose, and the effects of government's policy, the Court now moves on to a different phase. It starts the business of evaluating or assessing government's policy. To do this it adopts as its measuring rod (its scale) a test or standard of review. Chapter 5 will elaborate upon these tests. In the simplest terms, the standards of review "test" the constitutionality of the policy, asking the question whether it was rational or

necessary for the government to treat different groups of people differently in order
to achieve its purpose, and whether the purpose is legitimate. If the answer is no to
this test question, then the policy is unconstitutional.

*Problem 5.*   The last step is the application of the test or standard of review to determine whether government's policy is constitutional. This is no mechanical step, as
determining whether a policy's purpose is, for example, compelling, important, or
merely legitimate is a difficult problem in judgment. And, in fact, the Court has said
little about how it goes about deciding this question. Similarly, there is no simple
way to determine whether the classification established by government's policy was
"necessary," or substantially related to its purpose, or merely "rationally related" to
its purpose. The Court's decisions addressing affirmative action in admissions in colleges and professional schools illustrate the difficulties involved in both these steps.[9]
But this is the language that the Court has chosen to use in justifying its equal protection decisions. It is language that may, in fact, cover up or fail to reveal adequately
what in fact the justices were thinking about when they reached their decision.

## THE COURT AS SUPERVISOR OF GOVERNMENT'S RELATIONSHIP WITH RELIGION (THE FIFTH FEATURE)

The First Amendment specifies that "Congress shall make no law respecting an
establishment of religion, or prohibiting the free exercise thereof." Interpreting these
clauses and deciding on government's proper relationship to religion is one of the
more sensitive political problems the Court has faced over the years. The difficulty
the Court faces is closely tied to the fact that the two religion clauses are in tension
with each other. A too careful concern with avoiding governmental support of religion runs the danger of infringing upon the free exercise of religion. For example, a
governmental refusal to provide religious services in the context of a prison runs the
danger of denying the prisoners their right to the free exercise of religion. But a vig-
orous effort to defend the free exercise of religion runs the risk of forcing government
to support and aid religion. For example, seeing to it that prisoners do get to practice
their religion by arranging religious ceremonies, providing daily time for prayers, providing a religiously acceptable diet, or allowing the wearing of religious garb deeply
involves the government in supporting religion (*Cutter v. Wilkinson* [2005]). Nevertheless, the Court in *Cutter* upheld the law that required these religious accommodations
because the law only served to "alleviate exceptional government-created burdens on
private religious exercise [by those forcibly incarcerated in the government's prisons]."
   Over the years the Court has sought to resolve this tension between the clauses
in different ways. Sometimes the Court has given the establishment clause a "strong"
interpretation declaring that the clause creates a "wall of separation" between government and religion. Until recently this has been the dominant conception, but even

[9] *Grutter v. Bollinger*, 539 U.S. 306 (2003); *Gratz v. Bollinger*, 539 U.S. 244 (2003).

under this interpretation of the clause various forms of aid have been permitted (e.g., the loaning of secular textbooks to students attending private religious schools). More recently in a number of decisions the Court has adopted a "weaker" interpretation of the establishment clause, an interpretation that permits government to provide more forms of aid to parents and religious organizations as long as the aid is provided without discrimination—provided with an even hand to all parents and all organizations even if they are religious organizations. And when government makes facilities available for use by some civic groups it may not single out religious groups for exclusion even if their use of the facilities approaches the holding of religious ceremonies.

As for the free exercise clause, it also has been given stronger and weaker interpretations by the Court. Under a strong interpretation religious practices are protected from both the intentional restriction of religion and laws that have the unintended effect of restricting religion, unless rigorous enforcement of the law despite this effect is necessary to achieve very important government purposes. Under the weaker interpretation religion is only protected against intended restrictions of religion. We thus have had periods when the Court has combined strong interpretations of the establishment and free exercise clauses.

Today the Court embraces a weaker interpretation of both clauses. Accordingly, today's Court has upheld various forms of aid that flow without discrimination to all students (and their parents), regardless of whether they are attending private religious schools, and upheld general laws enforced evenhandedly even if those laws have a severe impact on the free exercise of religion. And some displays of the Ten Commandments are permissible whereas others are not, depending, on whether the display creates the undeniable impression that the government is promoting religion (*Van Orden v. Perry* [2005]; *McCreary v. A.C.L.U.* [2005]).

## CONSTITUTIONALITY OF FEDERAL AND STATE LAW: AN ADDENDUM

In order to be constitutional, a governmental policy must have been enacted in conformity with the requirements of the Constitution. What follows is one way to summarize those basic requirements.

For a *federal* law or policy to be constitutionally permissible under the federal Constitution, it must

1. be enacted according to the proper steps and procedures. If, for example, a particular law was enacted by Congress, the passage of the law must have conformed to the processes established in the Constitution for the enactment of legislation; and
2. be authorized by either
   a. explicit powers delegated by the text of the Constitution, or
   b. the powers reasonably implied by the text of the Constitution, or
   c. the residuum of inherent power on which government may call to preserve the polity; and

   3. violate neither
      a. any of the specific prohibitions of the Constitution's text, nor
      b. any of the rights properly implied in the Constitution.[10]

In addition, those who take a broad view of the Constitution would be inclined to add one or the other of the following additional requirements at this point:

      c. the sovereignty of the states, and/or
      d. any of those "natural rights" that people have irrespective of the form of government that surrounds them and that are arguably incorporated into the Constitution itself and just as binding as the document's plain words.

The criteria for finding a *state* law, policy, or practice constitutional under the federal Constitution are different. In order to be constitutionally permissible under the federal Constitution, a state policy, law, or practice must not

   1. be preempted or superseded by any federal statute or other federal action with the force of law, nor
   2. exceed limits on state authority by invading the powers granted to the national government, nor
   3. violate either
      a. any of the specific prohibitions of the constitutional document, or
      b. any of the rights properly implied in the Constitution.

And, as noted above, those who take a broad view of the Constitution would add an additional requirement at this point:

      c. any of those "natural rights" that people have irrespective of the form of government that surrounds them and that are arguably incorporated into the Constitution.

For a law, policy, or action to be constitutional it must meet all the relevant criteria. Failure of a federal or state statute, for example, to meet any of the relevant criteria means that the statute is unconstitutional.

# Practice Pointers

   1. When reading Supreme Court opinions, identify in the specific constitutional provision(s) applied to the issues before the Court the exact words or phrases interpreted by the Court in rendering its decision.
   2. Attorneys attacking the constitutionality of a law or policy may argue that it violates several constitutional provisions (e.g., the law exceeds both Congress's grant of power under the interstate commerce clause and under

---

[10] Adapted from Walter F. Murphy, James E. Fleming, Esq., and William F. Harris II, *American Constitutional Interpretation* (Mineola, N.Y.: Foundation Press, 1986), pp. 31–32.

Section 5 of the Fourteenth Amendment). They may also argue that a policy violates elements within the same constitutional provision (e.g., the law violates both the free speech clause and the free exercise clause of the First Amendment).

3. Some constitutional provisions are very precise (e.g., to be president, a person must be 35 years old). Other provisions are more vague (e.g., private property may be taken with "just compensation" but only for a "public purpose"). Scholars, attorneys, and justices often wrestle with the question of what approach should be taken in interpreting such provisions. Here are some approaches to choose from: (a) stick to the literal or ordinary meaning of the words and phrases; (b) look at the problem that motivated the adoption of the text in the first place and interpret the text strictly in light of that problem; (c) assume the framers deliberately adopted broad phrasing for future issues they had not specifically contemplated; or (d) interpret imprecise phrasing as evidence that the framers intended to allow for evolving meaning over time. (See Chapter 4.)

*Chapter*

3

# Opinion Writing
# in the Supreme Court

This chapter continues the discussion of judicial opinion writing by looking at the practice from the perspective of a Supreme Court justice. The assumption is that understanding the problems of a justice in writing Supreme Court opinions helps one to read and understand the opinions themselves.

## WRITING A SUPREME COURT OPINION:
## THE GENERAL PROBLEM

Courts, including the Supreme Court, could operate by simply declaring a winner in the dispute before them—"petitioner wins"—without offering any explanation or justification for the decision. But were the Supreme Court to operate this way, lower courts and future Supreme Courts would be left with no guidance. In the absence of an opinion we would be left to guess the principles of law at work; we would have little by which to guide our future behavior; we would remain uncertain regarding what the Court will do in new cases involving similar but not identical disputes. When the decision is of great political significance, but unaccompanied by a persuasive opinion, the Court's decision may continue to rankle significant portions of the population, making acceptance of the result more difficult. Written constitutional opinions can and do have an important educational and moral function that would obviously be lost if the Court merely declared winners and losers without explanation. Constitutional litigation is not a boxing match in which the judges announce the victor, leaving the loser to declare without insight into the decision, "I was robbed."

These comments help set the stage for the problem facing the justices. The justices are expected to write opinions that explain the dispute before them, that are persuasive justifications of the decisions reached so that the country *believes* what the Court asserts, and are clear regarding what the country must, must not, or may *do*. All this must be accomplished within certain constraints and expectations that sharply limit the ways in which a justice may go about offering such a justification. It is these constraints and expectations that work to make a judicial opinion different from the explanations and justifications one might offer when settling a dispute among children, or which a philosopher might offer in reaching a conclusion on a moral issue. In the absence of these constraints and expectations, the justices' opinions could look like any other justification—moral, theological, political, economic, or practical. In other words, it is these constraints and expectations that lead a justice to write a *legal* opinion. This is not to say that a legal opinion is amoral, or apolitical, or otherwise impractical. It is to say that the constraints and expectations bearing down on the justices lead them to use a special legal language, certain kinds of materials, and certain modes of reasoning and analysis. The justices consequently produce opinions written in a way that reflects a long tradition of judicial craftsmanship.

Let us examine this tradition by beginning with some general requirements an opinion writer has to satisfy. The opinion would have to have a name—for example, *Brandenburg v. Ohio* (1969)—with the name of the petitioner listed first. A justice is then expected to provide a description of the facts of the case (who did what to whom, when, how, why, etc.), including mention of the relevant statutes, regulations, policies, decisions, or actions that were involved in the dispute and might be the subject of the constitutional challenge. Readers of an opinion also want to know what the complaint stated—exactly what the complaining party said had been done that was unconstitutional, which constitutional provision(s) allegedly had been violated, and what argument was offered to support the claim of unconstitutionality. Next the readers will want to know what the government said in response—what it said by way of fending off the constitutional challenge. At this point in the opinion the justice would be in a position to identify the issues at stake—the questions raised by the competing arguments. The competing parties suggest different answers to these questions and the opinion writer must provide a judicial answer. Last, the readers will want to know what the trial court and the intermediate court of appeals decided.

I will now illustrate what has been said to this point. Brandenburg had been arrested for giving a speech advocating white racism and suggesting the need for violence to protect the interests of the white race. He delivered his speech at a KKK rally at which some members of the audience carried weapons. Brandenburg was charged with violating Ohio's Criminal Syndicalism statute "for advocating the duty, necessity, or propriety of crime, sabotage, violence, or unlawful methods of terrorism as a means of accomplishing industrial or political reform." At his trial on the "criminal syndicalism" charge, Brandenburg claimed that the arrest and enforcement of this statute were a violation of his First Amendment right to engage in freedom of speech; thus he asked that the charge be dismissed. Brandenburg was in fact fined $100 and sentenced to one to ten years' imprisonment. The Supreme Court of Ohio dismissed Brandenburg's appeal on the grounds that there was no substantial constitutional question in the case. Brandenburg sought review in the Supreme Court.

Brandenburg argued that prior Supreme Court cases relevant to this sort of problem established the principle that government may criminally punish a person for delivering a speech advocating the use of force only when there is a clear and present danger of lawless action. He argued that his speech was not likely to produce such action. The prosecutor, however, saw in Brandenburg's speech a clear threat of lawless action.

The issues in the case on appeal to the Supreme Court, thus, were (1) the appropriate test for determining the constitutionality of the state's conviction and (2) the application of that test to this case (i.e., whether the speech Brandenburg gave created a clear and present danger of lawless action).

The materials in the previous paragraph appear in the Supreme Court's opinion before it turns to the central issues and offers a justification for the reversal of the appellate court decision. It is at this point in the opinion that the real demands of judicial craftsmanship arise. Let us turn to these constraints and expectations before returning to the drafting of the opinion in *Brandenburg*.

## CONSTRAINTS AND EXPECTATIONS

It should go without saying that the decision should be the "correct" decision; as a substantive matter the opinion should be one that gains critical and popular assent. But this essential point aside, the point being addressed here is that the style or the manner of writing up and justifying a legally correct resolution of the dispute should satisfy certain constraints and expectations.

• If the opinion is to be the majority opinion and authoritatively establish constitutional doctrine, it must gain the assent of at least five of the nine participating justices. Note: The guidelines that follow apply to majority, plurality, concurring, and dissenting opinions.

• The opinion should be directed to resolving only the dispute and the issues before the Court. The opinion should not examine a wide range of unrelated First Amendment free speech issues. But the opinion should cover the necessary topics for resolving a dispute of this sort. (See Chapter 2.)

• The justices often say the statutes should be interpreted, if possible, to avoid constitutional difficulties.

• The justices should craft the opinion in a way to provide guidance for future federal and state court judges, as well as lawyers and the populace at large.

• The decision should have the appearance of being determined by considerations external to a justice's personal desires and will. The arguments the justices offer should be arguments based on law, doctrines, principles, and values that are not just a matter of personal preference and desire. It is the law that justices are expected to pronounce, not their colleagues' personal preferences in the dispute. "Integrity is defined, in part, by the strength to adhere to one's principles even when they lead to results one finds personally objectionable."[1]

• The opinion should make use of, or take account of, those "materials" the legal community (and society) accepts as the appropriate materials for writing opinions and developing legal arguments. For example, the opinion should take relevant precedent into account.

---

[1] Edward Lazarus, *Closed Chambers* (New York: Penguin Books, 1999), p. 303.

- The opinion should not use other "materials" the legal community (and society) considers inappropriate bases upon which to build a legal argument. For example, an opinion that was based on the Bible or the Koran would be viewed as not having used appropriate legal materials.

- The justices should write the opinion so that it is persuasive. It must offer a set of reasons and logically constructed arguments for the result reached.

- The justices need to pay attention to the stability of the law, thus, to the doctrine of *stare decisis*. (See Chapter 6.)

- A justice will want to draft an opinion that is not obviously inconsistent with views he or she personally expressed in previous opinions, or obviously inconsistent with precedent in general, unless the opinion specifically overrules precedent. Justice are also open to criticism if they vary their method of constitutional interpretation (see Chapter 4) from case to case in what may appear to be an all too transparent effort to reach predetermined results. The effort by a justice to be consistent over time helps in avoiding pure subjectivity. Furthermore, the views the justices express in this opinion should be ones with which they can live in the future.

## Crafting the Opinion

It is frequently the case that even the justices in the majority disagree among themselves over how the justification of the result, which they agree upon, should be phrased. Consequently the justices will have to compromise, to engage in some bargaining over the crafting of the majority opinion. (Recall at this point Chapter 1's description of the opinion-writing process.) As a consequence, some things may be deliberately phrased in general or ambiguous terms to ensure agreement among the five justices. Furthermore, arguments one justice may have wanted to include in the opinion may have to be dropped. Yet other points and arguments a justice personally did not want to use may have to be included.

This bargaining process can produce opinions that upon careful analysis can be shown to be internally contradictory, or take the form of a large umbrella under which the justices with different views can comfortably fit. Thus the final majority opinion may include not one central argument justifying the result, but several different arguments not inconsistent with each other, but not fully integrated either. Sometimes this umbrella is constructed by "arguing in the alternative." That is, the opinion may mount one argument in support of the result, and then move on to say something like the following: "Even if we do not rely on our previous argument, we conclude that the decision below should be reversed (or affirmed) for the following reasons." (For the reader of such an opinion the problem then becomes which of these several arguments is the central point of the opinion; which of these arguments establishes the basic doctrine, rules, and principles to be relied upon and used to resolve the next dispute.)

A disagreement among the signers of an opinion is sometimes signaled when the opinion says the following: "Assuming for the sake of argument that 'X' is true, nevertheless . . ." Or the opinion might say, "We need not resolve question 'Y' to reach a decision in this case." Yet another signal occurs when the opinion says something like: "Our analysis shows that the law would survive (be struck down) under either test."

## Addressing Only the Dispute before the Court

For reasons of constitutional doctrine, as well as traditional legal practice, the justices must decide only the actual dispute brought to them for review. The Supreme Court is not permitted to provide "advisory opinions" on constitutional issues that have not yet become the subject of a real dispute between real parties with something at stake; it may not provide legal advice on issues not the subject of dispute between the parties before the Court. Thus when the justices write opinions they are expected to pay close attention to the specific issues this dispute raises. Anything they write on issues not specifically in dispute in the case will be viewed as without official legal significance, will be understood to be nothing more than their personal opinion and not official doctrine or law.

In fact, anything that justices do to justify the result and that subsequent judges and lawyers conclude was not truly *logically* necessary to resolve the dispute may be viewed as merely a gratuitous comment, extraneous material with virtually no legal weight (such statements are called **dicta**). A justice may, nevertheless, wish to add such comments to his or her opinion for rhetorical purposes, or perhaps in order to send a message about his or her viewpoint and attitude on a problem. Though such a message is not "law," is not legally binding on the parties, and cannot be cited by other judges or lawyers as official Supreme Court doctrine, it may nevertheless serve the useful purpose of providing some guidance as to future directions the Court may take. (And gratuitous comments, "dicta," always stand a chance of becoming actual doctrine if supported in the future by at least five justices.)

## Providing Clear Guidance

The justices have a responsibility to provide guidance to future courts, but not by merely writing dicta. The justices must tread a narrow line between resolving only the specific issues before them, yet also lay down some general principles of law, some rules, some factors or guideposts that will indicate how they would approach resolving similar problems should they arise in the future. But the justices would not be living up to the ideal of the rule of law if their guidelines were so vague that they were not constrained by their own precedent, or if others could not understand what was or was not permitted. (Note: A judicial statement can be precise and be dictum; vague, yet not be dictum; or because of its vagueness, amount to dictum.)

There is a kind of paradox at work here. Out of the specific dispute before them, the justices are expected to generate general and *clear* principles, or guidelines, germane to resolving similar disputes. Let us return to the *Brandenburg* case. The opinion would provide little guidance and assistance if the rule the Court were to announce in this case was only the following: "In the future Brandenburg may not be prosecuted under the Ohio syndicalism statutes when he gives a speech identical in content to the one he delivered, to an identical crowd, in the same field, and under the same circumstances." Though such a rule addresses the dispute in that case, it is so specific that it is of limited future use. To provide more guidance an opinion should lead to a conclusion stated in more general terms, which can be applied or used in conjunction with a wider range of similar incidents. For example, the opinion might say the following: A speech that advocates the violent overthrow of the government in the abstract, at some indefinite point of time in the future, and that is delivered to a crowd of people indisposed to taking immediate action, is an example of speech protected by the First Amendment; such a speech may not be the subject of prosecution under criminal syndicalism statutes. (Note, however, that Brandenburg might have been prosecuted under a "disturbance of the speech" statute, but this issue was not before the Court, and any comments the Court might have made about the constitutional permissibility of prosecution under such a law would have been mere dicta.)

Now, if the Court phrases the rule in a case more broadly, some readers of the opinion may argue that this general rule should be considered dictum, because such a general rule would not have been necessary to resolve the dispute. Suppose a justice were to write that the appeals court is reversed because all speeches advocating the violent overthrow of the government are constitutionally protected from criminal prosecution. Such a rule would resolve the dispute before the Court; it would also provide guidance for the future. But such a rule would be considerably broader than necessary to resolve this particular dispute and hence would be viewed with suspicion by future judges and lawyers. They would suspect that in fact the correctly phrased version of the rule of this case was something narrower, *despite* what actually appeared in the opinion. Of course, when it is to the legal advantage of lawyers or judges to rely on the broadly stated principles in an opinion, they will do so. It is at this point that a dispute may arise over exactly how the opinion should be interpreted (see Chapter 6).

Broader formulations of the basic principle of the case help make the decision useful for resolving future disputes, but broad formulations also may be too general or vague to provide much guidance and may amount to dictum. (Note: The interest in providing guidance to the other branches of the federal government, as well as to state and local governments, rests on the assumption—an assumption that has been challenged—that these other parts of the government have an obligation to accept the Court's ruling as binding their future conduct, that is, that the Court is the supreme interpreter of the Constitution.) The craft of writing an opinion is a demanding one and carries grave responsibilities.

Furthermore, the justices do disagree on the question of how clear and precise a particular ruling must be. Such a disagreement is illustrated by the dispute among the justices regarding whether the majority provided adequate future guidance in determining whether a punitive damages award is to be considered constitutionally excessive. The majority said the constitutionality of a punitive damage award was to be determined by: "(1) the degree of reprehensibility of the defendant's misconduct; (2) the disparity between the actual or potential harm suffered by the plaintiff and the punitive damages award; and (3) the difference between the punitive damages awarded by the jury and the civil penalties authorized or imposed in comparable cases" (*BMW of North America v. Gore* [1996]). Justice Scalia attacked these guidelines, saying they "mark a road to nowhere; they provide no real guidance at all." He further noted that nowhere did the majority say that these were the only guideposts. "In other words, even these utter platitudes, if they should ever happen to produce an answer, may be overridden by other unnamed considerations. The Court has constructed a framework that does not genuinely constrain, that does not inform state legislatures and lower courts—that does nothing at all except confer an artificial air of doctrinal analysis upon its essentially ad hoc determination that this particular award of punitive damages was not 'fair.'"

## Justiciability and the Political Question Doctrine

Closely related to the goal of providing clear legal guidance is the doctrine that the Court will not even decide a case having concluded that there are no "judicially discoverable and manageable standards for resolving it" (*Baker v. Carr* [1962]). For many years the Court, based on this principle (and other considerations), refused to hear challenges based on the equal protection clause of the Fourteenth Amendment that electoral districts of unequal population size were unconstitutional. Once the Court formulated the "one person–one vote, one vote–one value" standard it was able to adjudicate claims that electoral districts of unequal population size violated this "judicially manageable standard" (*Reynolds v. Sims* [1964]). Today, the requirement that the Court be able to discover judicially manageable standards serves to block claims that political gerrymandering violates the equal protection clause (*Veith v. Jubelirer* [2004]). Political gerrymandering involves dividing geographical areas into equal population-sized electoral districts but often with an irregular shape in order to give one political party unfair political advantage, through the dilution of the opponents' voting strength, in the election of representatives.

## Providing a Persuasive Justification

In addition to providing legal guidance for future cases, the justices must offer a *logical* and *plausible* argument in support of the conclusion. The next chapters will delve more deeply into the construction of such arguments; suffice it to say here that such an argument begins with premises or assumptions that are *plausible* or *true*, and then with the tools of logic moves toward the conclusion.

Again let us return to the *Brandenburg* case. The argument could begin with a discussion and analysis of precedent—prior Supreme Court opinions from which the justices extract the following premise: (1) A person may be subjected to the criminal syndicalism statutes only if his or her "advocacy is directed to inciting or producing imminent lawless action and is likely to incite or produce such action." (Assume that this rule is in fact a plausible reading of prior Supreme Court opinions.) The opinion at this point will turn to the next premise—the meaning and interpretation of this first premise. The justices will at this point discuss the first premise and conclude that it means that a speech does not incite lawless action if it merely advocates the historical necessity of the violent overthrow of the government at some indefinite point in the future, and if there is little likelihood of imminent lawless action when such a speech is delivered to a crowd friendly to such a message.

Having established the more purely legal premises of the argument, the justices now turn to the facts of the case. After a review of the facts of the case, the justices agree with Brandenburg that (2) his speech advocated the violent overthrow of the government only in the abstract, and that the crowd he addressed was not primed for immediate action.

The justices thus reach their conclusion (3) that Brandenburg's right of freedom of speech was violated and that the conviction and opinion of the appeals court should be reversed. (Notice that this argument is in the form of a simple syllogism: (1) If A, then B. (2) It is the case that A. (3) Therefore, B.)

Be forewarned that this is a particularly simple example of legal reasoning. Many opinions will require the justices to mount more complex arguments involving chains of arguments (i.e., opinions in which one argument leads to a conclusion that then serves as the premise for the next argument that leads to a conclusion, which, in turn, is used as the premise for the next argument). In addition, as we shall see in Chapter 7, these linked syllogisms are used in conjunction with certain styles of justification (e.g., balancing).

## The Use of the Proper Legal Materials

By now you may have detected something new about the writing of a Supreme Court opinion. The justification should be phrased in such a way that it has the appearance of being based on considerations, rules, principles, and doctrines external to the justice. The justices should present their justifications as if they were based on THE LAW, and not on their personal preferences and desires. The expectation, if not the reality, is that justices of the Supreme Court are discoverers and interpreters of law, not dictators imposing their personal will. This means that the tone and the style of writing used in the opinions will appear impersonal and legalistic. The justices' opinions use personal pronouns, as in the phrase "We conclude that . . ."; but such phrasing is always meant to mean, "We, acting dispassionately, disinterestedly, objectively, logically, and scientifically, conclude that the law requires us to reach this conclusion."

In building a chain of syllogisms the justices are expected to rely upon and make reference to certain kinds of "legal" materials while avoiding use of or reliance upon other materials. The kinds of material the justices use include the following:

1. The text of the Constitution: specific words, phrases, and the surrounding language
2. Evidence of the intent of the drafters and ratifiers of the Constitution regarding the meaning of the words, and/or the specific effects or consequences of the text
3. The structure and implicit premises or "tacit postulates" (or "essential postulates," or "fundamental postulates") of the Constitution that order the relationship among the branches of the federal government, between the

federal government and the states, between governments at all levels and the individual

4. The abstract fundamental purposes and values that a justice says are embodied in a constitutional provision
5. Precedent—prior opinions of the Supreme Court
6. Evidence on American traditions, customs, practices, legal history, and history regarding Congress's understanding of the Constitution
7. Social science and other systematically collected and analyzed data that were not necessarily the subject of adjudication by the parties
8. Evidence on contemporary morality and attitudes
9. Considerations of practicality and prudence

The justices may also on occasion draw on legal commentary found in the scholarly journals, and evidence and analysis produced by social scientists. It is from these kinds of material that the justices are expected to construct the premises of their arguments.

There are major disputes raging among the justices, lawyers, and legal philosophers over which of these materials has priority in a situation in which one set of materials points toward one conclusion, and another set points toward a different conclusion. The disputes also include questions about how these materials are to be used and what constitutes an abuse of the materials. We shall return to these matters in Chapter 4.

Just as there are materials the justices arguably may legitimately rely on in crafting a justification, there are certain materials that today they would be expected *not* to use: (1) bald expressions of personal preference, values, positions, or personal intuition; (2) claims, for example, that God, one's parents, spouse, or the president told one what to do; (3) the Bible; (4) natural law; (5) the platform of a political party; (6) the writings of one's favorite philosopher; (7) the fact that a justice personally likes or feels sorry for the petitioner or respondent.

Some old opinions used these materials. Consider how strange they would sound today.

- It is against all reason and justice, for a people to entrust a Legislature with such powers; and, therefore, it cannot be presumed that they have done it (*Calder v. Bull* [1798]).
- I do not hesitate to declare that a state does not possess the power of revoking its own grants. But I do it on a general principle, on the reason and nature of things: a principle which will impose laws even on the Deity (*Fletcher v. Peck* [1810] [Johnson, J., concurring]).
- We think ourselves standing upon the principles of natural justice, upon the fundamental laws of every free government, upon the spirit and letter of the Constitution of the United States (*Terrett v. Taylor* [1815]).

In another case, denying Mrs. Bradwell's application to become a lawyer, the Court wrote: "[T]he civil law, as well as nature herself, has always recognized a wide difference in the respective spheres and destinies of man and woman. . . . The paramount destiny and mission of woman are to fulfill the noble and benign offices of wife and mother. This is the law of the Creator" (*Bradwell v. Illinois* [1873] [Bradley, J., concurring]). Though much is said about how the justices simply act upon their personal ideology, we would be very surprised if we found a majority opinion that simply said: "We like liberalism, you like conservatism. We win, 6 to 3. Statute invalidated."[2]

On occasion some justices on the Court rely on materials that the other justices believe should not be used. In one case striking down the criminalization of gay sodomy, and in another case barring the use of the death penalty to punish criminals under the age of 18, the majority opinion made reference to the laws of other countries, finding in those materials "confirmation" of the majority's position (*Lawrence v. Texas* [2003]; *Roper v. Simmons* [2005]). The use of these materials led dissenting Justice Scalia to write in *Roper*, "I do not believe that approval by 'other nations and peoples' should buttress our commitment to American principles any more than (what should logically follow) disapproval by 'other nations and peoples' should weaken that commitment."

Despite these strictures Justice Thomas has been known to make statements that have the appearance of a personal commentary. In his dissent from the Court's upholding of the University of Michigan law school's affirmative action plan, Justice Thomas wrote: "The Law School tantalizes unprepared students with the promise of a University of Michigan degree and all the opportunities it offers. These overmatched students take the bait, only to find they cannot succeed in the cauldron of competition" (*Grutter v. Bollinger* [2003]).

### Stability in the Law

As discussed in Chapter 6, stability in the law is important; thus, the opinion will want to conform to the principle of *stare decisis*. But in addition to writing opinions the justices want to express positions and viewpoints on the law that are consistent with their own prior opinions, unless they have consciously changed their minds. Few things would bring a justice into more disrepute than the production of a set of opinions expressing conflicting viewpoints; a justice's motives, if not his or her very rationality, would be questioned. The justices may expect to serve on the Court for many years, so they will also want to write the opinion they are currently working on in such a way that they can live with it in the future. Now, when all five of the justices involved in writing the majority opinion have these same concerns and interests, and each justice has a different prior set of opinions that he or she has written, it becomes even more obvious how difficult it may be to reach agreement, how much bargaining and compromising may have to occur to craft a single opinion all five of them can sign.

---

[2] Cf. John Hart Ely, "Foreword: On Discovering Fundamental Values," *Harvard Law Review* 92 (1978): 5, 34.

# CONCLUSION

It may take many months for five or more justices to craft a majority opinion they all can sign. The opinion must be one they all can live with, yet it must be internally logical, coherent, and persuasive. It must have the appearance of being an inevitable conclusion based only on those materials a justice is expected to rely upon, despite the fact that it is the product of considerable argument and debate. It must address only the specific questions before the Court, yet also provide guidance for the future without running so far afield as to fall into the trap of producing mere dictum. And, of course, the decision should be the "right" decision, justified by reasons that are seen as sound and takes into account the goal of stability in the law. Being a Supreme Court justice is hard work.

## Practice Pointers

1. Advocates before the Court seek not only to persuade the justices but also to provide legal arguments that the justices will incorporate into their opinions. Advocates must anticipate what a justice will require in order to write an opinion that is (a) favorable to their client; (b) useful as a precedent in future disputes; (c) consonant with prior precedent; and (d) based on appropriate legal materials.
2. Attorneys arguing cases before the Supreme Court should be familiar with the positions taken by each of the sitting justices in similar cases. The advocate can then tailor his or her argument so as to appeal to individual justices, who hopefully will take those arguments into account in writing their opinions. Keep in mind that the advocate's goal is to secure the agreement of five justices that his or her client should prevail.
3. An excellent way to learn to apply precedent and to make persuasive legal arguments is to start with a hypothetical issue that has not yet been decided by the Court and then to develop the arguments that could be made to the Court on both sides of the issue. This is the function of moot courts in law schools. It is also the basic structure of many law school examinations.

# PART 2

A Supreme Court opinion is in many ways like a house. A house can be constructed of many kinds of materials—bricks, mortar, wood, copper pipes, electrical wiring, roof and bathroom tile, and plastic. Similarly, a Supreme Court opinion is constructed from legal materials, for example, the text of the Constitution, and precedent. However, just as using sawdust as landfill to support the foundation of the house is to risk subsidence of the house, there are materials that the justices generally avoid in the construction of their opinions—for example, the latest public opinion poll. And just as there are appropriate and inappropriate uses of housing materials (building a chimney out of wood is inappropriate), so are there principles that guide the use of the legal materials of which an opinion is built.

Chapters 4, 5, and 6 discuss the building materials of which opinions are made and the disputes that exist regarding the selection of these materials. Chapter 4 pays special attention to the conflict regarding the use of the "intent of the framers" in interpreting the Constitution. Chapter 5 turns to what are called tests or standards of review and their use in the process of discovery and the process of justification.

Chapter 6 turns to the use of precedent. If we return to the house construction analogy, a precedent is like an existing building that the justices now consider emulating in the construction of a new building. But before deciding to emulate the old construction, a justice has to decide whether the precedent (the old building) is a suitable model for the new problem. He or she must come to a thorough understanding of the precedent before relying upon it. Thus Chapter 6 discusses the problem of extracting the central meaning from the precedent, which itself may be long and complex.

Another way to think about precedent is as a house to which the justices plan on adding an addition. Following this analogy, the precedent is to be incorporated into the new structure, creating yet a larger and more complex facility. A house is not simply a collection of building materials. To make a house, the various materials have to be related to each other according to a systematic plan, a blueprint. Chapter 7 turns to the understanding of the blueprint that underlies precedent and that must also underlie the new opinion. This blueprint is called in this chapter the "strategy of justification," and it is this strategy that guides the assembly of the materials discussed in the previous chapters into a coherent whole. Thus in writing an opinion (or any other legal argument), the writer must think about the general strategy of justification if the materials with which the writer is working are to be properly assembled. You also will have to consider your own strategy of justification when called upon to write a legal paper for your course.

# Chapter 4

# The Legal Materials Used in Building a Constitutional Opinion

This chapter examines the legal materials that are used in conjunction with the strategies of justification. For example, the strategy of deduction must begin with a premise (see Chapter 7). This premise must be grounded in something, namely, appropriate legal materials such as the text of the Constitution, the intent of the framers, or precedent. It follows that in order to understand fully a constitutional opinion one needs to pay close attention to an opinion's use of these materials.

The materials in question are:

1. The text of the Constitution: specific words, phrases, and the surrounding language
2. Evidence of the intent of the drafters and ratifiers of the Constitution regarding the meaning of the words, and/or the specific effects or consequences of the text
3. The structure and implicit premises or "tacit postulates" (or "essential postulates," or "fundamental postulates") of the Constitution that order the relationship among the branches of the federal government, between the federal government and the states, between governments at all levels and the individual
4. The abstract fundamental purposes and values that a justice says are embodied in a constitutional provision
5. Precedent—prior opinions of the Supreme Court
6. Evidence on American traditions, customs, practices, and history regarding Congress's understanding of the Constitution
7. Social science and other systematically collected and analyzed data that were not necessarily the subject of adjudication by the parties
8. Evidence on contemporary morality and attitudes
9. Considerations of practicality and prudence

To begin, it is useful to draw a distinction between two types of constitutional problems. First are those problems that arise in the absence of any precedent, and second are those that arise against a background of previous Supreme Court opinions. Problems of the first kind obviously can draw only on materials 1–3 and 6–7; these problems are discussed in this chapter. Chapter 5 discusses tests, or standards of review, and Chapter 6 discusses problems that arise in connection with the use of precedent.

Having drawn this sharp distinction, I will now blur it by noting that even if a problem arises against a background of existing precedent, sometimes it is useful to treat it as if the case were without precedent. Thus opinion writers may write their opinions by dealing with the problem before them as if there were no precedent, and then, having looked at the problem in this way, they may turn to providing a separate justification in terms of precedent.

## CONSTITUTIONAL INTERPRETATION (OR NOT)?

There are those who have rejected the very idea that the opinions of the Court are the product or should be the product of an exercise in *interpretation*. A school of thought, the legal realists, say that what the justices do is merely disguised politics and policy making and that this is unavoidable. A sitting judge on the Seventh Circuit Court of Appeals offers a related but different perspective. Judge Posner rejects the idea that "the judge has some kind of moral or even political duty to abide by constitutional or statutory text, or by precedent." Instead he embraces an approach called "pragmatism." "[Pragmatism] encourages the thought that the object of adjudication should be to help society to cope with its problems, and so the rules that judges create as a by-product of adjudication should be appraised by a "what works" criterion rather than by the correspondence of those rules to truth, natural law, or some other high-level abstract validating principle. . . ."[1]

Whereas legal realism and pragmatism seem to reject the idea of interpretation altogether, another approach, which can be called "textualism," focuses in a rigid way on the text of the Constitution itself, an approach that says that when the words of the Constitution have a plain meaning, that meaning must be followed regardless of any unfortunate consequences. But few people take this approach to the Constitution seriously. "If simply reading the Constitution the 'right' way were all the justices of the Supreme Court had to do, the only qualification for the job would be literacy, and the only tool a dictionary."[2]

These views aside, the actual practice among the justices has been to accept the proposition that what they are doing is "interpreting" the Constitution in a way that takes into account the text but also something more. But there has been a dispute among the justices reflected in their opinions regarding how they should go about the business of interpreting. (There is also a cottage industry among legal scholars

---

[1] Richard A. Posner, "Pragmatism Versus Purposivism in First Amendment Analysis," *54 Stanford Law Review* 737 (2002).

[2] Lawrence H. Tribe, *God Save This Honorable Court* (New York: Signet, 1985), pp. 5–51.

debating how the justices should carry out the practice of interpreting the Constitution.) The two main camps into which the Justices fall have been dubbed "**originalism**" and "**nonoriginalism.**" Originalism interprets the text by relying on historical evidence regarding the intent of the framers, or the understanding of the ratifiers or the generally understood meaning of the text at the time of adoption. Nonoriginalism takes the view that constitutional interpretation should not be limited to the intention of the framers, the understandings of the ratifiers, or evidence regarding the original meaning of the text. Nonoriginalists allow for the historical materials the originalists rely on exclusively to be supplemented. Thus Justice Brennan, who falls into the nonoriginalist camp, has been described as embracing "constitutional functionalism." He thus looks at the text, and asks, why is this provision here? What general public values was the text written to serve? As Justice Brennan put it: "But the ultimate questions must be: What do the words of the text mean in our time? For the genius of the Constitution rests not in any static meaning it might have had in a world that is dead and gone, but in the adaptability of its great principles to cope with current problems and current needs."[3]

## ORIGINALISM

### History and Concept

Explicit statements in support of originalism appear in almost all time periods. An early endorsement of originalism appeared in 1838 when the Court wrote, "The solution of this question must necessarily depend on the words of the Constitution; the meaning and intention of the convention which framed and proposed it for adoption and ratification to the conventions . . . in the several states . . . together with reference to such sources of judicial information as are resorted to by all courts in construing statutes, and to which this Court has always resorted in construing the Constitution" (*Rhode Island v. Massachusetts* [1838]). In 1925 the Court wrote that "the Fourth Amendment is to be construed in light of what was deemed an unreasonable search and seizure when it was adopted" (*Carroll v. United States* [1925]). Justice Harlan, himself not a very consistent originalist, issued one of the most forceful statements of originalism in 1970: "When the Court disregards the express intent and understanding of the framers, it has invaded the realm of the political process to which the amending power is committed, and it has violated the constitutional structure which is its highest duty to protect" (*Oregon v. Mitchell* [1970] [Harlan, J., concurring in part and dissenting in part]).

Originalism has its roots in a strict notion of the rule of law that itself rests on an important insight: a government strong enough to carry out its required functions can pose a threat to the liberty of its citizens. Accordingly, the framers sought to

---

[3] William J. Brennan Jr., "The Constitution of the United States: Contemporary Ratification," 27 *S. Tex. L. Rev.* 433 (1986), p. 437.

minimize this threat by instituting a government that was to operate within confines established in a basic written document, the Constitution. As noted in Chapter 1, it was to the courts that the task fell of policing the other branches of government in order to assure they stayed within the boundaries of the fundamental law. But, advocates of this perspective note, if the Supreme Court is to carry out its function of containing the other branches without itself operating as an illegitimate dictator, it must also operate within and be restrained by the Constitution.[4] If the Court, in policing the boundaries of the other branches of government, was not enforcing a body of law independent of the subjective will of the justices, the Court itself would be illegitimate. How, after all, in a democracy can a nonelected Court be justified, unless it functions to implement a body of law (i.e., the Constitution, which itself was democratically adopted)?

The legitimacy of judicial review thus depends on the Constitution to serve as an effective restraint on the justices. And if the Constitution is too plastic, too open to being used to legitimate current political fashion, it would have no more power to restrain than a rope of sand. We would lose both the possibility of a government under law, and the legitimacy of the institution of judicial review. Putting the Constitution into written form was meant to establish an explicit and permanent set of powers, rights, and duties. As Justice Joseph Story wrote in his *Commentaries*, the Constitution "is to have a fixed, uniform, permanent construction. . . . The meaning of the constitution is fixed when it is adopted, and it is not different at any subsequent time when a court has occasion to pass upon it."[5]

In response to the Warren Court's generous expansion of constitutional rights (which are classic cases of the practice of nonoriginalism as discussed later), academic lawyers and politicians called for a new approach to constitutional interpretation, which was dubbed originalism. In the 1980s, originalism largely took the form of seeking the original intent of the framers. This "psychological" version of originalism might thus rely on evidence regarding what was said during the Constitutional Convention. There are several difficulties with this approach: How does one really learn the subjective intent of a framer and how should the originalist compile the intentions of multiple framers who might approve a given text for different reasons. Further, the framers only proposed the text for consideration; they did not adopt it. Hence a second version of originalism focuses on the original understanding of the ratifiers. An additional problem is whether to focus on what framers or ratifiers intended to say (semantic intention) or on what they expected or hoped the provision would accomplish in terms of specific practices (expectation intention). And then there is this problem. Arguably the framers' expectation intention in writing the First Amendment was that writers and publishers would thereby be protected against government efforts to impose licensing requirements on them, but

---

[4] Perhaps the most accessible and powerful statement of originalism is to be found in Robert Bork, *The Tempting of America* (New York: Free Press, 1990).

[5] Joseph Story, *Commentaries on the Constitution of the United States* (Boston: Hillard, Gray, and Co., 1833), vol. 1, §426, p. 55.

what the framers *said* and *intended* to say was that speech was to be protected against "abridgement"—hence protected against a far broader range of restrictions than only licensing. In the face of a possible conflict between the text of the amendment and historical evidence regarding the immediate problem they were most concerned with solving, which takes priority? Many advocates of originalism have moved to a third approach—original meaning—which seeks to capture the general public meanings of the text at the time of adoption, a meaning that may not be contradicted by later or subsequent meanings.

## Originalism at Work

Here are several examples of originalism in operation. The first examples involve the finding of the meaning of word used in the text of the Constitution. Article 1, Section 3, Clause 6, confers upon the Senate the "sole power to try all impeachments." One issue that arose in *Nixon v. United States* (1993) was the meaning of the term "try." The petitioner argued that the words imposed a requirement on the Senate that all impeachments must be in the nature of a judicial trial. Hence, it was impermissible for the Senate to delegate to a committee of senators the task of receiving evidence and taking testimony; this was a task the Senate as a whole had to do. To support this claim the petitioner referred to a dictionary published in 1796 in which the word *try* was defined to mean "to examine as a judge; to bring before a judicial tribunal." The Court, however, concluded that the framers did not intend to use the word *try* in such a limited way. It noted that another dictionary published in 1787 defined the term to mean "[t]o examine." Thus the Court said that the framers did not intend to impose any specific limitations on the Senate by the use of the word *try.*

And in a discussion of the takings clause that permits the taking of property (with compensation) for "public use," Justice Thomas examined the original meaning of the term "use" and concluded that private property could only be taken if the government or its citizens as a whole actually "employ" the taken property, as opposed to turning it over to a private developer (*Kelo v. City of New London* [2005]).

The Fourth Amendment uses the term "search," which required interpretation when the police used a thermal imaging device pointed at a private house from a public street to detect heat from lamps used to grow marijuana (*Kyllo v. United States* [2001]). The paradigmatic case of the search of a home with which the framers were concerned was the search that required an actual physical invasion—a trespass. This surveillance was not a physical trespass; nevertheless, Justice Scalia extended the Fourth Amendment to cover this situation:

> We think that obtaining by sense-enhancing technology any information regarding the interior of the home that *could not otherwise have been obtained without physical "intrusion into a constitutionally protected area, . . .* constitutes a search—at least where (as here) the technology in question is not in general public use. This assures preservation of that degree of privacy against government that existed when the Fourth Amendment was adopted. On the basis of this criterion, the information obtained by the thermal imager in this case was the product of a search. [Emphasis added.]

Justices Scalia and Thomas have also used originalism—albeit reaching different conclusions—regarding the original understanding as to what the First Amendment free speech clause prohibits or does not prohibit. In *McIntyre v. Ohio Elections Commission* (1995) the majority struck down, as inconsistent with the free speech clause of the First Amendment, an Ohio law that prohibited the distribution of anonymous political literature. Justice Scalia, who dissented, argued the Court should have used originalism. In adopting that approach, he noted that originalism is "simple of application" when the government conduct under attack is a violation of the Bill of Rights or the Fourteenth Amendment "shown, upon investigation, to have been engaged in without objections at the very time the Bill of Rights or the Fourteenth Amendment was adopted." Application is also simple "where the government conduct at issue was *not* engaged in at the time of adoption, and there is ample evidence that the reason it was not engaged in is that it was thought to violate the right embodied in the constitutional guarantee." But in the case before him, the challenged conduct—a law prohibiting the distribution of anonymous political literature intended to influence a vote or election—was not prohibited when the First and Fourteenth Amendments were adopted. Nor was there, in his view, evidence that it was not prohibited because there was a belief people had a constitutional right to distribute anonymous literature.

In this situation, the proponent of originalism is forced to turn not just to history but to "judgment as to whether the government action under challenge is consonant with the concept of the protected freedom." In exercising his judgment in this case, Justice Scalia turned to tradition and found that no fewer than 24 states prohibited the distribution of anonymous literature. This evidence convinced him that this kind of prohibition was consistent with the right of free speech. "Such a universal and long established American legislative practice must be given precedence, I think, over historical and academic speculation regarding a restriction that assuredly does not go to the heart of free speech."

Justice Thomas, also a practitioner of originalism, came to a different conclusion—finding the law unconstitutional. Justice Thomas reviewed the widespread practice at the time of the adoption of the Constitution of anonymous political writing: even *The Federalist* was published anonymously. This, coupled with vocal support for this kind of political activity, led him to the conclusion that the framers "shared the belief that such activity was firmly part of the freedom of the press." Justice Scalia, however, looked at the same body of evidence and concluded that although many people practiced anonymous electioneering, he could find no evidence that it was regarded as a constitutional right. The mere fact that it was not prohibited did not mean such a prohibition would have been regarded as unconstitutional. Hence, he turned to an examination, as noted above, of more recent tradition and concluded that states constitutionally could prohibit anonymous electioneering.

Originalism may require a justice to examine a specific piece of writing by one of the framers such as one of the Federalist papers written by James Madison, Alexander Hamilton, and John Jay in an effort to persuade the public to support the proposed Constitution. In *U.S. Term Limits, Inc., v. Thornton* (1995) the Court had to decide whether a *state* may bar a person who has served three terms in the U.S. House of Representatives or two terms in the Senate from appearing on the general election ballot. (Having served either three or two terms, respectively, the incumbent congressperson or senator would have to resort to a write-in ballot, which would reduce his or her chances of being reelected.) Article 1, Sections 2 and 3, specify certain qualifications, for example, a minimum age a person must satisfy to be eligible to be a representative or senator. The issue before the Court was whether these were only *minimum* qualifications, leaving the states with the discretion to add additional ones, or whether the states were without power to add additional qualifications such as not having served more than three terms in the House. In an effort to learn about the intent of the framers, both the majority and dissenting opinions turned to evidence from the post-Convention debates, specifically *Federalist* no. 52.

James Madison, who wrote *Federalist* no. 52, began his commentary by noting that Article 1, Section 2, of the Constitution stipulated qualifications to be a *voter*, that the voters in each state must simply meet the same qualifications they must meet in order to vote for representatives for the most numerous branch of the state legislature. Thus to vote for a U.S. representative one had to meet the same requirements, whatever they might be, as one had to meet in order to vote for a state representative. As these voter qualifications were generally found in the *state constitutions*, that meant state *legislatures* could not themselves control who could or could not vote for a U.S. representative. (Of course, the state constitution itself could be amended, and in this way the qualifications for who could vote in a federal election could also be changed.) Madison, thus, observed in *Federalist* no. 52 that by eliminating state *legislative* discretion regarding voter qualifications, the U.S. Constitution avoided making the federal government "too dependent on the State governments." The U.S. Congress, he noted, "ought to be dependent on the people alone."

Madison then turned to what the U.S. Constitution had to say about the qualifications one had to meet in order to be an elected representative. He observed that the qualifications needed in order to be a state representative were "less carefully and properly defined [compared to the qualifications needed to be a voter] by the State constitutions, and being at the same time more susceptible of uniformity, have been very properly considered and regulated by the convention." He listed those qualifications and argued, "Under these reasonable limitations, the door of this part of the federal government is open to merit of every description, whether native or adoptive, whether young or old, and without regard to poverty or wealth, or to any particular profession or religious faith."

The majority and dissent in *U.S. Term Limits* offered two very different interpretations of Madison's observations. Writing for the majority, which ruled that states may not impose term limits on U.S. representatives and senators, Justice Stevens said that *Federalist* no. 52 supported that conclusion. He stressed that Madison was concerned with assuring the uniformity of qualifications and avoiding a "patchwork of qualifications"; Madison wanted the door to remain open for service in these offices; thus Madison believed states could not add qualifications to those already listed in Article 1, Section 2. Justice Thomas, however, argued that Madison was concerned only about assigning state *legislatures* control over the qualifications; if it were *the people* of the state acting by amending their state constitution, then Madison would not object to the additional qualifications.

Originalism as practiced by Justices Scalia and Thomas has sometimes led to decisions that in ordinary political parlance would be called "conservative," for example, when the Court in *Bowers v. Hardwick* (1986) concluded that making gay sodomy a crime was constitutionally permissible. (This decision was reversed in *Lawrence v. Texas* [2003].) The originalists on the Court have also moved toward an interpretation of the Establishment Clause that permits government in an evenhanded way to support all religions. But as we saw earlier, originalism also protected a homeowner from a search conducted using a thermal imaging device and Justice Thomas voted to protect freedom of speech by agreeing that the law restricting the distribution of anonymous literature was unconstitutional.

Relying on originalism, Justice Thomas, in a concurring opinion that imposed limits on the free speech rights of students, said he would go further and simply overrule all prior decisions that had recognized students enjoyed the protection of the free speech clause of the First Amendment (*Morse v. Frederick* [2007]). His argument can be captured in syllogistic form:

1. If it had been the case when the public schools were formed in the nineteenth century that it was understood that students enjoyed free speech rights, the schools would have respected them and the courts would have enforced them.
2. The schools did not respect those rights and courts did not enforce them.
3. The schools were not places for "freewheeling debates or exploration of competing ideas." "[I]n the earliest schools teacher taught and students listened; teachers commanded and students obeyed."
4. Legally, school–student relationship was governed by the *in locis parentis* doctrine, which gave school officials control over student speech.

Therefore, the First Amendment does not extend to students the right of free speech in public schools.

Although his argument has *logical validity* it is not *sound*, because the first premise of Justice Thomas's argument is untrue: (a) The text of the First Amendment makes the amendment applicable to *Congress* not the states, and (b) the incorporation doctrine, which extended the First Amendment to the states, was only developed by the Court in the middle of the twentieth century. Further, Justices Alito and Kennedy in a *concurrence* rejected premise 4. "When public school authorities regulate student speech, they act as agents of the State; they do not stand in the shoes of the students' parents." But, of course, a different originalist argument might be both valid and sound.

## NONORIGINALISM

Nonoriginalism does not reject as wholly irrelevant the intent of the framers or the meaning of words as they were used at the time of the founding. Yet the nonoriginalist will argue that the inevitably incomplete and ambiguous historical record rarely yields a certain answer regarding the intent of the framers or the meaning of words.

Justice Brennan wrote that originalism, "was arrogance cloaked as humility. It is arrogant to pretend that from our vantage we can gauge accurately the intent of the Framers on application of principle to specific, contemporary questions."[6] Elsewhere he added, "A too literal quest for the advice of the Founding Fathers . . . seems to me futile and misdirected" (*Abington School District v. Schemmp* [1963] [Brennan, J., concurring]).

Nonoriginalist also argue that the Constitution should be adaptable to new circumstances, to new problems, to new moral ideas. Many believe with Chief Justice John Marshall that unless the Constitution can adapt to the crises of human affairs, it cannot endure for ages (*McCulloch v. Maryland* [1819]). Justice Douglas, in his opinion striking down the poll tax, wrote, "In determining what lines are unconstitutionally discriminatory, we have never been confined to historic notions of equality any more than we have restricted due process to a fixed catalog of what was at a given time deemed to be the limits of fundamental rights. . . . Notions of what constitutes equal treatment for purposes of the Equal Protection Clause do change" (*Harper v. Virginia Board of Elections* [1966]). And Justice Brennan, in an opinion dissenting from the majority's decision to uphold the Nebraska legislature's practice of opening each day's session with a prayer led by a chaplain paid with public tax money, wrote:

> Finally, and most importantly, the argument tendered by the Court is misguided because the Constitution is not a static document whose meaning on every detail is fixed for all time by the life experience of the Framers. We have recognized in a wide variety of constitutional contexts that the practices that were in place at the time any particular guarantee was enacted into the Constitution do not necessarily fix forever the meaning of that guarantee. To be truly faithful to the Framers, "our use of the history of their time must limit itself to broad purposes, not specific practices." (*Marsh v. Chambers* [1983])

In the case in which the Court upheld the Minnesota Mortgage Moratorium Law, despite the explicit language of the Constitution forbidding the impairment of contracts, Justice Hughes wrote that the notion that "great clauses of the Constitution must be confined to the interpretation which the framers, with the conditions and outlook of their time, would have placed upon them . . . carries its own refutation" (*Home Building & Loan Association v. Blaisdell* [1934]).

Let's turn now to a closer examination of nonoriginalism in action.

## Nonoriginalism and Original Intent

When nonoriginalists make use of original intent they characteristically understand that intent to be directed toward broad functional purposes and values. The way Justice Brennan spoke of intent was in terms of a "national commitment" to certain broad values. In an important free speech case he described the First Amendment as

---

[6] William J. Brennan Jr., "The Constitution of the United States: Contemporary Ratification," 27 *S. Tex. L. Rev.* 433 (1986): 435.

part of a "profound national commitment to the principle that debate on public issues should be uninhibited, robust, and wide-open . . ." (*New York Times v. Sullivan* [1964]). In another case in which the Court had to decide whether the Constitution requires that welfare recipient be afforded an evidentiary hearing *before* termination of benefits ("Yes") he wrote that, "From its founding the Nation's basic commitment has been to foster the dignity and well-being of all persons within its borders" (*Goldberg v. Kelly* [1970]).

## Nonoriginalism and the Constitutional Text

Nonoriginalism has not only served to expand the scope of individual rights but also the constitutional grant of power to Congress to regulate interstate commerce. Most commentators have concluded that as originally understood the commerce clause did not empower Congress to regulate the production of goods, for example, manufacturing, and agriculture within the states.[7] But as noted in Chapter 2 the power to regulate interstate commerce is now understood to reach even the amount of wheat a farmer grows for the exclusive private consumption by his family.

The Court has interpreted the term "liberty" in the Fourteenth Amendment to include a variety of rights not expressly mentioned in the Constitution. A now notorious example of the first point can be found in the Supreme Court's decision in *Lochner v. New York* (1905). In that case a majority of activist nonoriginalist justices struck down a New York law that prohibited the employment of bakery employees for more than ten hours a day or 60 hours a week. The Court ruled that the term "liberty" in the Fourteenth Amendment's due process clause (no state shall deprive any person of life, liberty, or property without due process of law) included the notion of freedom of contract. The Court saw this law as an interference with the liberty of contract. In effect the Court concluded that the amendment protected the liberty to purchase and sell labor services regardless of the unequal bargaining position of employer and employee.

In a case striking down a law making homosexual sodomy a crime the Supreme Court wrote, "Freedom extends beyond spatial bounds. Liberty presumes an autonomy of self that includes freedom of thought, belief, expression, and certain intimate conduct" (*Lawrence v. Texas* [2003]).

Let us take the example of the free speech clause of the First Amendment. The term "speech" could be narrowly confined to oral and printed expression, but nonoriginalist justices say "speech" extends to a wide range of "expressive activities." In *NAACP v. Button* (1963), Justice Brennan extended the protection of the free speech clause to the NAACP's activities in sponsoring litigation. (Justice Harlan's dissenting opinion argued that litigation was "conduct" and not "speech," therefore not an activity covered by the First Amendment.) To take another example, nonoriginalists on the Court have said that sleeping overnight in a park to demonstrate the plight of

---

[7] Albert S. Abel, "The Commerce Clause in the Constitutional Convention and in Contemporary Comment," 25 *Minn. L. Rev.* 432 (1941).

the homeless is a form of "speech." A majority of the Court refused to accept the truth of this proposition; the majority opinion written by Justice White merely said it would accept this proposition provisionally, only for the sake of argument. Justice White went on to uphold the National Park Service regulation prohibiting camping in certain parks even when done as part of a political demonstration (*Clark v. Community for Creative Non-Violence* [1984]).

## Using Implicit Premises

One of the most noted nonoriginalist decisions is *Baker v. Carr* (1962), which drastically modified the "political question" doctrine so as to make the federal courts available to review the apportionment of representation in state legislatures. Prior decisions had held that the apportionment of state legislatures was a "political question" not appropriate for judicial action. In *Baker*, Justice Brennan's majority opinion reversed direction, thereby dramatically altering the relationship between the Supreme Court and the states. The nonoriginalist activists felt impelled to act because the state legislatures themselves would not act; those possessing disproportionate power in the legislatures simply had no incentive to give it up. Then, having decided that the "political question" doctrine did not in fact bar federal court review of state legislative apportionment, in *Reynolds v. Sims* (1964) the majority took the next step and struck down as unconstitutional the apportionment of the Alabama legislature. The opinion rested in part on a set of new principles that Chief Justice Warren said were fundamental principles of representative government. Here are examples of the principles he found implicitly embedded in the Constitution:

- Undoubtedly the right of suffrage is a fundamental matter in a free democratic society.
- As long as ours is a representative form of government, [the] right to elect legislators in a free and unimpaired fashion is a bedrock of our political system.
- Logically, in a society ostensibly grounded on representative government, it would seem reasonable that a majority of the people of a state could elect a majority of that state's legislators.
- Since achieving fair and effective representation for all citizens is admittedly the basic aim of legislative apportionment, we conclude that [equal protection] guarantees the opportunity for equal participation by all voters in the election of state legislators. (*Reynolds v. Sims* [1964])

Warren did not trace these principles back to a specific provision in the Constitution, or to historical evidence of the framers' intent. The principles are simply discerned as logically necessary. Based on such general principles, the chief justice concluded that "the weight of a citizen's vote cannot be made to depend on where he lives," and, thus, a "State must make an honest and good faith effort to construct districts [that elect representatives to the legislature] in both houses of its legislature, as nearly of equal population as is practicable."

The dissenters rejected the fundamental principles Warren said were implicit in the Constitution. They viewed the majority opinion as nothing less than the imposition of the justice's own particular theory of democracy.

Justice Breyer, as noted earlier, has staked out a position on the appropriate approach to Constitutional interpretation that echoes the Court's position in *Reynolds v. Sims*, but he argues the framers wrote the Constitution with general intent to promote "active liberty," by which he means the right of people to participate in self-government. Justice Breyer thus calls for interpreting the specific provisions of the Constitution as designed to further this larger objective. Hence any ruling of the Court to uphold or strike down a policy must examine the consequences of that ruling for realizing the larger goal behind the Constitution. He thus would have the Court examine cases arising under such disparate parts of the Constitution as the free speech clause, the commerce clause, and the equal protection clause in terms of the consequence of the ruling for advancing or inhibiting the general goal of promotion of active liberty. Whether his approach is best characterized as originalist or nonoriginalist is an interesting question.

## Working with Tradition

Tradition is arguably useful to shed light on the meaning of the Constitution because it tells us what "society"—or at least a large proportion of the society—has considered to be within the power of government to do or not do. If many supposedly reasonable people believe that, for example, doing "X" is within (or not within) the power of government, it would seem to follow that the justices ought to pay attention to these views. Some philosophers of law even argue that these long-standing understandings and practices should be understood to be "law," and thus properly may be relied upon by a justice in reaching a decision.

Where is evidence of "tradition" to be found? One source is to be found in the **common law** that serves as a kind of background to which the Constitutional text "refers." Conflict over the proper use of the common law in interpreting the Fourth Amendment arose in *Georgia v. Randolph* (2006), in which the Supreme Court ruled that the police violated the prohibition against unreasonable searches when they searched a house having gotten permission to do so from the wife only and not from the husband, who was present at the scene at the time of the search. In a concurring opinion Justice Stevens, in rejecting an originalist approach, noted that "*if 'original understanding' were to govern the outcome of the case*" the search was clearly invalid because, at the time the Fourth Amendment was written, under the common law only the husband would have held the property rights in the home, hence only the husband would have had the legal power to consent or not to consent to the warrantless search. Justice Scalia in his dissent rejected Steven's characterization of how originalism worked. Yes, using originalism the Fourth Amendment should be interpreted, said Justice Scalia, against the background law of property rights. But he added:

> As property law developed, individuals who previously could not authorize a search might become able to do so, and those who once could grant such consent might no longer have that power. But changes in the law of property to which the Fourth Amendment referred would not alter the Amendment's meaning: that anyone capable

of authorizing a search by a private party could consent to a warrantless search by the police.

Here is another example of a dispute over the use of tradition. The case is *Michael H. v. Gerald D.* (1989), in which Justice Scalia, the originalist, was sharply attacked for his interpretation of tradition by a nonoriginalist justice, Justice Brennan. Michael H. alleged that he had had an adulterous relationship with Carole D., and that he was the natural father of Victoria. Victoria now lived with Carole D. and Gerald D., husband and wife. Michael sought visitation and other rights with respect to Victoria. But California courts rejected his claims, relying on the presumption established in California law that a child born to the wife is legitimately the child of that marriage. The California courts stuck to this presumption even though blood tests established a 98.07 percent probability that Michael H. was in fact the father. The California courts stated that the state law's presumption was really a "substantive rule of law" (i.e., the operative California law favored preserving the family unit of husband and wife; the integrity of a family like that of Carole and Gerald could not be impugned; and somebody like Michael was not entitled to parental prerogatives, even if he was the natural father).

Michael claimed that he had a constitutional right as her father to his relationship with Victoria and that California law violated his constitutional right. Such a constitutional right is not expressly mentioned in the Constitution; thus Scalia tried to determine whether "tradition" recognized Michael and Victoria as a family unit. His examination of tradition led him to the conclusion that historically this kind of relationship had not been treated as a family unit; hence Michael did not have a protected constitutional right. "[O]ur traditions have protected the marital family (Gerald, Carole, and the child they acknowledge to be theirs) against the sort of claim Michael asserts." The California decision was upheld.

It was in this context that Scalia made his comments about the proper methodology for discovering and interpreting tradition. Scalia's approach was one of looking to tradition to see whether, specifically, an *adulterous natural father's* parental prerogatives had historically been protected. Hence he examined our traditions by focusing on this narrow question, rather than on what tradition had to say about the prerogatives of "natural fathers" more generally, or of "parents." He supported his focus by arguing that he wanted to avoid, if possible, having to work with tradition broadly defined, for example, rights of natural parents generally, "because general traditions provide such imprecise guidance." To have the justices, he argued, speculate about how general traditions apply to specific problems allows the justices to dictate rather than discern society's own views. The problem with using tradition too broadly defined, he noted, was illustrated in this very case. He noted that both Justice O'Connor and Justice Brennan would have preferred to look at tradition in more broadly defined terms, yet using a broader conception of tradition each came to an opposite result, with O'Connor concurring in the Scalia judgment and Brennan dissenting. Hence, Scalia concluded that to look at tradition in a general and abstract way left "judges free to decide as they think best when the unanticipated occurs," but a "rule of law that binds neither by text nor by any particular identifiable tradition, is no rule of law at all" (*Michael H. v. Gerald D.* [1989]).

Justice Brennan attacked Scalia's methodology on several fronts. First, he charged that Scalia "pretends that tradition places a discernible border around the Constitution." Tradition cannot control judicial discretion, Brennan argued, because reasonable people can disagree (1) about the content of a particular tradition, (2) about which traditions are relevant, (3) about when a tradition is firm enough to be relied upon, and (4) about when it has become too obsolete to be relevant. Second, he argued that the particular way of using tradition—looking at whether a specific variety of parenthood has been protected—had never before been used by the Court and was misguided. We ought to limit the role tradition plays in constitutional interpretation.

> In [Scalia's] constitutional universe, we may not take notice of the fact that the original reasons for the conclusive presumption of paternity are out of place in a world in which blood tests can prove virtually beyond a shadow of doubt who sired a particular child and in which the fact of illegitimacy no longer plays the burdensome and stigmatizing role it once did. [In] construing the Fourteenth Amendment to offer shelter only to those interests specifically protected by historical practice, moreover, the plurality ignores the kind of society in which our Constitution exists. . . . The document that the plurality construes today is unfamiliar to me. It is not the living charter that I have taken to be our Constitution; it is instead a stagnant, archaic, hidebound document steeped in the prejudices and superstitions of a time long past. (*Michael H. v. Gerald D.* [1989])

## Drawing on New Materials

The extensive use of statistical data in constitutional debates began with Louis Brandeis. As an attorney in the earlier part of the century Brandeis gained fame for his arguments before the Court in support of liberal social legislation, for example, regulations limiting the hours that an employer could require women to work. Brandeis argued that this legislation was "reasonable," and he proved it by marshaling statistical evidence establishing the existence of a social problem the legislation was designed to address. Hence there came into existence the "Brandeis brief." These briefs were short on technical legal argument and long on statistical data elaborating on the social problem it was the purpose of the law to correct.

Though Brandeis used such data to defend liberal social legislation against the threat posed by a conservative activist court, in more recent years activists have used data and the analysis of social scientists to attack governmental policies. A sophisticated example of this practice can be found in a dissenting opinion by Justice Blackmun. His opinion uses complex social science studies to prove that the likelihood of a criminal defendant's being given the death penalty dramatically changed depending on the race of the victim. For example, the data showed that a killer of a white person had a significantly higher chance of receiving the death penalty than did the killer of a black person. The less activist majority rejected the argument that these data demonstrated an equal protection violation (*McCleskey v. Kemp* [1987]).

Reliance on evidence of contemporary social values has characterized a number of the opinions written by nonoriginalist activist justices. In *Furman v. Georgia* (1972) a majority of the Court, in a one-paragraph per curiam opinion, declared that the death penalty policy of the states in three cases was "cruel and unusual punishment" in violation of the Eighth Amendment. Three justices agreed with this conclusion, because the administration of capital punishment had been arbitrary and capricious, not because the penalty was unconstitutional per se. Justice Brennan went further in a concurring opinion. He took the position that the death penalty was never a permissible form of punishment. He argued, among other things, that the death penalty was contrary to contemporary community values. And to prove his point he used evidence of the infrequent use of the death penalty; he argued that this was an "objective indicator" that despite public opinion polls showing support for the penalty, the penalty today was contrary to modern values. In his willingness to rely on contemporary community values Justice Brennan was following in the tradition of other justices such as Chief Justice Warren, who commented on the words "cruel and unusual punishment" by noting that "[t]he Amendment must draw its meaning from the evolving standards of decency that mark the progress of a maturing society" (*Trop v. Dulles* [1958]).

In his concurring opinion in *Furman*, Justice Marshall took a very different approach to the same question. He argued that "polling" data should be ignored because most people were not fully informed "as to the purposes of the penalty and its liabilities." He said that if people were to be presented with evidence on how, for example, the penalty is imposed in a discriminatory manner, and on the number of innocent people killed, he was convinced that "the average citizen would . . . find it shocking to his conscience and sense of justice. For this reason alone capital punishment cannot stand."

Relying both on "evolving standards of decency" and an examination of the historical common law at existence at the time of the drafting of the Eighth Amendment the Court concluded that the Eighth Amendment prohibits a state from inflicting the death penalty on a person who at the time the penalty would be imposed was mentally ill in a way that deprived him of the mental capacity to understand that he is facing execution as punishment for a crime (*Ford v. Wainwright* [1986]). This case opened the door to finding that the amendment was violated when Texas sought to execute a convicted killer who was competent to stand trial but who subsequently came to believe he was being executed not because of the crime he committed but to stop him from preaching (*Panetti v. Quarterman* [2007]).

In addition to turning to new statistical data and contemporary values, some justices have been willing to rely on the Ninth Amendment ("The enumeration in the Constitution, of certain rights, shall not be construed to deny or disparage others retained by the people"). For most of the history of the Court this amendment was rarely referred to—it was cited in only three cases. But in the Connecticut contraception case (see Chapter 8) a majority of the Court resurrected the amendment. Today, a leading liberal scholar on constitutional law says that the Ninth Amendment "at least states a rule of construction pointing away from the reverse incorporation view that only the interests secured by the Bill of Rights are encompassed within the Fourteenth Amendment, and at most provides a positive source of law for fundamental but unmentioned rights."[8]

---

[8] Lawrence Tribe, *American Constitutional Law*, 2d ed. (Mineola, N.Y.: Foundation Press, 1988), pp. 774–775.

## The Broad Invocation of American Values

The broad invocation of American values not supported by a careful interpretation of historical texts such as Madison's notes on the Constitutional Convention or *The Federalist* is not a common feature of judicial writing. But occasionally the justices do support their judgments by broad appeals to these values. Justice Brandeis supported his conception of the free speech clause by arguing, "Those who won our independence believed that the final end of the State was to make men free to develop their faculties; and that in its government the deliberative forces should prevail over the arbitrary. They valued liberty both as an end and as a means. They believed liberty to be the secret of happiness and courage to be the secret of liberty" (*Whitney v. California* [1927] [Brandeis, J., concurring]). Here is another example. The Supreme Court has addressed in a series of cases the constitutionality of multi-million dollar punitive damage awards and has concluded that the Constitution does impose a limit on the size of those awards (a limit to be determined case by case). The majority based its conclusion that such limits exist on the premise that "elementary notions of fairness enshrined in our constitutional jurisprudence dictate that a person receive a fair notice not only of the conduct that will subject him to punishment, but also of the severity of the penalty that a State may impose" (*BMW of North America v. Gore* [1996]).

In two controversial decisions the Court went beyond an examination of evolving standards within the United States to consider the laws of other countries. In a case striking down a Texas law prohibiting gay sodomy the Court took note of changes in the law of other nations decriminalizing sex between people of the same gender (*Lawrence v. Texas* [2003]). Thus in striking down a law that permitted the imposition of the death penalty on perpetrators under 18, Justice Kennedy wrote,

> It is proper that we acknowledge the overwhelming weight of international opinion against the juvenile death penalty, resting in large part on the understanding that the instability and emotional imbalance of young people may often be a factor in the crime. . . . The opinion of the world community, while not controlling our outcome, does provide respected and significant confirmation for our own conclusions. . . . It does not lessen our fidelity to the Constitution or our pride in its origins to acknowledge that the express affirmation of certain fundamental rights by other nations and peoples simply underscores the centrality of those same rights within our own heritage of freedom. (*Roper v. Simmons* [2005])

## Considerations of Practicality

The justices, both originalists and nonoriginalists, make use of arguments regarding what is practical and not practical. These problems can be of several kinds. When the Court refused to strike down Texas's system of school finance, the majority opinion noted that the Court was being asked to address a problem that was beyond its expertise and specialized knowledge (*San Antonio Independent School District v. Rodriguez* [1973]). Besides worrying about the Court's own institutional competence, the justices also consider the practical impact of the ruling they are being asked to make. In deciding that Paula Corbin Jones's civil suit against President

Clinton was not to be automatically deferred until Clinton left office, the Court addressed the question whether its ruling would "generate a large volume of politically motivated harassing and frivolous litigation" (*Clinton v. Jones* [1997]). The majority was not persuaded this was a real risk, but Justice Breyer, although concurring, argued that it ought to be within the Court's discretion to postpone such a suit if there was evidence that the suit would interfere with the president's ability to carry out his official duties. Justice Breyer has in fact said that "the real-world consequences of a particular interpretive decision, valued in terms of basic constitutional purposes, play an important role in constitutional decisionmaking."[9] Considerations of practicality are also attributed to the framers and ratifiers. For example, the majority opinion deciding that Congress did not have the authority to abrogate state sovereignty by authorizing suits against the state in state courts to enforce federal rights argued that the framers were concerned that private suits against nonconsenting states for money damages could damage the financial integrity of the states. The majority then went on to discuss a broader range of practical implications if they ruled that Congress did have such authority (*Alden v. Maine* [1999]).

As noted earlier, the Court in *Georgia v. Randolph* (2006) ruled that the police violated the prohibition against unreasonable searches when they searched a house having gotten permission to search only from the wife and not from the husband, who also was present at the scene. Then the Court went on to consider this question— should police be required to seek out potentially objecting cotenants who were not physically present at the moment of the search in order to obtain their consent for the search? No. "There is no ready reason to believe that efforts to invite a refusal would make a difference in many cases, whereas every co-tenant consent case would turn into a test about the adequacy of the police's efforts to consult with a potential objector."

## LIBERALISM AND CONSERVATISM

What is the association, if any, between originalism and conservatism, nonoriginalism and liberalism? Technically speaking there is no link. Originalism and nonoriginalism are approaches to Constitutional interpretation based on values and considerations that are not designed to be "result oriented." That is to say, the arguments for embracing originalism are not arguments that say, "Adopt originalism because it will be a cover for rationalizing the conservative results you want to achieve." It is true that in many areas of constitutional law the justices who embrace originalism would reach decisions that conservatives embrace, for example, in regard to criminalization of gay sodomy (*Lawrence v. Texas* [2003]). And justices who embrace originalism do reach conclusions that liberals could applaud. Justice Scalia wrote the majority opinion in a case that concluded the use without a warrant

[9] Stephen Breyer, "Madison Lecture: Our Democratic Constitution," 77 *New York University Law Review* 245 (2002).

of a thermal imaging device directed at a home from a public street to detect the use of heat lamps for growing marijuana was a search that violated the Fourth Amendment (*Kyllo v. United States* [2001]). Justice Stevens, widely viewed as a liberal judge and proponent of nonoriginalism, dissented. And in *McIntyre v. Ohio Elections Commission* (1995), Justice Stevens's majority opinion protected freedom of non-speech in striking down a law that prohibited the circulation of anonymous leaflets in connection with political campaigns. Justice Thomas, a strong adherent of originalism, concurred, whereas Justice Scalia, also a strong proponent of originalism, dissented.

## JUDICIAL ACTIVISM AND DEFERENCE

The charge of "judicial activism" is frequently used to attack justices who have reached decisions with which one disagrees. Hence Democrats have charged the Court with judicial activism in striking down federal statutes as violations of the Eleventh Amendment. And Republicans have charged the Court with judicial activism in striking down state antiabortion laws. Adherents both of originalism and nonoriginalism have been characterized as practitioners of activism. Similarly, conservatives and liberals have been charged with being activist judges.

But what is the definition of "judicial activism"? Professor Graglia has offered this definition: "By judicial activism I mean, quite simply and specifically, the practice by judges of disallowing policy choices by other governmental officials or institutions that the Constitution does not clearly prohibit."[10] But the cases that reach the Supreme Court are typically hard cases in which the meaning of the Constitution is in dispute; hence under this definition the avoidance of judicial activism could mean almost never striking down the law or policy—a virtual abdication of the power of judicial review.

Other definitions of judicial activism have been identified by a legal scholar.[11] One definition is that a judge is judicially active when he or she ignores or disregards precedent. Another is that the judge is "legislating from the bench." Finally, judicial activism can mean that the judge has engaged in "result-oriented" judging. Activism might also be understood as a judicial attitude that "I'm in charge, and I will seek to be a player equal to the other branches in shaping policy." Given the various possible definitions of the term "judicial activism," the vagueness of the definitions and the difficulty of establishing the charge (when has a judge disregarded precedent?), it is not a particularly useful term for describing or understanding the Supreme Court justices and their opinions.

---

[10] Lino A. Graglia, "It's Not Constitutionalism, It's Judicial Activism," 19 *Harvard Journal of Law and Public Policy* 293 (1996).

[11] Kennan D. Kmiec, "Comment: The Origin and Current Meanings of 'Judicial Activism,'" 92 *California Law Review* 1441 (2004).

Perhaps the most notorious example of judicial activism is the decision in *Dred Scott v. Sandford* (1857)—a decision that is almost universally criticized and was centrally important in helping to precipitate the Civil War—in which the Court decided that Scott, a slave, was not a "citizen" of the United States and, therefore, had no right to sue in federal courts. By barring his suit, the Court prevented Scott from making the legal claim that he was no longer a slave because at one point in his life his master had taken him into free territory and this had had the legal effect of liberating him. Chief Justice Taney concluded, using historical references, that the framers never intended for blacks to be citizens of the United States, regardless of whether they became free or not. His approach to constitutional interpretation was an example of pure originalism.

> No one, we presume, supposes that any change in public opinion or feeling should induce the Court to give the words of the Constitution a more liberal construction in their favor than they were intended to bear when the instrument was framed and adopted. Such an argument would be altogether inadmissible in any tribunal called on to interpret it. If any of its provisions are deemed unjust, there is a mode prescribed in the instrument itself by which it may be amended; but while it remains unaltered, it must be construed now as it was understood at the time of its adoption. It is not only the same words, but the same meaning. (*Dred Scott v. Sandford* [1857])

The Court's decision was also an example of nondeference in its willingness to take on issues not necessary for the Court to address, for example, the question of Congress's authority to adopt the Missouri Compromise, which barred slavery in the territories.

# Practice Pointers

1. If an advocate wishes to tailor an argument to appeal to a particular justice, the advocate needs to consider whether that justice is an **originalist** or **nonoriginalist**. The advocate can then offer arguments consistent with that justice's approach to constitutional interpretation.
2. Your understanding of originalism can be sharpened by researching the debate among legal scholars over the original intent of the framers in adopting the Fourteenth Amendment as it bears on the constitutionality of the "separate but equal" doctrine in public schooling. First, read *Brown v. Board of Education* (1954). Then ask whether, contrary to the Court's opinion, the decision can be defended on originalist grounds. In that connection read: Michael W. McConnell, "Originalism and the Desegregation Decisions," 81 *Virginia Law Review* 947 (1995); Michael J. Klarman, "Reponse: Brown, Originalism, and Constitutional Theory: A Response to Professor McConnell," 81 *Virginia Law Review* 1881 (1995); Michael W. McConnell, "Reply: The Originalist Justification for Brown: A Reply to Professor Klarman," 81 *Virginia Law Review* 1937 (1995). Also look at

Earl M. Maltz, "Remark: A Dissenting Opinion to Brown," *Southern Illinois University Law Review* 93 (1995).

3. If the framers and ratifiers of the Fourteenth Amendment approved of segregated schools, the decision in *Brown* contradicted their intentions. Scholars have debated what a "better" or "stronger" nonoriginalist opinion in *Brown* would look like, an opinion that relied less on the kind of social science evidence seemingly depended upon by the Court. Your skills at writing nonoriginalist opinions will be strengthened by reading the hypothetical opinions printed in: Jack M. Balkin, *What* Brown v. Board of Education *Should Have Said* (New York: New York University Press, 2001).

# Chapter 5

# Tests or Standards of Review

This chapter will first introduce the general idea of a **test or standard of review** (terms that can be used interchangeably); second, it will review specific examples of these tests from the five different areas of constitutional law reviewed in Chapter 2. In Chapter 6 you will be introduced in more detail to the use of these tests in the writing of a judicial opinion. Suffice it to say here that these tests often perform the function of a premise in a legal argument as illustrated by the following:

> *Premise:* To be consistent with the First Amendment's prohibition against the establishment of religion, a policy must not be adopted whose purpose is to promote religion. (Hence the *test:* Was this policy adopted for the purpose of promoting religion?)
>
> *Second Premise:* Evidence from the record of the case shows this law was not adopted with the purpose of promoting religion.
>
> *Conclusion:* Therefore, at least insofar as this test is concerned, this policy is constitutionally permissible.

CAVEAT: Although tests are frequently used by the Court in the process of discovery and justification, they are not used in all cases.

## TESTS IN GENERAL

### Tests and the Burden of Proof

In constitutional law, a test is, first, a criterion that a policy must meet in order for it to be constitutionally permissible. For example, one simple criterion used in some areas of constitutional law requires that in order for the policy to be constitutionally permissible (1) it must serve a purpose that is *legitimate* and (2) it must employ means that are *rationally related* to that legitimate purpose. Determining whether the policy is directed to a purpose that is legitimate, by means that are rationally related to that purpose, involves inquiry and judgment, of course.

A second feature of these tests is that they specify who has the burden of proof—who must convince the Court that the policy meets or does not meet the test. In some cases this burden of proof (which can also be called the "risk of nonpersuasion") lies with the party attacking the constitutionality of the law. In these situations, unless the party convinces the Court that the law is unconstitutional, the Court will uphold the policy. That is, in these cases the policy is *presumed* to be constitutional unless and until the Court has been convinced otherwise.

In other cases the burden of proof rests with the government that adopted the policy. In these situations the Court will presume that the policy is unconstitutional unless and until the government can convince the Court that the policy is permissible.

## Selection of the Appropriate Test

Selection of the appropriate test for use in the case before the Court is, of course, the first or preliminary step. As indicated, different areas of constitutional law use different tests; thus the very first step the justice has to take (a step you also must take in thinking about a legal problem) is to decide which area of constitutional law is involved in the conflict; for example, is this a commerce clause case, or an equal protection case, or does it perhaps have elements of both? There may be only one appropriate test to use in that category of case, but sometimes the justice may have to choose from among a number of different tests that are used in that particular area of the law. Cases that arise under the equal protection clause of the Fourteenth Amendment, for example, might use any of three tests. Thus a justice (or a lawyer, legal scholar, or student of the law) must also look to precedent for guidelines for selecting the appropriate test. As we shall see below, equal protection precedent provides a set of additional guidelines for test selection. Once the test has been selected, the justice applies it in the process of discovery and the process of justification.

## Where Do the Tests Come from in the First Place?

We have been assuming to this point that a justice need only look at precedent to determine the appropriate test. But we need to ask, Where did the test come from the first time it appeared in a Supreme Court opinion? These tests are not found in the Constitution. The tests are judicial creations, and the Court with fair regularity has changed, modified, reinterpreted, and discarded them. Arguments over the derivation and choice of a test, as well as over the interpretation and application of a test, are one vehicle (rhetorical mode) judges use to express their disagreements. Majority and dissenting opinions often reflect disagreements about the formulation, selection, and interpretation of a test, as well as its application to the case at hand. The justices are today in a two-front prolonged struggle over the meaning of the tests used to implement the establishment clause of the First Amendment. The justices disagree both over whether the tests (discussed below) should be abandoned, and how these tests are to be applied in a particular case. (*McCreary County v. A.C.L.U.* [2005]; *Van Orden v. Perry* [2005]).

When it comes to constructing or designing a test in the first place, many considerations enter that are rarely discussed in Supreme Court opinions. The more a justice believes that one of the other branches of government is going to make a constitutional error, the more likely the justice will opt for a tough test that places the burden of persuasion that the policy is constitutional on that branch. The lower the probability of such an error, the weaker will be the test the justice favors, and the justice will be inclined to place the burden of persuasion on the party attacking the policy. Another consideration is the role the Court should play vis-à-vis the other branches of government. The more a justice is uncomfortable with a court that closely scrutinizes the activities of the other branches of government, the more a justice will be inclined to place the burden of proof on the party attacking the policy and require that party to meet a very heavy burden in proving the law to be unconstitutional. Justices, however, who see the Court as playing an important role in shaping policy despite its nonelected status will tend to be more willing to adopt the view that the government has the burden of proof to convince the Court that the policy is constitutionally permissible. A final consideration in test construction is the workability of the test. Vague, amorphous, and elastic tests may amount to tests in appearance only; such a test is of little practical use in the process of discovery and provides little in the way of strong justification in the process of justification.

When, after experience, a test proves to be unworkable the Court will drop reliance upon it. In *Agins v. City of Tiburon* (1980) the Court ruled in a challenge based on the takings clause of the Fifth Amendment ("nor shall private property be taken for public use, without just compensation") that the application of a zoning ordinance to a particular piece of property effects a taking if the ordinance does not *substantially advance* legitimate state interests. Then in *Lingle v. Chevron* (2005), the Court abandoned the "substantially advances" test because it was "regrettably imprecise" and because the test did not require exploration of the magnitude or character of the burden the challenged regulation imposed on the private property. Nor did it require how the regulatory burden was distributed among property owners, as a consequence it did not determine whether the regulation had an effect comparable to a physical invasion of the property or its appropriation by the government. In addition to its doctrinal inadequacies, the test could lead to a review of a vast array of regulations of private property—"a task for which the courts are not well suited."

If the Justices are unable to develop a satisfactory test they may conclude that the case is **nonjusticiable** and the issue in the case should be classified as a **political question.** Claims that a state has politically gerrymandered its electoral districts to favor one political party in such a way that the voters of another political party have had the value of their vote consistently degraded have raised such a problem for the Court. A plurality of the Court today will refuse to hear all such cases on grounds that there are no judicially discernible or manageable standards for determining whether, and when, the way district boundary lines have been drawn have improperly diminished the influence of one political party on the state's political process (*Veith v. Jubelirer* [2004]). Justice Kennedy agreed with the dismissal of the case in *Veith* but held to the belief that it might be possible in the future that the Court would discern workable principles for such cases. Hence he was unwilling to agree with the plurality that all claims of gerrymandering should be declared nonjusticiable.

### Tests and Judicial Activism: Deference and Nondeference

Chapter 1 discussed judicial activism. Tests to an important extent determine whether the Court will be an activist Court in particular cases. When the test used by the Court in a particular case places the burden of proof on the government to establish that the statute, policy, or action of an official is constitutionally permissible, the Court is more likely than not to end up striking the policy down, especially if the burden placed on the government is a difficult one to satisfy. When the test used by the Court has these characteristics the Court ends up scrutinizing the policy with great vigor and without much deference toward the other branch of government. For example, the tests relied upon by the Court in freedom of speech cases reflect a posture of nondeference whereas the tests relied upon by the Court in cases addressing the constitutionality of statutes regulating business reflect a strong posture of deference. It might be noted that the "congruence and proportionality" test used in connection with examining Congress's power to enforce the Fourteenth Amendment has drawn the ire of members of Congress as not being sufficiently deferential to Congress. But note that Justice Scalia's attack on the test is grounded, not on its failure to defer to Congress, but on the lack of clarity and precision of the test.

## SELECTED EXAMPLES OF TESTS

### Congressional Power

In developing tests for use in connection with deciding cases dealing with the scope of congressional power the Supreme Court has looked at the text to determine whether the power is express or implied and whether it is checked or limited by the existence of another grant of authority (e.g., by a grant to another branch of the federal government, by state sovereignty, by the "dormant commerce clause"). The Court has thus examined the semantic and expectation intentions of the framers, precedent, and the practical consequences of recognizing or denying the existence of the power.

In the opinion dealing with whether Congress had the authority to establish a national bank, Chief Justice Marshall promulgated the following test of the scope of Congress's authority: "Let the end be legitimate, let it be within the scope of the constitution, and all means which are appropriate, which are plainly adapted to that end, which are not prohibited, but consistent with the letter and spirit of the constitution, are constitutional" (*McCulloch v. Maryland* [1819]). This test is still cited today by the Court in cases involving challenges to Congress's authority. Different tests come into play in connection with such constitutional problems as Congress's authority to regulate interstate commerce and Congress's taxing and spending power.

One of the most important powers of Congress is the power to regulate commerce among the several states (U.S. Constitution, Article 1, Section 8). In recent years the Court has interpreted this power as granting Congress the authority to regulate the use of the channels of interstate commerce, to regulate and protect the instrumentalities of interstate commerce, and to regulate any activity that "'substantially affects' interstate commerce" (*United States v. Lopez* [1995]). As interpreted by the Court, to meet this test the legislation must regulate "economic" or "commercial" activity, and this activity must then "substantially affect" interstate commerce. Hence legislation that regulates noncommercial activity, for example, possession of a firearm in a school zone, is beyond the power granted by Article 1, Section 8, just as would be the regulation of an economic activity that did not substantially affect interstate commerce. Using these concepts the Court upheld a federal law that had the effect of prohibiting the possession, obtaining, or manufacture of cannabis for personal medical use (*Gonzales v. Raich* [2005]). Obtaining and using cannabis for medical use was not itself a "commercial" activity but it was an "economic" activity.

Section 5 of the Fourteenth Amendment gives Congress "power to enforce, by appropriate legislation, the provisions of this article." As discussed in Chapter 2, the Court in recent years has cut back the scope of this power. The test adopted by the Court to determine whether the legislation exceeds Congress's power requires that "there must be a congruence and proportionality between the injury to be prevented [by the legislation] or remedied and the means adopted to that end" (*City of Boerne v. Flores* [1997]). Justice Scalia, who originally had agreed to the test, now would abandon it. He would, under a different test, have struck down the law.

> I joined the Court's opinion in *Boerne* with some misgiving. I have generally rejected tests based on such malleable standards as "proportionality," because they have a way of turning into vehicles for the implementation of individual judges' policy preferences. I yield to the lessons of experience. The "congruence and proportionality" standard like all such flabby tests, is a standing invitation to judicial arbitrariness and policy driven decisionmaking. Worse still, it casts this Court in the role of Congress's taskmaster. Under it, the courts (and ultimately this Court) must regularly check Congress's homework to make sure that it has identified sufficient constitutional violations to make its remedy congruent and proportional.

## State Regulation of Interstate Commerce

Recall from the discussion in Chapter 2 that the Supreme Court has promulgated the following test for use in cases in which a state law that affects interstate commerce has been challenged as a violation of the "dormant commerce clause."

> Where the statute regulates evenhandedly to effectuate a legitimate local public interest, and its effects on interstate commerce are only incidental, it will be upheld unless the burden imposed on such commerce is clearly excessive in relation to the putative local benefits. If a legitimate local purpose is found, then the question becomes one of degree. And the extent of the burden that will be tolerated will of course depend on the nature of the local interest involved, and on whether it could be promoted as well with a lesser impact on interstate activities. (*Pike v. Bruce Church, Inc.* [1970])

This test indicates, roughly speaking, that if a state law regulating interstate transportation is to be upheld, it must (1) regulate evenhandedly (not discriminate against out-of-state commerce), (2) serve a legitimate local public purpose (e.g., not be designed to promote racial segregation), (3) have only an incidental impact on interstate commerce (its effect must be slight), and (4) the burden on interstate commerce must not be excessive in relation to the local benefits (the local benefits must out-weigh the harm done to interstate commerce).

The *Pike* test is an example of a test that is under attack today. Justice Scalia is today engaged in efforts to get the other members of the Court to abandon the test announced in the *Pike* case (*Tyler Pipe Industries, Inc., v. Washington Department of Revenue* [1987]; *Goldberg v. Sweet* [1989]).

## Cases Involving the Fifth Amendment Takings Clause

The Fifth Amendment commands that private property shall not "be taken for public use without just compensation." The Supreme Court has thus had to decide when the governmental policy amounts to a taking. There is no dispute that a physical invasion of land is a taking. But what if a regulation eliminates all economic value or only partially reduces the economic value of the land; has a taking occurred in either circumstance? One famous test developed by the Court to answer these questions states that "while property may be regulated to a certain extent, if regulation goes too far it will be recognized as a taking" (*Pennsylvania Coal Co. v. Mahon* [1922]). A taking is automatically invalid if it is not "for public use." But what constitutes "for public use"? In a case in which the long-owned private homes of relatively poor people were taken by the state and turned over to a private developer, the Court found the taking was "for public use" (*Kelo v. City of New London* [2005]). Relying on the "test" whether the taking served a "public purpose," the Court concluded that the taking in this case for economic development was a public purpose. (Of course, the losing plaintiffs in the case had now to be provided "just compensation.")

## Cases Involving Individual Rights

The Supreme Court's individual rights opinions fairly bristle with myriad tests and standards of review. For example, the Court has said that a search without a warrant does not violate an individual's Fourth Amendment protection against unreasonable searches and seizures if the area searched is not one with regard to which (1) the person exhibited an actual expectation of privacy, and (2) that expectation was one that society was prepared to recognize as reasonable. Relying on this test, the Court said that the police may conduct warrantless searches of garbage bags left on the public sidewalk (*California v. Greenwood* [1988]). In another example, the Court has said it will determine whether a punishment violates the prohibition against "cruel and unusual punishments" by taking into account (1) the gravity of the offense and the harshness of the penalty, (2) the sentences imposed on other criminals in the same jurisdiction, and (3) the sentences imposed for commission of the same crime in other jurisdictions (*Solem v. Helm* [1983]).

The Court's free speech opinions rely on different tests depending on the free speech problem involved. I shall take note of only three. The Court has ruled that the right of free speech does not extend to the selling of obscenity. According to the famous (infamous?) definition of obscenity developed by the Court, to decide whether a publication is obscene a court must look at "(a) whether 'the average person, applying contemporary community standards' would find the work, taken as a whole, appeals to the prurient interest, (b) whether the work depicts or describes, in a patently offensive way, sexual conduct specifically defined by the applicable state law, and (c) whether the work, taken as a whole, lacks serious literary, artistic, political, or scientific value" (*Miller v. California* [1973]).

Regarding the regulation of "commercial speech" (e.g., an advertisement for a product), the Court has written that commercial speech that concerns an unlawful activity or is misleading is not protected by the First Amendment. But if the speech is about a lawful activity and is not misleading, then state regulation is permissible only if the regulation meets a three-part test: (1) the government interest in regulating the speech must be substantial; (2) the regulation must directly advance the governmental interest; and (3) the regulation must be no more extensive (no tougher) than is necessary to serve the interest (*Central Hudson Gas v. Public Service Commission* [1980]). In subsequent cases the Court interpreted test 3 to mean that government must use means that are narrowly tailored to achieve the desired objective. Government is not, however, required to use the least restrictive means (*Board of Trustees of State University of New York v. Fox* [1989]).

Finally, in deciding cases in which, for example, a person has been charged with breach of the peace by giving a speech, the test states that government may prohibit advocacy only when "such advocacy is directed to inciting or producing imminent lawless action and is likely to incite or produce such action" (*Brandenburg v. Ohio* [1969]).

In opinions involving the regulation of business and cases involving the right to "privacy," the Supreme Court uses yet a different set of tests or standards of review. (Lawyers and legal scholars call both these kinds of cases "substantive due process" cases.) These cases involve challenges based on the "due process" clause of the Fourteenth Amendment and involve rights and values that are not expressly mentioned in the clause, but that the Court has seen fit to protect (e.g., privacy and the right to use contraceptives). The two tests the Court relies on in this area are the "rational basis test" (most frequently used in opinions dealing with economic and business regulation) and the "strict scrutiny test" (used in privacy and other lifestyle cases).

The rational basis test as it operates today imposes on the person challenging government's law, regulation, or policy the burden of persuading the Court of either of two points: (1) that the law or policy does not serve a "legitimate" purpose, or (2) that the law or policy is a means that is "not rationally related" to that purpose. (Because the burden of persuading the Court of the unconstitutionality of the law is on the challenger, it is said that the law comes to the Court with a presumption of its being constitutional. In order to win, the challenger must rebut this presumption.) Thus, an opinion justifying striking down a law on the basis of this test will conclude either that government's purpose was illegitimate or that the means chosen to seek the purpose were not rationally related to the end, or both. I hasten to add that if the Court uses this standard of review, it is in fact very unlikely that the government will lose the case and the challenger win. Almost without fail, when this test is used the law will be found to be constitutionally permissible. In other words, this test is a "lenient" test, and when the Court uses it, the Court defers to the legislature's judgment. A Court that behaves in this way is also said to be acting with "restraint."

The Court's opinions dealing with "privacy"—use of contraception, abortions, the right to marry—employ a "strict scrutiny" test. When the Court uses this test, it says that it is the government that must convince the Court both that (1) its policy serves a purpose that is not just legitimate but also compelling, and (2) the means are "necessary" for the achievement of that purpose. Now it is said that the law that comes before the Court is presumed to be unconstitutional. If the law is to survive and not be struck down, government must persuade the Court of the two points in the test.

If this is the test used in the opinion, it is unlikely that the Court will uphold the law. This is a "tough" test; hence its name. To use the test suggests that the Court is looking very closely at the law and the justification offered for invading the constitutional right; not many justifications will be accepted as sufficiently strong. A Court using this test is a more "activist" Court.

With these two tests available—the rational basis and the strict scrutiny tests—how does the Court explain its choice of one or the other? I now come to the Court's need to develop a test to choose a test. Roughly speaking, the Court has said it will use the strict scrutiny test when the individual right involved in the dispute is a "fundamental" right, that is, an especially important right; if the right is a mere ordinary constitutional right, then the Court will use the rational basis test. Thus some constitutional rights have been designated as fundamental (e.g., the right to privacy, the right to use contraception, the right to an abortion, the right to marry). If the opinion writer classifies the right as fundamental, then the opinion goes on to say that its infringement will be assumed to be unconstitutional and the government must persuade the Court not to strike down the law. In other words, the government must show that the strict scrutiny test is satisfied. But if the opinion writer does not classify the right as fundamental (e.g., the right to run a business, or the right to engage in homosexual sodomy), then the opinion moves on to use the rational basis test. Now it is the person challenging the government's policy who must persuade the Court of the failure of the law to satisfy the rational basis test.

This discussion hardly exhausts the tests involved in individual rights cases. Other tests deal with such topics as the right to free exercise of religion, impairment of contracts, waiver of one's right to have an attorney present when being questioned by the police, right to a hearing before being dismissed from government employment (procedural due process), right not to be subjected to ex post facto lawmaking and bills of attainder.

## Equal Protection

Speaking roughly, the Court tends to use a different test or standard of review in connection with different kinds of equal protection cases. That is to say, the Court's opinions can be classified into three groups:

### Group 1

- Cases in which a racial criterion is used to the disadvantage of a racial minority
- Cases in which a racial criterion is used as part of an affirmative action plan

- Cases in which the difference in treatment affects a fundamental right/interest and may also have an impact on the poor
- Cases in which the criterion is phrased in terms of illegitimacy or citizenship[1]

The cases that fall into the first group are decided by the Court using the strict scrutiny test. When this test is used, the government's policy is presumed unconstitutional unless the government can satisfy its burden of persuasion. The government must prove that the classification used serves a compelling purpose and that the classification was necessary to realize that purpose. This is the toughest of the tests and when it is used the conclusion is almost invariably that the law is unconstitutional. (A plurality of the Court has said that the Constitution is color-blind, hence any racial criterion is unconstitutional unless it serves one or two special goals—even then, the use of the criterion must meet the strict scrutiny test. See Chapter 9.)

*Group 2*

- Cases in which a gender criterion is used to the disadvantage of women or men
- Cases in which a gender criterion is used as part of an affirmative effort to help women

The opinions in group 2 use what is called the middle-level test. The government must persuade the Court that (1) its policy based on gender serves an "important" purpose, and (2) the criterion used and the difference in treatment are "substantially related" to the purpose. When this test is used, the government's policy is presumed unconstitutional unless the government can satisfy its burden of persuasion, which is now lighter than under the previous test. When this test is used there is a greater likelihood that the law will be found to be permissible than when the strict scrutiny test is used.

*Group 3*

- All other cases, such as those involving the regulation of business, or the use of age as a criterion. In rough terms, the opinions in group 1 use an equal protection version of the strict scrutiny test.
- As with the other strict scrutiny test, the burden of persuasion is on the government. For the law to be upheld government must convince the Court that (1) its policy serves a "compelling" purpose, and (2) the criterion used, the classification scheme, and the differences in treatment are "necessary" to serve that purpose.

The group 3 opinions use the equal protection version of a rational basis test. The person challenging the law must convince the Court either that (1) the purpose

---

[1] One might wonder why cases that involve differences of treatment based on gender or handicap are not included in this group of cases. This is an important question that has been the subject of dispute among the justices.

of the law is not legitimate, or that (2) the criterion and classification scheme are not "rationally related" to the purpose. The use of this test means government's policy is presumed to be constitutional unless the complaining party can convince the Court otherwise. When this test is used there is virtually no probability that the law will be found to be unconstitutional.

These three tests mark different degrees of judicial activism. When the toughest test is used the Court will write an opinion that involves a searching examination of the law, whereas when the weakest test is used the opinion will reflect a willingness to accept legislation that may have many flaws in it.

## Establishment and Free Exercise Tests

Recall from Chapter 2 that the Supreme Court has struck a delicate balance between the establishment and free exercise clauses of the First Amendment. The Court has sought to strike this balance using certain tests. The derivation of the tests used in conjunction with the "establishment clause" opinions has been the subject of much controversy both on and off the Court. The text, the framers' intent, the theory and principles of the First Amendment, tradition, contemporary values, precedent, and practical considerations have all figured into the debate over the development, interpretation, and application of the tests. It is these debates that characterize many of the recent majority and dissenting opinions.

One set of tests in dispute in connection with the establishment clause are the so-called Lemon tests (the opinion in which they appeared was *Lemon v. Kurtzman* [1971]). To survive a challenge based on the establishment clause, (1) the policy must have a secular purpose; (2) its primary effect must be one that neither advances nor inhibits religion; and (3) the law must not foster excessive governmental entanglement with religion. Today the entanglement test has been collapsed into the second, primary effect test, as but one aspect of the inquiry into the primary effect of the policy (*Agostini v. Felton* [1997]).

Although the Court has stayed with the first and second test, over the years the interpretation, especially of the second test, has evolved. Thus in reading these establishment clause opinions one has to be sensitive to the particular version of the test being used in the case. Different justices use different versions of this same test, reflective of deep disagreements over the meaning of the establishment clause. Justice Souter believes the clause establishes a principle of "no aid" to religion. But he recognizes that "there is no pure aid to religion and no purely secular welfare benefit"; hence the Court's task is to realistically assess the effect of a particular form of aid (*Mitchell v. Helms* [2000]). To that end, he says the Court needs to look at a number of factors: the evenhandedness of the aid, the type of aid recipient, the direct- or indirectness of the distribution, the content of the aid, its potential divertibility to religious purposes, the degree the aid supplants religious school expenses, and the substantiality of the aid. This version of the test places sharp limits on government aid.

Other justices who reject the "no aid" principle offer a different interpretation of the test. Justice Thomas interprets the second test to mean that aid is permissible if it does not result in governmental indoctrination, does not define its recipients by reference to religion, or does not create excessive entanglement. As a practical matter Justice Thomas finds these elements are satisfied when the aid is offered on a neutral basis to both public and private schools (religious and nonreligious), and is secular in content (e.g., computer equipment). If it meets this test, even if the aid is diverted to religious purposes, the aid is permissible.

Justice O'Connor staked out a position between Justices Souter and Thomas. Although she accepts Justice Thomas's formulation of the second test, she does not accept the view that the test is automatically satisfied if aid is offered on a neutral basis. She would look into additional factors such as whether in fact the aid was diverted for religious purposes; thus she rejects Justice Souter's concern with the mere potential for diversion and rejects Justice Thomas's position that aid provided on a neutral basis may be diverted to religious purposes.

Further complicating establishment clause litigation is the fact that the justices have introduced yet other tests to flesh out and accompany the Lemon tests. For example, some justices have embraced the endorsement test as a way of clarifying and making Lemon tests more specific. (This test requires the Court to determine whether government intends to convey a message of endorsement or disapproval of religion.) But as it turns out, this effort to achieve greater precision has led to further disputes regarding the endorsement test itself—when it should be used and its meaning (*Capital Square Review and Advisory Board v. Pinette* [1995]).

The justices have also divided over the use of the Lemon tests to decide cases regarding public praying and displays of religious materials. In a case dealing with display of the Ten Commandments inside a courthouse, the majority relied heavily on the first Lemon test—the purpose test that it understood to mean that the "government may not favor one religion over another, or religion over irreligion . . ." (*McCreary v. ACLU* [2005]). The dissent agreed this was a "valid principle where public aid or assistance to religion is concerned, . . . but it necessarily applies in a more limited sense to public acknowledgment of the Creator." And Justice Thomas, concurring in a companion case, said the Court should abandon the Lemon tests; he would find an establishment clause violation only if the state imposed mandatory observance or mandatory payment of taxes for religion (*Van Orden v. Perry* [2005]).

Turmoil, though not quite as extensive, has also marked the use of tests in connection with the free exercise clause. Free exercise cases generally involve a state law or policy that does not discriminate on the basis of religion but has an especially acute impact on a religious person or group. The affected person or group now asks to be exempted from the law's coverage. For example, the state's policy may say that no one may collect unemployment compensation who voluntarily leaves a job. Now the question arises whether this policy may be constitutionally applied to a person who leaves a job in a munitions factory because of religious objections to war. Must this person, in the name of the free exercise of religion, be excused from the state's policy and be allowed to collect unemployment compensation?

Between roughly 1963 and 1990 the Supreme Court used the following approach to resolve these kinds of cases. Take, for example, *Thomas v. Review Board of Indiana Employment Security* (1980). The burden was first placed on the religious objector to establish (1) that his or her claim for an exemption was based on a religious belief and not on a mere philosophical or other nonreligious belief; (2) that the religious claim was sincerely held; and (3) that continued enforcement of the policy would have a real impact on his or her free exercise of religion. The Court said that only if it were convinced of these points would it listen to what the government must establish. If the religious objectors were convincing, the burden of persuasion would switch to the government, which would have to meet the terms of a strict scrutiny test in order to avoid the granting of an exemption. In 1990 the Court adopted a new approach. Thus today in most free exercise cases the Court asks whether the law was adopted with the intent of burdening freedom of religion or whether this burden was merely an incidental effect of a generally applicable and otherwise valid provision. Religious objectors must comply with valid and neutral laws of general applicability even if the burden on the free exercise of religion is severe (*Employment Division, Department of Human Resources v. Smith* [1990]).

## TESTS AND THE ILLUSION OF CERTAINTY

Although tests are useful both in the process of discovery and in the process of justification, they are not easy to use—their use is not like working with an algorithm. The use of tests in an opinion may create the illusion that the basis of the decision has been spelled out, but a closer look may reveal that the Court has not in fact really informed us of the basis of its decision. For example, in a decision upholding a school's policy of random drug testing of all pupils engaged in competitive extracurricular activities, including the school choir, the majority opinion used a balancing test that took into account factors such as the degree of the drug problem the school faced, the privacy expectations of the students, the invasiveness of the drug test, and so forth (*Board of Education of Independent School District No. 92 of Pottawatomie County v. Earls* [2002]). The opinion describes each factor on the two sides of the metaphorical scale and then announces the result without providing a true calculation of why the factors on the side favoring the school outweighed the factors on the other side favoring the student plaintiffs.

The difficulty of working with tests is evidenced by frequent complaints from dissenting justices that the majority misused a particular test. For example, many of the tests noted above call for an examination of the relationship of the means to the purpose. Thus various tests call for a "rational relationship"; a means that does not sweep too broadly; a means that is substantially related to the end; a restriction that is no greater than necessary; a means that is "narrowly tailored"; a means that "directly advances" the purpose; or a means that is "necessary." You will note that the justices disagree over the application of these tests and that they offer little additional assistance in the opinions regarding how they used or how others should use these tests. An example of such a dispute arose in an affirmative action case in which the majority and the dissent disagreed over whether the way the Michigan University Law School pursued the goal of diversity was "necessary" (*Grutter v. Bollinger* [2003]). The same dispute arose in *Parents Involved in Community Schools v. Seattle School*

*District No.1* (2007) regarding the view of a race-based student assignment plan in public elementary and high schools. (See Chapter 9.)

As noted above, the equal protection cases that fall into group 1 use a test that requires the government to serve a "compelling state interest." The Court has never specified a definition regarding what constitutes a "compelling state interest." As a consequence, there was a sharp disagreement between the majority and dissent in the University of Michigan Law School case over whether the school's goal—student body diversity—was a "compelling state interest." Similarly, in the substantive due process area, the Court has not provided a precise definition of what constitutes a "fundamental right."   .

# Practice Pointers

1. An efficient way to become familiar with constitutional law is to learn the tests that the Court has developed to justify decisions.
2. To further your understanding, you need to develop an understanding of the function and purpose of such tests. Tests help the Court distinguish when a mere infringement of a right amounts to a constitutional violation, that is, when an infringement is permissible and when it is not. And the strict scrutiny test is used when government has used a racial classification scheme in a law or policy. In such a case, strict scrutiny is employed to distinguish between legitimate and illegitimate uses of a racial classification.
3. When you make a constitutional argument based on precedent, you will need to fully understand what test was relied upon in the precedent, and, in addition, how that test was applied (e.g., which party had been given the burden of proof and what that burden was).
4. In reading precedent, note any disputes among the justices regarding the appropriate test to be used, and note any disputes regarding the application of the test.
5. When reading opinions regarding the jurisdiction of the federal versus state government, pay attention to the terminology used by the Court and how the Court classifies the particular government activity being challenged.
6. Pay attention to the similar (but not identical) tests used in conjunction with "substantive due process" cases and equal protection cases. Understanding the differences between these similar sets of tests will give you a firm grasp of the difference between substantive due process and equal protection cases.
7. Note that in an "establishment clause" challenge, the plaintiff seeks to have the impugned law or policy struck down as a whole. In a "free exercise" challenge, the plaintiff may either be seeking to have the law struck down because it arguably was adopted with the intent of suppressing a religion, or seeking to obtain an exemption from the law or policy that is having an incidental but significant negative impact on the free exercise of religion.

# Chapter 6

# Precedent

Precedent is an important building material for the writing of judicial opinions and almost any other legal argument. Precedent is itself embodied in a legal opinion; thus legal opinions are used to create new legal opinions. A justice, as well as any person writing a legal argument, seems unavoidably to encounter what appears to be a vicious circle—to write an opinion one needs to understand a prior opinion, but to understand a prior opinion one needs to know how to write an opinion. There is a way out of the circle, which this chapter provides by examining the concept of a precedent's *ratio decidendi*.

The interpretation of precedent by formulating its *ratio decidendi* is both a skill and an art, in which the justices are very adept. This chapter will examine the basic approach the justices use in developing the *ratio decidendi* of a precedent, as well as discuss the principle of **stare decisis**—the principle that guides the justices in deciding whether to follow or overrule a precedent.

## A TERMINOLOGICAL INTERLUDE

There are a number of terms that frequently occur in constitutional law: (1) principles; (2) doctrines; (3) tests or standards of review; (4) rules; (5) the holding or the *ratio decidendi*; and (6) policy. Let's begin with the term "policy." Policy making may be viewed as the process by which goals and the means to the goals are simultaneously considered and decided upon. Those who engage in policy making may (are expected to?) engage in compromise and bargaining with a view to reaching mutually agreed-upon solutions. In constitutional parlance, policy is something that only the legislature produces. Courts, it is frequently said, should not engage in policy making. Courts, in theory, should only find, interpret, and apply the law.

The terms "principles," "doctrines," "rules," "tests," and "standards of review" are frequently used interchangeably. For example, the following formulation can be referred to as a principle, rule, doctrine, or test: Pursuant to its authority to regulate interstate commerce, Congress may regulate labor relations even at a "local" manufacturing plant, when it is part of an interstate manufacturing and sales company, because labor disruption at such a plant has "a most serious effect upon interstate commerce" (*National Labor Relations Board v. Jones & Laughlin Steel Corp.* [1937]).

This might also be termed the "holding" or the *ratio decidendi* of *Jones & Laughlin*. This rule also provides a "test" for deciding future cases, namely, a regulation is permissible under the commerce clause if it regulates an activity that has a "substantial economic effect" upon interstate commerce.

But while terms such as "rule" and "principle" are often used interchangeably, they can also be used with different meanings and implications. For example, the term "principle" sometimes means something very fundamental and enduring. Principles, in the grand sense of the word, tend to be cast in general value-laden terms that require further elaboration and interpretation. For example, it might be said that the principle embodied in the equal protection clause of the Fourteenth Amendment is that all people should be treated with equal dignity and respect. But we also say that the Constitution embodies other "principles" that are less obviously moral statements (e.g., the principle of separation of powers).

Chapter 5 spoke of "tests" or "standards of review." Recall that these are judicially created criteria that the Court says a governmental policy must satisfy in order to be constitutional. For example, a policy that treats different businesses differently is constitutional if "the classification is rationally related to a legitimate purpose." (This is the rational basis test used in equal protection cases.) Tests derive from or are based upon principles, which presumably are more fundamental and enduring.

"Rules" also derive from fundamental principles, and rules are typically formulated in more precise or narrow language than fundamental principles. For example, based in part on the principle of separation of powers, the Supreme Court has developed certain rules (or doctrines) that it uses to guide its decisions regarding whether to hear a case. One is the rule that the Court will not render advisory opinions on questions submitted to it by a president seeking legal advice.

The *ratio decidendi* of an opinion is (1) the **material** facts of the case, plus (2) the conclusion whether or not the government's policy is constitutional. (The *ratio decidendi* can also be called the holding.) For example, in *Zobel v. Williams* (1982), Alaska distributed its surplus tax revenues, derived from the taxation of its booming oil industry, to state residents in the form of a dividend that varied from resident to resident depending upon the length of time the resident had lived in Alaska after it had become a state. The Court concluded that this policy violated the equal protection clause of the Fourteenth Amendment. Thus the *ratio decidendi* in the case can be stated as follows: It is a violation of the equal protection clause for a state to redistribute surplus tax revenues to residents according to a formula that allocates the revenues proportionately in terms of the length of time the resident was in the state after it became a state. Note that the **material** facts of the case may include both the **adjudicated** facts and the **background** facts relied upon by the Court. (See Chapter 1.)

The holding, *ratio decidendi*, rules, and principles of these opinions are not something to be "discovered," but something that is creatively formulated through an interpretation of the opinion. Take, for example, the formulation of the holding. As indicated, the formulation of the *ratio decidendi* requires a determination as to what are the "material" facts of the case. One says a fact was "material" to the decision if one is prepared to show that it was "necessary" or "sufficient" to the conclusion. If one is prepared to show that the fact had a "causal" effect on the conclusion regarding constitutionality or unconstitutionality, then one is prepared to claim that fact was "material."

Back to *Zobel*. In reaching its decision the Court rejected Alaska's argument that the length of residency was a measure of a resident's contribution to the state, and that the state could apportion the surplus funds in terms of a resident's contributions to the state. In other words, the Court also "held" (ruled, or concluded) that rewarding citizens differentially for undefined past contributions of various kinds to the state is not a "legitimate state purpose." Let me now suggest a yet more generalized version of the *ratio decidendi*: It is a violation of the equal protection clause of the Fourteenth Amendment for a state to treat its bona fide law-abiding residents differently based solely on an assessment as to who is a more worthy citizen.

To summarize, the terms "principle," "holding," "rule," "test," and "*ratio decidendi*" are sometimes used interchangeably. Second, there are occasions when these words do not mean precisely the same thing. For example, as noted, the holding or *ratio decidendi* is often used in its technical meaning, namely, it is a rulelike statement formulated by combining (1) the material facts of the case with (2) the decision on whether the government's policy was constitutional or not.

Third, in justifying the "holding" or *ratio decidendi*, the Court will announce "principles," "rules," "tests," or "standards of review" that it then uses in justifying its *ratio decidendi*. Hence, it is often said that the opinion "held" (ruled, or concluded) that in the future all problems of type X will be analyzed in terms of test H. These principles, rules, tests, and standards of review also carry precedential weight and are used by future courts in the justification of decisions they reach. These principles, rules, tests, and standards of review can in turn be used as part of a strategy of deduction; they may themselves be applied by further deduction, or may require balancing. In short, precedent can be used directly in an analogical argument, but in addition there are materials to be found in precedents that can be used in conjunction with deduction and balancing. Precedent has multiple uses.

The Court frequently uses the *ratio decidendi* from a precedent in conjunction with an argument based on **analogy**. For example, using *Zobel* as an analogy, one could argue that it would be unconstitutional for a state to apportion the size of a *tax exemption* in terms of the length of time a person resided in the state. Similarly, again by analogy, it arguably would be unconstitutional to give to longtime residents the opportunity to cast a vote worth five times the vote cast by a new arrival. Of course, one can always question whether the analogy is appropriate, and one might even ask whether these two conclusions are sound.

# THE ENGLISH DOCTRINE OF PRECEDENT

## The *Ratio Decidendi, Obiter Dictum*, and Distinguishing Cases

The doctrine of precedent that influences American law has its origin in English common law. English common law courts express the justifications for their decisions in terms of reliance upon previous decisions. English courts do this in the name of the doctrine of precedent, which says that two cases must be decided the same way if their "material" facts are the same. The reasons for this doctrine are several: It is only fair that like cases should be decided alike; it is rational to decide like cases alike; and adhering to precedent helps to assure stability in the law, stability that allows people to make plans.

Here is a simple example of the doctrine of precedent in operation. In what we shall call case B, the defendant threatened to bring criminal charges against the plaintiff, a foreign servant girl, if she did not provide certain information (*Janvier v. Sweeney* [1919]). The defendant's threat was an empty lie because he knew that any charges he might bring against the girl were baseless. Nevertheless, the girl became ill from the distress caused her by the threat. The girl became the plaintiff in a suit by bringing a suit against the defendant. The court's opinion can be summed up in a syllogism that goes roughly as follows:

> *Legal Premise:* Where the defendant has willfully told the plaintiff a lie that is likely to so frighten the plaintiff as to cause the plaintiff physical distress, the defendant is liable. (Premise based on precedent in prior case A.)
>
> *Factual Premise:* The defendant in this case told the plaintiff a lie that was likely to, and in fact did, so frighten the plaintiff as to cause the plaintiff physical distress (based on facts determined at the trial).
>
> *Conclusion:* The defendant is liable.

Our concern is how the judge in case B went about developing his argument, and more specifically, how he went about establishing the legal premise that began his justification. Before we turn to the examination of the syllogism, it is useful to note that the syllogism is the preeminant example of "deductive" reasoning, which will be examined in more detail in Chapter 7. Notice that the syllogism takes the following general form:

> *Legal Premise:* If A, then B, that is, if the defendant did X, then defendant is liable.
>
> *Factual Premise:* It is the case that A is true, that is, the defendant did X.
>
> *Conclusion:* Therefore B, that is, the defendant is liable.

We now need to ask where the judge obtained the first premise. (The second premise was established by the trial in the trial court.)

*Step 1.*    First, judge B undertook a search for relevant precedent—precedent with material facts similar to the case before him. This search brought him to *Wilkinson v. Downton* (1897). The defendant in *Wilkinson*, as a practical joke, told the plaintiff that her husband had been seriously injured in an accident and had been sent with two broken legs to the Elms hospital at Leytonstone. This false statement so shocked the plaintiff that it produced vomiting, other serious physical consequences, and weeks of suffering. Previous to this "joke" she had not been in ill health, nor had she ever exhibited any predisposition to nervous shock. The judge in *Wilkinson* (case A) noted that the defendant willfully did an act calculated to cause physical harm to the plaintiff, and that this was a proper legal basis on which to sue as there was no justification for the lie.

*Step 2.*    Judge B recognized that the facts of case A were similar to, but not identical with, the facts of the case with the foreign servant girl. Thus his second step was to decide whether the facts were similar enough in important respects that case A should be treated as precedent for case B, or whether case A was **distinguishable** from case B. In fact he concluded that case A was *analogous* to case B; thus he decided not to distinguish case A, and used it to justify his decision in case B. (The judge in case B could have **distinguished** case A from B, and written an opinion saying prosecutors should be allowed to use threats of prosecution as a means of gathering information.)[1]

*Step 3.*    The third step was to determine the *ratio decidendi* of the decision in case A. We know already that judge B interpreted the decision in case A to stand for the *ratio decidendi* stated above as the legal premise of the syllogism (let us call it version 1). But how did judge B decide that this legal principle was the *ratio decidendi* of case A? The answer is that it took an act of *interpretation* to settle upon this particular version of the *ratio decidendi*. Here is another possible version of the *ratio decidendi* of case A.

> Where the defendant has willfully lied to the plaintiff by saying that a close family member has suffered a grievous injury, and this lie causes such distress that the plaintiff suffers severe physical distress for a period of weeks, the defendant is liable. (version 2)

This is a *narrower* version of the *ratio decidendi* because this rule would only cover cases in which the deliberate lie was about the well-being of a family member and the effect of the lie showed up as physical symptoms. If this were the "holding" of case A, then the court in case B would have a harder time using the precedent to justify a decision in favor of the servant girl.

But, as we saw, judge B chose to interpret case A as establishing a more abstract and general *ratio decidendi*. Yet how did judge B conclude that the more general *ratio decidendi* was the better interpretation? And why did judge B not interpret case A to stand for an even more abstract or general rule, namely, that any false statement told to anybody that causes any degree of mental distress is a basis for liability (version 3)?

In English practice, interpreting a case and choosing among possible versions of the *ratio decidendi* are guided by an important rule: "Courts do not accord to their predecessors an unlimited power of laying down wide rules."[2] Based on this principle, a British judge would reject version 3 as an unnecessarily broad description of the holding of case A.

As for version 2, though it is a plausible candidate, judge B might conclude that the first version best fits what he understands precedent A to have said; that is to say,

---

[1] Suppose, however, that the only precedent the judge in case B could find was in cases in which the plaintiff deliberately inflicted physical harm by hitting the defendant. These cases, involving a "battery," are *distinguishable*. Hence, finding no case like case B, the judge would have two choices: He could conclude that the plaintiff could win her suit as there is no binding rule that he could use to write a justification in support of the plaintiff, or he could "extend" the battery cases, using them to justify a decision that essentially made "new law."

[2] Glanville Williams, *Learning the Law*, 11th ed. (London: Stevens and Sons, 1982), p. 75.

the judge might conclude that, according to precedent A, even lies *not* told about family members were harmful and a basis for suit.

Before moving on to step 4, I would like to interject a comment about the concept of *obiter dictum*, or just plain **dictum**. Dictum takes several forms. It can be an "aside," a "remark by the way," on a point of law not necessarily involved in the case before the court. For example, judge A noted that the plaintiff also sued the defendant for "deceit" as well as for intentionally inflicting emotional harm. To prove deceit the law requires that the plaintiff establish that the defendant lied, that the defendant intended the plaintiff to act on the lie, that the plaintiff relied on the lie, and that in so acting the plaintiff was injured. But judge A noted that the injury to the plaintiff did not arise because she "acted" on the basis of what the defendant said. Her shock and physical distress were simply a spontaneous reaction to the lie. Thus, judge A hinted, without actually deciding, that a suit for deceit would fail. But he did note that the plaintiff had another basis upon which to collect damages for the harm done, namely, her claim of infliction of emotional suffering. Accordingly, judge A's comments on the claim for "deceit" were dictum, a statement about the law unnecessary to the actual decision in case A.

One also finds dictum in an opinion when a judge makes what appears to be a legal ruling but his comments are based on hypothetical facts, facts not proven in the case. For example, suppose that judge B had said that he would have ruled differently if the defendant had lied to the plaintiff to force her to provide information necessary to protect the national security. This "exception" to liability for deliberately causing emotional distress would not be law, would not be binding on future courts, because it was not an issue argued before the court and the pronouncement of such an exception would have been unnecessary to the actual decision before the court in case B.

Finally, we can identify as dictum a holding or rule that is phrased by the judge in a manner that is unnecessarily broad for the purposes of the case he or she is deciding. Version 3 of the holding of the case discussed above, for example, covers problems and issues not actually before the court in case A; hence this version is broader than necessary to describe the case. Accordingly, a judge who announced this as the holding of his or her decision could be said to have announced mere dictum.

*Step 4.* The last step judge B took in writing the opinion was to **apply** the *ratio decidendi* of case A to the facts of case B. Thus judge B concluded that the lie told to the foreign servant girl was the sort of lie likely to cause emotional distress, and the distress felt by the foreign servant girl was of a magnitude sufficient to allow recovery of damages. As I indicated above, judge B did make such findings of "fact," as reflected in the second, or factual, premise of the syllogism.

## THE THEORY OF THE DOCTRINE OF PRECEDENT

The doctrine of precedent requires that a judge determine the *ratio decidendi*. By imposing this requirement on future courts the doctrine assumes that there really is a *ratio decidendi* to be "discovered." Stated differently, the doctrine of precedent presupposes that the legal meaning of a prior opinion is not simply a rule subjectively read into the precedent by the judge in case B. That is, the doctrine assumes that judge B is not wholly free to imaginatively develop any version of a *ratio decidendi* he may want.

The doctrine of precedent also assumes that future courts are bound by the *ratio decidendi*. That is, when the precedent is relevant, these future judges must follow the precedent, even if they personally do not like the decision to which they are driven. Regardless of personal ideology, as noted earlier, like cases, as a matter of fairness and rationality, should be treated alike.

Additional considerations other than fairness and rationality also support adherence to the doctrine. Besides the fact, as noted earlier, that the doctrine of precedent preserves the predictability and stability of the law, it also improves the efficiency and speed of judicial decision making, as it is easier and faster to reach decisions in cases based on preexisting rules than to invent new rules each time a dispute comes to court.

One should now be able to predict some effects of the doctrine of precedent. The doctrine of precedent tends to make the law change slowly, a step at a time, incrementally. It limits sudden changes of direction or new doctrines. And it points to a set of special criteria for the selection of judges. That is, judges should be people who can be dispassionate and fair in interpreting and applying precedent. Under this system a judge's personal ideology becomes a matter of lesser importance than in a system in which judges are expected to "make" law. Finally, one would expect to find in the opinions of the judges operating under this system extensive and careful analysis of precedent.

# THE DOCTRINE OF PRECEDENT (*STARE DECISIS*) IN THE SUPREME COURT

## The Legal Status of the Doctrine of Precedent

Let us begin with an obvious, but important, point. Because the Supreme Court is the *supreme* court, there is no higher court whose precedents it must follow. This also means that a nineteenth-century Supreme Court has no greater legal authority than a twenty-first-century Court merely because it sat earlier in history.

Now let us turn to a more fundamental observation. The basic starting point of all constitutional justifications must be the Constitution itself. Thus, to paraphrase Chief Justice Marshall's opinion in *Marbury v. Madison* (1803):

> It is a proposition too plain to be contested that either the Constitution controls any Supreme Court act repugnant to it, or the Court may alter the Constitution by an ordinary judicial opinion. Between these alternatives there is no middle ground. But certainly those who framed the Constitution contemplated that as the fundamental law of the nation, an opinion of the Court repugnant to the Constitution is void.

Given these assumptions, it follows, as night does the day, that the Supreme Court cannot and should not be bound to follow a precedent that it has itself concluded is not a sound interpretation of the Constitution. Stated differently, the justices are in a sense duty bound to *overrule* their own precedent if they conclude upon further reflection that a decision was wrong. Justice Brennan wrote, "[W]hen a Justice perceives an interpretation of the text to have departed so far from its essential meaning, that Justice is bound, by a larger constitutional duty to the community, to expose the departure and point toward a different path.[3] Then there is this: "[I]n cases involving the Federal Constitution, where correction through legislative action is practically impossible, this Court has often overruled its earlier decisions. The Court bows to the lessons of experience and the force of better reasoning, recognizing that the process of trial and error, so fruitful in the physical sciences, is appropriate also in the judicial function" (*United States v. Scott* [1978], quoting from *Burnet v. Coronado Oil & Gas Co.* [1932] [Brandeis, J., dissenting]). Similarly, the Court has written that "in constitutional questions, where correction depends upon amendment and not upon legislative action, this Court throughout its history has freely exercised its power to reexamine the basis of its constitutional decisions" (*Smith v. Allwright* [1944]), and:

> *Stare decisis* is a cornerstone of our legal system, but it has less power in constitutional cases, where, save for constitutional amendments, this Court is the only body able to make needed changes. (*Webster v. Reproductive Health Services* [1989])[4]

Yet the Court finds itself on the horns of a dilemma. To overrule precedent undermines the principles behind the doctrine of precedent: the principle of fairness, predictability, and stability in the law, and the rule of law itself. The Court acknowledged this problem when it wrote, "[A]rguments continue to be made, in these cases as well, that we erred in interpreting the Constitution. Nonetheless, the doctrine of *stare decisis*, while perhaps never entirely persuasive on a constitutional question, is a doctrine that demands respect in a society governed by the rule of law. We respect it today and reaffirm *Roe v. Wade* [1973]" (*City of Akron v. Akron Center for Reproductive Health, Inc.* [1983]). In a similar vein Justice Marshall wrote:

> [T]oday's decision is supported, though not compelled, by the important doctrine of *stare decisis*, the means by which to ensure that the law will not merely change erratically, but will develop in a principled and intelligent fashion. That doctrine permits society to presume that bedrock principles are founded in the law rather than in the proclivities of individuals, thereby contributes to the integrity of our constitutional system of government, both in appearance and in fact. . . . [E]very successful

---

[3] William J. Brennan Jr. "The Constitution of the United States: Contemporary Ratification, 27 *S. Tex. L. Rev.* 433 (1986): 444.

[4] The Court's attitude toward the doctrine of *stare decisis* is different regarding decisions interpreting a federal statute. The Court has written, "The burden borne by the party advocating the abandonment of an established precedent is greater where the Court is asked to overrule a point of statutory construction. Considerations of *stare decisis* have special force in the area of statutory interpretation, for here, unlike in the context of constitutional interpretation, the legislative power is implicated, and Congress remains free to alter what we have done" (*Patterson v. McLean Credit Union* [1989]). See also *Booth v. Maryland* (1987) and *Smith v. Allwright* (1944).

proponent of overruling precedent has borne the heavy burden of persuading the Court that changes in society or in the law dictate that the values served by *stare decisis* yield in favor of a great objective. [Here] we have been offered no reason to believe that any such metamorphosis has rendered the [rule] of reversal outdated, ill-founded, unworkable, or otherwise legitimately vulnerable to serious reconsideration. (*Vasquez v. Hillery* [1986])

The justices also consider overruling precedent when the precedent has proved to be unworkable; when related principles of law have developed in a way to leave the original rule in the precedent but in reality render it a mere remnant of a doctrine that has already been abandoned; and when facts that were relied upon in the precedent have changed or come to be seen so differently that the original rule has lost its justification (*Planned Parenthood of Southeastern Pennsylvania v. Casey* [1992]).[5]

The Court is also constrained in overruling precedent by the understanding that it may work a special hardship when people have come to rely on the rule's continued application, such as when people in business plan and invest in a commercial venture on the assumption that the "rules of the game" will not change in the middle of the game (*Planned Parenthood of Southeastern Pennsylvania v. Casey* [1992]).

Some justices have also expressed a concern that overruling too frequently would undermine the legitimacy of the Court—"frequent overruling would overtax the country's belief in the Court's good faith. . . . There is a limit to the amount of error that can plausibly be imputed to prior courts." In refusing to overrule the Court's controversial abortion decision in the face of political pressure, these same justices wrote that "to overrule under fire in the absence of the most compelling reason to reexamine a watershed decision would subvert the Court's legitimacy beyond any serious question" (*Planned Parenthood of Southeastern Pennsylvania v. Casey* [1992]).

Nevertheless, criticism of the Court's first decision holding that a state may make it a crime to engage in homosexual sodomy was a factor in the decision of the Court to overrule that precedent (*Bowers v. Hardwick* [1986]; *Lawrence v. Texas* [2003]). It was not the only factor. In overruling *Bowers*, the majority in *Lawrence* said that the original decision misinterpreted the concept of liberty in the Fourteenth Amendment; misinterpreted the legal history regarding the making of sodomy a crime; that other precedent served to undermine *Bowers*; and that *Bowers* could be overruled because people had not come to rely upon it, that is, stability in doctrine was not necessary here.

Clearly the justices face a difficult choice in choosing between announcing a ruling the current majority thinks is correct versus preserving stability. The dilemma can be illustrated by considering the decision of the Court in *Brown v. Board of Education* (1954) to overrule its decision in *Plessy v. Ferguson* (1896). In *Plessy* the Court had upheld the policy of racial segregation as long as the separate facilities

---

[5] For example, in *Adarand Constructors, Inc., v. Pena* (1995) the Court specifically overruled a recent affirmative action decision, *Metro Broadcasting, Inc., v. FCC* (1990), on the basis that the decision represented a "surprising turn" and was inconsistent with its other affirmative action decisions.

98    CHAPTER 6 / PRECEDENT

and services were equal. Yet a half century later the Court came to the conclusion that the separate-but-equal doctrine was not consistent with the equal protection clause. But a vast social, political, and legal system with enormous political support had developed a reliance on the doctrine of separate but equal. The Court, of course, in this case proceeded to overrule *Plessy* despite strong countervailing considerations that pointed toward not disturbing the status quo.

## Overruling Precedent

Even people who are only casually familiar with the history of the Supreme Court are aware that the Court has famously overruled precedent. Perhaps the most frequently cited example is the Court's overturning of the doctrine of separate but equal. In fact the practice of explicitly overruling precedent occurs with some regularity. In 1932, Justice Brandeis noted 28 instances in which the Court had overruled or qualified constitutional decisions (*Burnet v. Coronado Oil & Gas Co.* [1932] [Brandeis, J., dissenting]). Professor Maltz writes:

> Even Justice Brandeis would have no doubt been surprised at the lack of respect among succeeding justices for the doctrine of *stare decisis*. In the twelve-year period from 1937 to 1949, for example, the Court overruled earlier constitutional decisions in twenty-one cases [footnotes omitted]—nearly as many as in the 140 years preceding *Coronado Oil & Gas*. By 1959, the number of instances in which the Court had reversals involving constitutional issues had grown to sixty; in the two decades which followed, the Court overruled constitutional cases on no less than forty-seven occasions. It seems fair to say that if a majority of the Warren or Burger Court has considered a case wrongly decided, no constitutional precedent—new or old—has been safe.[6]

The meandering course of constitutional doctrine was no more vividly on display than in *Chimel v. California* (1969), an opinion dealing with the proper scope of a search incident to a lawful arrest. The Court in *Chimel* concluded that an arresting officer constitutionally may search, without a warrant, the area within the arrestee's immediate control in order to remove weapons the arrestee might try to use, or to seize evidence he might try to conceal or destroy. In justifying this conclusion the Court reviewed the relevant precedent. Its review identified five previous changes of doctrine (its decision in *Chimel* represented a sixth change), and at one point the Court said about these changes that precedents "were thrown to the winds."

The cavalier attitude of one justice toward precedent can be illustrated with the opinions of Justice William Douglas. Justice Douglas wrote the majority opinion in *Skinner v. Oklahoma* (1942), which struck down an Oklahoma statute providing for compulsory sterilization after the third conviction for a felony involving moral turpitude, but excluding such felonies as embezzlement. His opinion contained a long

---

[6] Earl M. Maltz, "Some Thoughts on the Death of *Stare Decisis* in Constitutional Law," *Wisconsin Law Review* (1980): 467. In a more recent opinion Justice Rehnquist noted that, over the past 20 terms, the Court overruled in whole or part 33 of its decisions (*Payne v. Tennessee* [1991]).

passage that made the claim that procreation was one of the basic civil rights of man—a claim he made without citing a single precedent or any other source material. And in *Harper v. Virginia Board of Elections* (1966), Justice Douglas wrote the majority opinion striking down the poll tax, a small fee a voter had to pay before being allowed to vote. His opinion brushed past the two previous cases in which the Court had upheld the poll tax. He made no reference to the doctrine of precedent. Instead, after a cursory summary of a number of other opinions, he announced that the earlier poll tax cases were now overruled. His reason was simply stated: "Notions of what constitutes equal treatment for purposes of the Equal Protection clause do change."

In short, it is the rare justice who consistently takes an existing precedent as settled law and follows it despite the fact that it means he must adopt a conclusion with which he personally disagrees. Justice Scalia has written, "[I] would think it a violation of my oath to adhere to what I consider a plainly unjustified intrusion upon the democratic process in order that the Court might save face" (*Booth v. Maryland* [1987]).

There are several basic reasons why the justices do overrule precedent. Finely Peter Dunne, newspaper man and humorist, offered perhaps the most famous explanation: "No matter whether the Constitution follows the flag or not, the Supreme Court follows the election returns." This arguably too cynical view of the Court points to another more fundamental and plausible explanation. Presidents are often elected after a dramatic change in public opinion and culture, leading to the nomination and confirmation of justices with views of the Constitution's meaning different than their predecessors, hence leading to a change in doctrine. It is also the case that a particular precedent may have proved to be difficult to interpret and implement in a consistent way or was proven to lead to unfortunate consequences, hence the Court may adopt a new doctrine. And of course the Constitution may have been formally amended pursuant to Article V, forcing the Court to abandon precedent based on the older text. And justices may reject precedent because they sincerely believe it was based on an incorrect method of constitutional interpretation.

## EXPANDING AND NARROWING PRECEDENT

Overruling precedent is the most dramatic way of changing constitutional doctrine. The Court also reinterprets precedent sometimes to expand and sometimes to narrow the precedent. (The consequences of expanding and narrowing precedent can vary, as discussed below, depending on whether the precedent was one that originally struck down a governmental policy or upheld a governmental policy.) The Court has several methods of (re)interpreting precedent.

### Drawing a Factual Distinction

Let's look more closely at the craft of distinguishing precedent and reading it narrowly. A justice distinguishes a precedent by pointing to a *material* fact in the precedent, which the justice argues makes that precedent different from the case currently before the Court, hence inapplicable to the case at hand. Distinguishing cases is both easy and hard. It is easy in the sense that every case can be distinguished from every other case because no two cases are identical in all particulars (e.g., the names of the parties are different, the people involved in the case are not the same people). But we would destroy the idea of precedent if we were to take seriously the notion that *Haydn v. Mozart* was to be distinguished from *Monk v. Ellington* simply because the people involved were different. Should we distinguish the first case because it involved classical composers and the second jazz composers? White composers *versus* African American composers? Probably not, because the practice of distinguishing cases involves distinguishing cases based on differences in *material* facts.

A dispute over distinguishing precedent arose in *Clinton v. Jones* (1997), which began when Paula Corbin Jones brought a suit to recover damages against President Clinton for sexual harassment he allegedly committed prior to his becoming president. In response to the suit President Clinton argued that the Constitution required the federal courts to defer such litigation until his term ended. In ruling against the president the majority opinion had to deal with a precedent that arguably supported the president's position. The precedent was the decision in *Nixon v. Fitzgerald* (1982), which dealt with the question whether a "whistle blower" could seek civil damages against President Nixon and other officials after he was fired following his testimony before a congressional committee. The Court ruled that the president was absolutely immune from civil liability for his official acts. "Because of the singular importance of the President's duties, diversion of his energies by concern with private lawsuits would raise unique risks to the effective functioning of government." The majority opinion in *Clinton v. Jones* distinguished *Nixon v. Fitzgerald* by noting that the *Nixon* decision involved presidential immunity from suits for money damages arising out of the president's official acts but the case before the court in *Clinton* involved unofficial conduct. The grant for immunity with regard to official acts was based on the desire to avoid rendering the president "unduly cautious in the discharge of his official duties." And of course this rationale provided no support for immunity for unofficial conduct.

## Narrowly Interpreting the *Ratio Decidendi*

*Wisconsin v. Constantineau* (1971) involved a statute that provided that certain public officials could forbid in writing the sale or gift of alcoholic beverages to a person who drank excessively (as defined in the law). The chief of police of Hartford, without any notice or hearing, posted a notice in liquor stores that Constantineau was not to be sold any liquor. Justice Douglas found that this "posting" was degrading, and he concluded it was unconstitutional. He wrote, "Where a person's good name, reputation, honor, or integrity is at stake because of what the government is doing to him, notice and an opportunity to be heard are essential." Thus the Court seemed to say that before government could publicly brand someone with a stigmatizing label, there had to be a hearing, an opportunity for the person to defend his or her good name and prevent the "posting."

The next case to arise was *Paul v. Davis* (1976), in which the chief of police of Louisville, Kentucky, distributed a flyer to merchants alerting them to active shoplifters, and Paul's name was on the list. (Paul had been charged with shoplifting, but the case had been filed away and had never gone to trial.) Paul argued that the distribution of the flyer was unconstitutional under the ruling in *Wisconsin v. Constantineau*. Justice Rehnquist, writing for the majority, said the *Wisconsin* case should be read *narrowly*. Thus Justice Rehnquist declared that the *Wisconsin* case involved two *material* facts: (1) a stigma was imposed on Constantineau, and (2) he was also denied the opportunity to buy liquor. Thus Justice Rehnquist concluded that it was not the stigma standing alone that Constantineau suffered that led to the declaration of unconstitutionality; also necessary to the declaration of unconstitutionality was his loss of the right to buy liquor. In other words, Justice Rehnquist concluded that the loss of the right to buy liquor was a *material* fact in the *Wisconsin* case. The *Wisconsin* case, he said, stood for the following *ratio decidendi*: The right to a hearing may be invoked only when the stigma government has imposed is accompanied by a loss of some more tangible interest such as employment or a right a person previously had (e.g., the right to buy liquor). He thus *distinguished* the shoplifting case from the *Wisconsin* case on the ground that Davis had only been stigmatized and that alone was not sufficient to trigger a right to a hearing. Rehnquist "limited" the *Wisconsin* case to its set of facts (i.e., interpreted narrowly, and thus kept the restraints on government to a minimum).

The dissenting opinion of liberal Justice Brennan said the majority had "discredited the clear thrust" of the *Wisconsin* case and expressed the belief that "today's decision must surely be a short-lived aberration." (More about the liberal response below.)

In a free speech case the majority of the Court struck down a federal law that made it a crime to possess or distribute computer-generated images of a child engaged in sexual activity (*Ashcroft v. Free Speech Coalition* [2002]). In striking down the law, the Court distinguished it from an earlier case that upheld a law making it a crime to distribute materials depicting children engaged in sexual conduct (*New York v. Ferber* [1982]). The Court noted that in *Ferber* the focus was on the production of child pornography with actual children; thus the ban was justified to prevent harm to real children. Thus a ban on virtual child pornography could not be justified based on *Ferber*.

## Reducing an Announced Principle to *Obiter Dictum*

Reducing the precedential value of doctrine by declaring a principle found in the decision to be *obiter dictum* is another way of narrowly interpreting a precedent. The precedent given this treatment by liberal justices was *Pennsylvania Coal Co. v. Mahon* (1922). The case involved a Pennsylvania statute that prohibited the mining of coal in such a way as to cause the subsidence of, among other things, people's homes. The plaintiff in the case sought enforcement of the law against the coal company in order to protect his house from subsiding because of the coal mining under it. The coal company claimed that to enforce the law against it would be a "taking" of its property (the coal company had a deed giving it the right to remove all coal even if it hurt the surface structures) without just compensation in violation of the Fifth Amendment. The Supreme Court agreed.

Many years later the Court faced the question of what precisely was the *Mahon* holding. Here are two possible versions of the *ratio decidendi* of *Mahon*:

A. A regulatory law that goes "too far" in limiting the use by a property owner (the coal company) of its property is a "taking" even if it serves a public purpose. (The opinion in *Mahon* actually stated this rule. Note that to accept this rule as the holding could severely restrain government and improve the protection of private property against governmental control, depending on how the phrase "too far" was interpreted.)

B. A law that limits the use of one's property merely to protect the interest of one other private individual (the homeowner in *Mahon*) does not serve a sufficient public interest, thus constitutes a "taking." (This version of the *ratio decidendi* sharply limits the implications of *Mahon*. That is to say, to read the case this way means government may engage in extensive regulations so long as they are not intended to help single private individuals. This *narrow* version expands government's authority.)

In 1987 a liberal majority of the Court said it was version B that had been embraced in *Mahon* (*Keystone Coal Association v. DeBenedictis* [1987]). The liberals argued that it was only the narrow issue of the enforcement of the law to protect a single property owner that came up in *Mahon*. Hence the liberals in *DeBenedictis* said it was not necessary for the Court in *Mahon* to discuss the broader version of the *ratio decidendi* in order to decide the specific case before it. That is, *Mahon* involved only the enforcement of the law at the behest of a single homeowner. Thus those passages in *Mahon* that took up the broader *ratio decidendi* were merely *advisory* and without precedential value.

Note that by saying that *Mahon* was limited to a narrow problem and a narrow *ratio decidendi*, the liberal majority in *DeBenedictis distinguished* the two cases. The Court in *DeBenedictis* said these restrictions were constitutional, were not a "taking" without compensation, because, among other reasons, they served an important public purpose and were not merely directed to protecting the interest of a single property owner. This freed the liberal majority in *DeBenedictis* to reach a different conclusion from that reached in *Mahon*. In fact, the Court in *DeBenedictis* upheld another Pennsylvania statute that placed tough restrictions on coal mining for a variety of environmental reasons.

In sum, this section of the chapter has illustrated three ways of reading precedent narrowly: (1) elevating certain facts to the status of being material to the decision; thus any other case that did not involve those facts must be treated as a different problem and the principle announced in the precedent does not apply; (2) interpreting the rule of a precedent narrowly; and (3) determining that a particular rule was mere dictum.

## Rejecting a Fact as Material

Broadening the interpretation of precedent can be accomplished in different ways: one way is to reject as *not* material a fact that would, if it were material, tend to limit the meaning of the precedent. Recall the *Wisconsin* case involving the posting of lists of people who drank to excess and Justice Rehnquist's narrow interpretation of the case in which he stressed as *material* the loss of the right to purchase liquor. Now let us look at Justice Brennan's interpretation of the liquor case as he outlined it in the subsequent shoplifting case (*Paul v. Davis* [1976]). He attacked Rehnquist's narrow interpretation of the liquor case on two grounds. First, Brennan quoted passages from the *Wisconsin* opinion that seemed to indicate that the Court had been solely concerned with the stigmatizing effect of the posted list, and not the loss of the right to buy liquor: "The *only* issue present here is whether the label . . . is such a stigma . . . that procedural due process requires notice and an opportunity to be heard." Second, he said the reference in the *Wisconsin* opinion to the loss of liquor-buying rights was there only as part of a complete presentation of the facts and "nowise implied any limitation upon the application of the principles announced." In short, for Brennan the loss of the right to buy liquor in the *Wisconsin* case was *not* a *material* fact and not a basis upon which to *distinguish* it from the shoplifting case.

That is to say, Justice Brennan used the *Wisconsin* case as an analogy for deciding *Paul v. Davis*. He did this by abstracting and generalizing from the facts of the *Wisconsin* case, by downplaying some particulars of the *Wisconsin* case and thereby making it more generally applicable.

Here is another example of how precedent can be broadened by denying that certain facts were material to the decision. In 1988 the liberals and the conservatives once again clashed over the constitutionality of providing financial funds to various organizations, including religious organizations, for services and research related to teenage sexuality (*Bowen v. Kendrick* [1988]). Under the law authorizing the grants, religious organizations that received funds were not restricted from, for example, providing counseling on sexual matters from a religious perspective. The federal program was challenged on the grounds that the grant money would be used by religious organizations to promote their religiously based views on abortion, contraception, and related sexual topics. Chief Justice Rehnquist wrote the majority opinion, which upheld the law as written ("on its face") without reaching the question whether the law as implemented ("as applied") was constitutional. I will not explore every aspect of Rehnquist's opinion, but will instead concentrate on his interpretation of one precedent, which he used to support his conclusion that the funding program was constitutional.

Almost twenty years prior to the *Bowen* case, the Court upheld the provision of financial aid to colleges, including religious colleges, to assist in the construction of new facilities that could be used only for secular purposes (*Tilton v. Richardson* [1971]). (Incidentally, this decision stands in marked contrast to the Court's basic resistance to providing financial assistance to religiously affiliated elementary and secondary schools. I will not discuss these seemingly inconsistent results.) Chief Justice Rehnquist in *Bowen* interpreted *Tilton* as standing for the following propositions: (1) A general grant program may be established even if it is foreseeable that some proportion of the recipients would be religiously affiliated and pervasively sectarian. (2) Prior cases do not warrant creating the presumption that pervasively religious institutions are not capable of using federal funds in a secular manner.

Now let us look at how Chief Justice Rehnquist arrived at these propositions. To interpret *Tilton* in this way Rehnquist had to ignore the following facts and comments found in the *Tilton* opinion. That is, he overlooked them, and thus implicitly concluded that the following matters were not material to the decision in *Tilton*.

- The law that was upheld in *Tilton* specifically forbade using the federal funds to build buildings to be used for sectarian purposes.
- Religious indoctrination was not a substantial purpose or activity of the church-related colleges; hence it was not likely that religion would permeate the area of secular education.
- Colleges and universities stress the importance of academic freedom and free and critical responses from the students.
- The students served by colleges and universities were not impressionable, hence less susceptible to religious indoctrination.

If we take these comments of the *Tilton* Court into account, the *ratio decidendi* of the opinion is much narrower than as described by Chief Justice Rehnquist. For example, the more accurate formulation would look something like this. Financial assistance to religiously affiliated organizations is permissible *only if* the aid is limited to assisting secular activities and there is reason to believe, given the nature of the organizations assisted, that they do not have religious indoctrination as a substantial purpose, and their clients are not expected or likely passively to accept religious indoctrination. Clearly, if this were the *ratio decidendi* of *Tilton*, then the aid program in *Bowen* would be unconstitutional. But by giving *Tilton* a different interpretation, Rehnquist could use it to support his conclusion upholding the *Bowen* grant program. The liberals on the Court in their dissenting opinion obviously took a narrower view of *Tilton*.

Stated somewhat differently, Rehnquist chose to use precedent as a relevant *analogy* by ignoring certain facts of the precedent. He *generalized* and *abstracted* from the precedent in building his argument for upholding governmental authority. The liberals, on the other hand, chose to emphasize those facts in *Tilton* that Rehnquist chose to ignore.

## Expanding the Meaning by Generalizing the Material Facts

Closely related to the technique of rejecting a fact as material is the practice of generalizing those facts accepted as material. Here is an example of how one can generalize from a specific set of facts to a more general statement. Assume a 6-year-old boy took a book of fairy tales from another 6-year-old boy. The teacher concluded that this act was wrong. Here are different versions of the teacher's *ratio decidendi*. (1) Six-year-old boys should not steal the books of other 6-year-olds. (2) Children should not steal the belongings of other children. (3) People should not steal what is valuable to other people. In the same way, one can expand upon the meaning of a precedent. We can see this process at work in the way the majority opinion in *Lawrence v. Texas* (2003) interpreted precedent. The majority opinion in *Lawrence* (striking down a law making homosexual sodomy a crime) interpreted the precedent protecting a right to use contraception and terminate a pregnancy with an abortion as establishing the principle that the government cannot regulate with a criminal law personal relationships "absent injury to a person or abuse of an institution the law protects."

## Broadly Interpreting the Goal the Precedent Was Intended to Serve

There exists a different technique justices use for broadly interpreting a precedent. In *Weeks v. United States* (1914) the Supreme Court announced the "exclusionary rule"—the rule holding that evidence illegally seized by the police from the accused in violation of the Fourth Amendment may not be used in trial to prove the guilt of the accused. Many years after the announcement of this rule, the Court dealt with two issues regarding the scope of the rule: first, whether the exclusionary rule could be invoked to block introduction of evidence to a grand jury (as opposed to a criminal trial), and, second, whether the exclusionary rule applied to evidence seized by the police based on a search warrant issued by a magistrate—a search warrant that itself ultimately proved to be invalid but that the police relied upon in good faith (*United States v. Calandra* [1974]; *United States v. Leon* [1984]). The liberals, who were in the minority in both cases, answered yes to both questions by *broadly* interpreting *Weeks*. Though *Weeks* did not involve the precise issues of *Calandra* and *Leon*, the liberals said *Weeks* controlled in both cases. The strategy the liberals followed in giving *Weeks* a broad interpretation involved two steps.

1. They interpreted *Weeks* as having based the exclusionary rule on two goals: the goal to protect the integrity of the judicial system by not permitting it to use illegally seized evidence, and the goal of deterring the police by not letting them profit from their lawless behavior.

2. The liberals also said *Weeks* recognized that the Fourth Amendment privacy right was a personal constitutional right that included the right of the accused to exclude all illegally seized evidence.

Thus the liberals rejected the conservatives' interpretation of *Weeks*. As the conservatives read *Weeks*, the exclusionary rule's purpose was solely to deter the *police*, not to redress an injury to the privacy of the search victim. The exclusionary rule, said the conservatives, was a *remedy*, not a *right*, and the application of remedies in a particular situation depends on calculating the costs and benefits of using them. In both *Calandra* and *Leon* a conservative majority concluded that the costs of applying the exclusionary rule outweighed the benefits; hence illegally seized evidence may today be used in a grand jury proceeding and may be used in a criminal trial if the police acted in good faith on a warrant.

But let us return to the liberals' method for interpreting *Weeks broadly*. Most important, they found in *Weeks* two rationales for the exclusionary rule. The rule, they said, had to be understood in light of both these goals as well as the fact that it was a personal constitutional right of the accused. The twin goals of the rule, and its status as a personal right, made the rule applicable to every aspect of the criminal justice system. In short, the liberals broadened the application of the rule by viewing the rule as serving very broad goals and purposes. Interpreting a rule in this way is a classic method of assuring its broad application. In this instance the broad reading of the rule would have restricted the area of permissible governmental action (i.e., would have made more governmental policies unconstitutional).

Let's go back to *Clinton v. Jones*. Justice Breyer, in a concurrence that amounted to a dissent, agreed that the president should not enjoy automatic temporary immunity but that the president should be given the opportunity to convince the courts that in a particular case a postponement of the suit was needed. Justice Breyer supported his position in part by offering a different interpretation of *Nixon v. Fitzgerald* than the interpretation of the majority. The key to the *Nixon* case, he said, was a desire not to divert the president from his duties by having to respond to private law suits. Because distraction from duties was the key factor in *Nixon*, that case should be read to stand for the principle "that judges hearing a private civil damages action against a sitting President may not issue orders that could significantly distract a President from his official duties." Justice Breyer thus interpreted the *Nixon* case to stand for a different and somewhat broader principle than the principle embraced by the majority opinion.

## WORKING WITH CONFLICTING LINES OF PRECEDENT

Sometimes a case comes to the Court against a background of two different and conflicting lines of precedent and we find the majority distinguishing line A, but embracing line B, whereas the dissent embraces line A and distinguishes line B. This situation arose in *Jackson v. Metropolitan Edison Co.* (1974), a case in which a customer of a *privately* owned and operated electric utility brought suit against the company, claiming that her Fourteenth Amendment due process right had been violated when the company without proper notice and a hearing terminated her electrical service because she did not pay her bill. The problem the case posed was that the Constitution in general and the Fourteenth Amendment in particular are addressed to *government*, not to private, behavior. If that was all that had to be said, this *constitutional* suit against a private company would have been dismissed. But there are times when the government is sufficiently involved with the private sector that the Court is willing to say that what ostensibly seems like purely private behavior should in fact be deemed "state action"; thus the Constitution would be applicable to regulate the behavior. But when is private behavior not to be seen as purely private behavior (state action will be said to be present) and to be subjected to the restraints of the Constitution? In *Jackson* the majority ruled that the state action requirement was not present, but the dissent concluded that it was. To support their different conclusions the majority and dissent had both to confront the precedent.

The precedent involved several different lines of cases. One was the "public function" line of cases that, speaking roughly, established the proposition that private performances of "public functions" were subject to the Fourteenth Amendment (*Marsh v. Alabama* [1946]). The plaintiff argued that the electrical company provided an essential public service; hence it performed a public function. But the majority opinion rejected that argument by interpreting the precedent such as the

*Marsh* decision narrowly. The majority said the precedent stood for the proposition that there would be state action only if the private entity exercised powers "traditionally and exclusively reserved to the state." Because providing electricity was not a function "traditionally and exclusively" carried out by the state, the Metropolitan Edison Company had not been delegated a state power. Because it was not carrying out by delegation a power that was exclusively a state power, there was no state action and the Constitution did not apply. In dissenting, Justice Marshall interpreted the public function cases more broadly. He said that the precedent stood for the proposition that a service that is "traditionally identified with the state through universal public regulation or ownership" is state action; hence utility service is a public function and Metropolitan Edison Company is subject to the Constitution.

There was yet another line of cases with which the majority and dissent in *Jackson* wrestled. This line of cases stood for the proposition, roughly stated, that state action would be said to be present if the state was involved with the challenged action "to some significant extent." There were three precedents in this line that caused the majority and the dissent in *Jackson* some difficulties. In one of these cases the Court had concluded that state action was present. This was *Burton v. Wilmington Parking Authority* (1961), which involved a private restaurant that leased space in a publicly owned parking facility. The restaurant would not serve black people and the question was whether the equal protection clause was applicable—had the restaurant engaged in "state action?" The Court concluded "yes" because it found significant involvement between the government and the restaurant: the restaurant was leasing from the government; the building itself was dedicated to public uses; the building itself had been built with public money; the restaurant operated as an integral part of the building; the state could have affirmatively insisted that the restaurant not discriminate. In short there was a symbolic and symbiotic relationship here. The second precedent involved a private club that refused service to the black guest of a member (*Moose Lodge No. 107 v. Irvis* [1972]). Here the private club was involved with the state because it had a liquor license from the state and was subject to the state liquor registration scheme. Nevertheless, the majority opinion concluded that there was no state action—there was not the same symbiotic relationship as existed in *Burton*. The third precedent was *Public Utilities Commission v. Pollack* (1952).

Returning now to *Jackson*, the majority opinion distinguished *Burton* and embraced *Moose Lodge*. The majority in *Jackson* noted that there was a finding in *Burton* that the state had "so far insinuated itself into a position of interdependence with [the restaurant] that it must be recognized as a joint participant in the [discrimination]." But here the state was not a joint participant in the cutoff of services. The majority reached this conclusion even though the state fully regulated the rates that Metropolitan Edison could charge its customers, and despite the fact that after Metropolitan Edison had notified the state of the method it would use to terminate services to delinquent customers, the state had not blocked this procedure and in fact had given formal approval to it. The majority in *Jackson* held the state had not "put its own weight on the side of the proposed practice." The situation in *Jackson* was more like *Moose Lodge* where the mere fact the private club was subject to state liquor regulations was not enough to find state action. As a general position the majority said the precedent stood for the proposition that there is only state action when there is a "sufficiently close nexus between the State and the challenged action of the regulated entity so that the action of the latter may be fairly treated as that of the State itself." Here the state was not sufficiently connected with the cutoff of service as to be able to say that the cutoff was a product of state action.

In dissent Justice Marshall offered a different interpretation of *Burton* and concluded that it forced a different result in the *Jackson* case. Justice Marshall said (agreeing with Justice Stewart's concurrence in *Burton*) that the state in *Burton* by its inaction had placed its power, property, and prestige behind the discrimination. Here the state involvement was even greater because the state had granted approval to the company's mode of service termination, the very act being challenged in the case. He also noted that, in *Moose Lodge*, the Court had suggested that if the state had fostered or encouraged the racial discrimination that case would have come out differently. This, he noted, was a less rigid standard than the majority required. He thus disagreed with the majority that precedent supported its "nexus" standard.

In the third precedent, *Pollack*, the Court concluded that a bus company had engaged in state action when it operated a piped music system on its buses. (The plaintiffs in the case challenged the piped music on First Amendment grounds.) The majority in *Jackson* said that the material facts of the case were that this piped music system had been specifically approved of after a hearing by the District of Columbia Public Utilities Commission. The government had in fact placed its imprimatur on the piped music. But the *Jackson* majority then distinguished *Pollak* by noting that the state had not similarly placed its imprimatur on Metropolitan Edison's policy regarding the termination of service. The state had not "put its own weight on the side of the proposed practice by ordering it."

Justice Marshall in dissent disagreed with the majority that the hearing held in *Pollak* was a material fact of that case. "I am afraid that the majority has in effect restricted *Pollak* to its facts if it has not discarded it altogether."

## THE EFFECTS OF NARROW AND BROAD READINGS OF PRECEDENT

All the justices, regardless of political preference, use the techniques discussed in this chapter to step around precedent they find embarrassing, and to bring to their aid precedent they think useful. Both liberals and conservatives will interpret narrowly precedent with which they disagree and broadly the precedent with which they agree. The consequences of narrow and broad interpretations of precedent vary depending on whether the precedent was one striking down a government policy or upholding a government policy. The pattern here is captured in the next table.

Turning to cell I, the narrow interpretation of a precedent striking down a government policy has the consequence of expanding government power because the range of impermissible actions has been made smaller by the narrow interpretation. This is what happened in *Paul v. Davis*. The consequence of a broad interpretation

|  | Precedent Striking Down a Governmental Policy | Precedent Upholding a Governmental Policy |
|---|---|---|
| The Narrow Interpretation of Precedent | I<br>Limiting the Area of Impermissible Actions | II<br>Limiting the Area of Permissible Actions |
| The Broad Interpretation of Precedent | III<br>Expanding the Area of Impermissible Actions | IV<br>Expanding the Area of Permissible Actions |

of that same precedent (cell III) has precisely the opposite effect (i.e., the power of the government is reduced). This is what happened in *Weeks v. United States*.

Turning to cell II, the narrow interpretation of a precedent upholding government policy has the consequence of keeping government power somewhat limited (i.e., the area of permissible action is not expanded). If Chief Justice Rehnquist had read the decision in *Tilton* narrowly he would have limited the power of government to aid religious schools. But, instead he read *Tilton* broadly (cell IV) with the consequence that he expanded the power of government to aid private religious schools.

When confronted with a seemingly conflicting line of cases the justices can work a kind of magic, turning what might at first seem a potpourri of principles into a coherent body of law. They do this by narrowly interpreting some precedent and broadly interpreting other cases. In Chapter 9 we shall see a plurality of the Supreme Court narrowly interpret one case that upheld the use of race in making admissions decisions and broadly interpreting other cases that barred the use of race in making governmental decisions. This reading of the cases turned the admissions case into a kind of narrow exception to the color-blind principle announced in the broadly read cases. As a consequence, the area of impermissible actions was expanded and the area of permissible actions was narrowed.

# Practice Pointers

1. Legal advocates need to be able to formulate the *ratio decidendi* of all the precedent they are relying upon and the precedent they are distinguishing.
2. Much of the art of being an attorney is being able to offer an interpretation of a precedent in a way that the precedent serves the interests of your client. Learning how to interpret opinions "broadly" or "narrowly" is an essential skill for attorneys. The skilled advocate can take any precedent and offer both a broad and narrow version of the *ratio decidendi*.
3. Related to the broad and narrow reading of precedent is the art of distinguishing precedent. Precedent that is not favorable for your client you will want to distinguish. Other precedent you may wish to convince a court

is "on all fours" with the case before the court and should be followed. Thus a complete argument will distinguish unfavorable precedent and seek to extend favorable precedent to the case at hand.

4. A way for the Court to effectively overrule a precedent without saying so is to give it an extremely narrow interpretation or to distinguish it in a way that makes its application in the future constrained to a narrow set of circumstances.

# Chapter

# Strategies of Justification

# 7

Chapters 4, 5, and 6 examined the legal materials out of which a judicial opinion may be constructed. But having the materials at hand is insufficient for writing a persuasive opinion. The materials need to be assembled into a persuasive package, and this is where the **strategy of justification** comes in. Strategies of justification are the means by which coherence and logic are achieved in the part of the opinion justifying the decision. Following the statement of facts of the case, a review of the claims and counterclaims made by the parties to the case, a summary of the lower courts' decisions, and a statement of the issues on appeal—after all this has been done—the Supreme Court issues its ruling(s) on the issue(s), rulings that are then supported with an argument. This chapter outlines one generic or overall strategy of justification and several variations used in making those arguments.

## THE SYLLOGISM AND DEDUCTIVE REASONING

The syllogism was introduced in Chapter 6. At its simplest, the legal syllogism consists of a **legal rule** (premise 1), a **set of facts** (premise 2), and a **conclusion**. All judicial opinions have at their heart the syllogism or a set of linked syllogisms. Whether a justice is an originalist or nonoriginalist, a liberal or conservative, the syllogism is the basic tool of justification. For example, in generic form an originalist argument goes something like this:

*Premise 1:* The meaning of the Constitution is exclusively determined by the original understanding of the framers and ratifiers.

*Premise 2:* The framers' and ratifiers' semantic intention regarding the phrase "a well-regulated militia" in the Second Amendment was————.

*Conclusion:* Therefore, gun control legislation regulating gun ownership by private individuals is constitutionally (im)permissible.

Here is another example using a test discussed in Chapter 5:

*Premise 1:* A policy that treats people differently on the basis of race is a violation of the equal protection clause of the Fourteenth Amendment unless the difference in treatment both serves a compelling state purpose and is necessary to achieve that purpose. (This is the legal rule, or premise 1, in the syllogism.)

*Premise 2:* The affirmative action policy requiring contractors who do business with the city to subcontract at least 30 percent of the dollar value of each contract to minority contractors was not adopted for a compelling state purpose. Moreover, the 30 percent set aside was not necessary to achieve the state purpose. (This is the set of facts applied to the legal rule.)

*Conclusion:* This affirmative action plan violates the Fourteenth Amendment (*Richmond v. J. A. Croson Co.* [1989]).

For the syllogism to be acceptable it must be both **logically valid** and **sound**. Here is an example of an **invalid** syllogism.

*Premise 1:* If one is tried and convicted of burglary, one will go to jail.

*Premise 2:* Kent was sent to jail.

*Conclusion:* Therefore, Kent committed burglary.

This represents a logical fallacy because the conclusion does not necessarily follow from the premises. Kent might have gone to jail for reasons other than having committed a burglary. One will rarely if ever find in a Supreme Court opinion as blatant a logical fallacy. (There are other logical fallacies but an examination of them would take us beyond the scope of this book.) The more salient concern is with the **soundness** of the syllogisms used by the justices. A syllogism may be logically valid but nevertheless **unsound** because one or more of the premises are not supported by evidence. Consider the syllogism dealing with affirmative action. A justice writing an opinion would have to provide a basis for the first premise. That basis might be found in precedent, but if there were no precedent because this is the first time the Court had to deal with this problem, the premise then would have to be based on other materials (e.g., the text of the Fourteenth Amendment, the intent of the framers, or perhaps other general principles). Turning to the second premise, the justice would have to offer the basis for that premise. That is to say, the justice would have to explain why he or she concludes that policy was adopted for a "noncompelling" purpose and that the means involved was "not necessary" to achieve the purpose. For a more complex example of deduction in action see the addendum to this chapter.

## Deduction, Originalism, and Nonoriginalism: The Illusion of Certainty

Justification through use of a deductive argument is obviously a powerful tool of persuasion. But it is a tool that can be used to justify many different positions. Let's return to the example regarding the requirement of subcontracting to minority-owned businesses. A different justice might start with a different first premise (the legal rule), such as that the Fourteenth Amendment requires government to be wholly color-blind. Based on that premise, this justice would also find the policy unconstitutional but based on a different argument.

*Premise 1:* The Fourteenth Amendment prohibits government from distributing benefits or burdens based on race.

*Premise 2:* This policy distributes benefits based on race.

*Conclusion:* This policy violates the Fourteenth Amendment.

How might this justice justify this first premise? One line of argument might be that this is what the framers intended. In fact, in the case analyzed in Chapter 9, a central dispute between the majority and dissent was with regard to this first premise, with each group of justices using different evidence and analyzing the evidence they used in common differently.

Because evidence regarding original meaning and precedent is frequently open to varying interpretations, the legal premises of the justices' syllogisms are almost never free from being vulnerable to a challenge that the syllogism(s) they marshaled to justify their judgment are not sound. It is also often the case that the factual premises are themselves open to disagreement and challenge. Again in Chapter 9, you will see that justices disagree whether to characterize the racial percentages involved in the challenged policy as "quotas" or as mere targets or starting ratios. In short, although the justices may offer legal justifications that are logically valid, their justifications may not be sound.

## DEDUCTION AND THE ANALOGY

As noted above, the deductive argument can take on several forms. One form is the analogy. This mode of argument rests on the assumption that a result in case B (the case currently before the Court) can be justified by pointing to the fact that case A (the precedent) is like case B in "material" ways, and case A reached result X, the same result that should be reached in case B. Stated differently, if cases A and B are alike in "material" respects, then case B should be decided the same way as case A. This is true because of the maxim "like cases should be treated alike." And this maxim finds its force in the values of fairness and rationality (i.e., it is neither fair nor rational to treat like cases differently). Thus the deductive syllogism looks like this:

*Premise 1:* Like cases (analogous cases) should be treated alike.

*Premise 2:* Case B is like case A (is analogous to case A).

*Conclusion:* Therefore, case B should be decided the same way as case A.

The difficult step in reasoning based on analogy is determining whether case B is sufficiently *like* case A. As a practical matter no case is ever completely like another case in all respects. In other words every case can be distinguished from every other case. No case is precisely like every other case in every particular and we confront again the technique of distinguishing cases (see Chapter 6). For example, assume that in case A a man with blue eyes robs a grocery store of three apples and he is then convicted of robbery. In case B a woman with brown eyes robs a grocery store of two bananas. Are these cases alike in "material" respects, requiring that the woman in case B also be convicted of robbery? Is the color of eyes a significant difference? Is the gender of the robbers? Is it material that one stole three apples and the other two bananas? Presumably the answer to these questions is no. But what if someone forced the first person to steal some fruit by threatening his life, and the second person stole fruit as a prank? This would seem to be a relevant difference. Thus you can see that to make a persuasive argument on the basis of analogy, one must make a convincing argument that the cases are analogous on the "material" facts, that they are not distinguishable. For example, one must explain why eye color is not relevant but motivation *is* relevant in distinguishing the cases.

Now let's look at an example from the Supreme Court. Assume the Supreme Court has adopted the following rule: A state's prohibition of the importation of goods into its territory is impermissible if it is a protectionist measure, but permissible if the prohibition is directed toward legitimate local concerns. Using such a rule, the Court struck down a state's barring of the importation of out-of-state milk. The law was designed, said the Court, to protect the state's own farmers from out-of-state competition. However, the Court did uphold one state's quarantine of any other states' diseased goods. Now suppose New Jersey adopts a law that prohibits the importation of solid or liquid waste that the importer seeks to dump in New Jersey. Is this law more like the invalid "milk" law or more like the valid "diseased" goods law? Which is the better analogy? In *Philadelphia v. New Jersey* (1978) the Court concluded that the New Jersey law was more like the unconstitutional milk law. The solid and liquid waste, said the Court, did not pose the same immediate health threat as did diseased meat. In fact, New Jersey permitted its own solid and liquid waste to be disposed of in its landfills. The New Jersey law, concluded the Court, was an "obvious effort to saddle those outside the State with the entire burden of slowing the flow of refuse into New Jersey's remaining landfill sites."

Did the Court make the right comparison? Was the Court correct in saying that dumping toxic waste was not like trying to sell diseased meat? That diseased meat did raise a real issue of local concern, but that toxic waste dumping did not raise the same immediate health hazard? Is the *immediacy* of the health hazard the crucial, "material" factor that *distinguishes* the meat problem from the toxic waste problem? Is the fact that New Jersey permits its own toxic wastes to be disposed of within New Jersey material, showing the absence of a real health concern? Did New Jersey have any other choice regarding its own toxic waste? Why might the Court have been correct in saying the toxic waste issue was really more like the milk case? These are the kinds of problems one encounters when working with precedent.

# DEDUCTION AND BALANCING

## Introduction

The premises in the underlying syllogism may require a justice to assess the relative "weight" of competing interests, which leads to the justification of "balancing." The legal rule in such cases is usually phrased as a conditional sentence with outcomes presented in the alternative, that is, "if X then Y; if not X then Z." The syllogism then looks something like this:

*Premise 1:* If the interests of the individual outweigh the interests of the government, we will rule in favor of the individual; but if the interests of the government outweigh those of the individual, we will rule in favor of the government.

*Premise 2:* The interests of (the individual OR the government) are weightier.

*Conclusion:* Therefore we will rule in favor of (the individual OR the government).

Because this syllogism involves deduction and balancing we might call this form of argument deductive-balancing. But this cumbersome phrase will be simply reduced to "balancing" in what follows.

An opinion couched in language of balancing has the appearance of being impersonal, dispassionate, and disinterested. It also has the appearance of being practical as it seems to take into account the realities faced by the contending parties. Who can say that justice was not done when the Court considered all the factors and rendered what it considered to be its best judgment regarding what was best for the individuals involved and society? Finally, this strategy is especially practical when there is no precedent available for deciding the case. That is to say, balancing can be used in cases in which there appear to be no prior relevant analogies, when the Court must confront a problem for the very first time.

## Simple Balancing

It is important to note that sometimes this strategy is "disguised." That is, the idea of balancing is expressed in different ways in different opinions; it will not always be stated in precisely the form that holds that one side wins because its interests outweigh the other side's. It takes a bit of practice to recognize that a given justification is but a disguised version of balancing.

Let us turn to an undisguised version of balancing. The opinion might begin with an assessment of the "harm" produced by the policy. The amount or degree of harm affected by the policy can be understood as a "function of" the importance of the interests of the plaintiff times the degree of impact the policy has on those interests. Thus the opinion would address the following two points:

1. The interests of the plaintiff. The plaintiff could be an individual, as would be the case in an individual rights case; but the holder of these interests might also be a governmental official such as the federal district court that issued the subpoena to President Nixon in the "executive privilege case" discussed in Chapter 2 (*United States v. Nixon* [1974]).
2. The impact on those interests of the policy being challenged.
   Next the opinion would discuss the "benefits" of the policy; these benefits would be a function of the interests the policy sought to secure and the extent

to which the means chosen actually realized those interests. Hence the opinion would discuss:

3. The interests that the challenged policy seeks to realize.
4. The extent to which the challenged policy actually realized those interests.

Finally, the opinion would announce its conclusion as to whether the harm was greater than the benefits; whether, on balance, the policy was constitutional. The Court has used balancing in a variety of cases, for example, in deciding whether students involved in competitive extracurricular activities may be randomly tested for drugs (*Board of Education of Independent School District No. 92 of Pottawatomie County v. Earl* [2002]) and whether the criminally accused can be involuntarily administered antipsychotic drugs in order to render that defendant competent to stand trial for serious, but nonviolent, crimes (*Sell v. United States* [2003]).

## Problems in Using Simple Balancing

It is difficult for an opinion writer to provide an accurate and precise comparative assessment of the harms and benefits involved in a case because there is usually no common unit of measure in which to carry out the comparison (e.g., harms are worth $352 and benefits are worth $353). This means that sometimes the opinions do little more than fully describe the interests at stake in colorful and persuasive terms. Justice Frankfurter, for example, in the concurring opinion discussed above, simply analyzed the government's interests by describing at great length the size, organization, and threat posed by the Communist Party. Opinions may resort to a mere listing of the interests at stake on each side. Or the opinion writer may try indirectly to get at the importance of the interests by citing analogies. Thus in a case questioning the constitutionality of involuntary "stomach pumping" (vomiting induced with an emetic agent) undertaken to recover capsules the petitioner had swallowed, Justice Frankfurter wrote that this method of criminal investigation was "too close to the rack and screw to permit of constitutional differentiation" (*Rochin v. California* [1952]).

The use of the analogy to help pinpoint the degree of importance of an interest is tricky. As you know, simile and metaphor are literary or poetic devices used for illustrative effect. They are not intended to convey literal truth, only figurative meaning. "She sings like a bird" means *She sings well*, not *She chirps*. Is stomach pumping really like the rack and screw? Take another example. In *Wyman v. James* (1971), the Court considered whether a visit by a caseworker to the home of a welfare recipient was constitutionally permissible in the absence of a search warrant. Citing the text of the Fourth Amendment and precedent, the majority opinion emphasized the importance of privacy of the home. Yet, the opinion also invoked an *analogy*. The home visit, wrote the Court, was "akin" to the routine civil audits conducted by the Internal Revenue Service. This home visit was as administratively necessary as the audit, and both invaded a sphere of privacy. Yet if those audits could be constitutionally required, so could this visit. The opinion concluded that the home visit was a reasonable administrative tool; it served valid purposes and was not an unwarranted invasion of personal privacy.

But an astute reader of this opinion would ask whether a visit in someone's home is really the same thing as looking at business records. Has not the home been traditionally considered a private sanctuary? A critic might say that the Court offered an unconvincing argument in support of its judgment.

How strong a state's interest is in its policy may be indirectly assessed by looking at the number of other states pursuing the same policy. If many states do the same thing, the interest is strong; if many do not, the interest is less important. Assessment of interests may take the opinion writer into a detailed examination of tradition, especially tradition embodied in the common law and other official policies. Thus in *Tennessee v. Garner* (1985), in considering whether it was constitutional for the police to use deadly force to stop a fleeing and unarmed criminal suspect, the Court looked to police practices generally, the old English common law rules on the matter, the modern trend in state law on the question, the modern trend in police policy around the country, and statistical data on the effect of crime rates when the police have followed a policy of limited use of deadly force.

Along with the problem of providing a precise assessment of the interests, opinion writers face the difficulty of how to characterize them. Take the Communist conspiracy case again. Is this a conflict between (1) the interest of individuals in being left alone to live their own lives and speak their own minds, as opposed to (2) the interest of the state in suppressing extreme political opinions? Or did that case involve (3) a conflict between the interest of individuals in advocating false, misleading, and immoral doctrines, and (4) the interest of those in power in suppressing political dissent in order to protect their political base? Or perhaps the conflict should be described as one between 1 and 4, or between 2 and 3. Thus for a legal argument to be persuasive it must use characterizations of the interests that are plausible, that seem to capture what really is at stake in the dispute.

A criticism that has been made of balancing is that it is so flexible and adaptive a strategy that the justices can use it to justify any conclusion they prefer for purely personal and subjective reasons. In the "stomach pumping" case noted above, Justice Frankfurter relied on an investigation of "the decencies of civilized conduct" as part of his assessment of the interests at stake. Justice Black, who agreed that stomach pumping was unconstitutional, disagreed with Frankfurter's strategy of justification. He demanded, "[W]hat avenues of investigation are open to discover 'canons' of conduct so universally favored that this Court should write them into the Constitution?" (*Rochin v. California* [1952]).

## Balancing and Deference to the Legislature

The previous sections described balancing at its simplest. As you might expect, the strategy may take on a more complex form. In one variation on the simple model, the opinion writer may announce that striking the balance is an effort best left to the judgment of the legislature, to another branch of government; accordingly, the writer says he or she will examine the balance struck by the legislature only to determine whether that balance was reasonable. Even if the opinion writer might have struck the balance differently, if the balance was reasonable the Court will accept it.

The writer thus concludes that the Court should *defer* to the judgment of the other branch of government.

Justice Frankfurter's concurring opinion in *Dennis v. United States* (1951) uses this strategy. The case involved a federal law that made it a crime to advocate knowingly the overthrow of the government or to organize a group that advocates the overthrow of the government. The petitioners challenged their convictions under the law on the grounds that the convictions violated their First Amendment right to freedom of speech. Justice Frankfurter's opinion, concurring in the judgment that the convictions be upheld, said that the primary responsibility of balancing the demands of free speech and the interests of national security belonged to Congress, and that the Court should set aside Congress's judgment only if there was no reasonable basis for it. After examining those interests, the Frankfurter opinion concluded that Congress had determined that the danger created by the advocacy of overthrow justified the restriction on free speech, and that it was not for the Court to second-guess the legislature.[1]

## Further Refinements Regarding Balancing (Optional Reading)

*Deduction to Produce a Balancing Test.*    A controversial example of a deduction that leads to balancing is the Court's deduction of the strict scrutiny test.[2] The Court said that when fundamental rights have been affected by government's policy, or when government has used a "suspect" classification (criterion), then "strict scrutiny of the classification which the state makes . . . is essential, lest unwittingly, or otherwise, invidious discriminations are made against groups or types of individuals in violation of the constitutional guaranty of just and equal laws" (*Skinner v. Oklahoma* [1942]). In adopting the strict scrutiny test the Court omitted making the link between, on the one hand, fundamental interests and suspect classifications, and on the other, the strict scrutiny test. (Note that a deductive argument could have been made by the

---

[1] Balancing can be used in two ways. First, it can be used simply to decide the case before the Court, with the understanding that if a similar case were to arise in the future, the Court would once again balance the factors in reaching a judgment. Second, balancing can be used to arrive at a principle or rule that, when used in future cases, would not involve the Court in further balancing. Let us illustrate the use of both strategies.

In *Argersinger v. Hamlin* (1972) the question was whether indigents charged with "petty offenses" had a right to a court-appointed attorney. The majority opinion used balancing to justify its conclusion that Argersinger's constitutional rights had been denied when he was not appointed an attorney for a trial involving a minor offense, namely, carrying a concealed weapon. But then the opinion concluded by announcing the following rule: "[A]bsent a knowing and intelligent waiver, no person may be imprisoned for any offense, whether classified as petty, misdemeanor, or felony unless he was represented by counsel at his trial." The concurring opinion, while agreeing that the conviction should be overturned, said that there should be no such absolute rule, that balancing should be used in each and every future case to determine whether the accused should be provided with a court-appointed lawyer. The concurrence then concluded with a sketch of the factors that should be weighed in these future cases.

[2] Recall that when this test is used it is the government that must carry the burden of proof; failure to meet this burden of proof means that the law will be struck down. The government must establish that the law is necessary to the achievement of a purpose that is compelling.

Court to justify the selection of this test.) Turning to the test itself, if one looks at it closely one could see it as embodying a disguised form of balancing. In other words, given the great importance of the individual interest at stake, or the suspect nature of the classification, the test involves the Court in discussing whether the reasons for this law are strong enough to justify the invasion of the interest, the imposition of a harm. That is to say, a case such as *Skinner* says that when the individual interests at risk are really important (i.e., a fundamental interest), then government's policy is constitutional only if it effectively serves a purpose so important as to outweigh the possible harm.

Let us look at another specific example. An argument using balancing followed by deduction characterizes many areas of constitutional law. One of the clearest examples of this mode of justification is found in *New York v. Ferber* (1982). At issue was a New York statute prohibiting the distribution of materials depicting children under 16 engaged in sexual conduct, regardless of whether the materials were "obscene" according to the technical definition of obscenity developed by the Supreme Court. The opinion reviewed the costs associated with the production of such materials (impact on the child's psychological and physical well-being); the benefits of child pornography (negligible); and the law's effectiveness in reducing the production of such materials (prohibiting distribution is the most expeditious if not the only practical way to protect children because it dries up the market for these materials). Based on this *balancing*, the opinion concluded that child pornography should be placed outside the protection of the First Amendment. The opinion went on to say that any law banning this material must meet certain tests in order to be constitutional:

1. The law may ban only visual depictions of specified sexual conduct involving children;
2. the term "sexual conduct" must be appropriately limited and described;
3. the prohibition need not be limited to that which is patently offensive or appealing only to prurient interests; and
4. the material at issue need not be evaluated as a whole.

Using these tests, the Court concluded (*deduced*) that New York's law was constitutional.

*Balancing Plus Balancing.*   The opinions that use the balancing-plus-balancing strategy of justification engage in balancing in order to produce a test that itself calls for specified balancing factors. We have already seen an example of such an opinion earlier in this chapter, the concurring opinion in *Argersinger v. Hamlin* (1972), dealing with the right to an attorney for trials for petty criminal offenses. Consider another example from the Court's opinions on freedom of speech. The question arose in *Connick v. Myers* (1983) and *Pickering v. Board of Education* (1968) whether citizens continue to enjoy their First Amendment free speech rights to criticize the government when they become employees of that same government. In approaching the question, the Court balanced (1) the interest of the individual in speaking out and the public interest in hearing what the individual has to say, against (2) the public interest in the continued smooth operation of government. Balancing these considerations led the Court to the following test: If the employee spoke out truthfully on a matter of "public concern" (a term the Court spent much time defining), then the speech activity may be the basis for disciplinary action only after weighing the following factors: (1) the impact of the speech on working relations with fellow employees; (2) the impact on the working relationship with the immediate superior; and (3) the seriousness or fundamental nature of the issues raised by the employee.

*The Analogy, Balancing, and Deduction.*    We have already seen how balancing and deduction can be combined into one overall argument. Analogy can also be used in conjunction with balancing and deduction. Take, for example, a deductive argument. For the argument to proceed, it is necessary to select the starting premise. Finding this premise may require the use of an analogy. Take the problem of whether sleeping in the park to demonstrate the plight of the homeless is a form of "speech." The opinion writer might seek to compare this kind of activity with picketing, an activity acknowledged to be a form of "speech" activity. Thus the question arises of whether sleeping in the park is sufficiently like picketing also to be called a "speech" activity. If the answer is yes, then the park-sleeping case should be decided using the tests, rules, doctrines, and principles taken from the picketing case. The deduction can then begin.

Here is another example. Consider one of the tests used in cases in which governmental assistance to private religious schools is challenged as a violation of the establishment clause of the First Amendment. (The establishment clause, let us say, prohibits most forms of governmental assistance to religion.) The test states that the primary effect of the aid must not be to advance or inhibit religion (first premise). Thus the opinion must resolve the question of whether the aid advances or inhibits religion. This becomes the first premise of our syllogism. To help reach a conclusion on whether the aid advances or inhibits religion, the opinion may consider analogies. Suppose that in a prior opinion the Court had concluded that lending textbooks directly to students attending private religious schools was permissible (did not advance religion). Also suppose the Court had held that the loan of wall maps to those same students did advance religion, and thus was impermissible. Now suppose the aid in the new case involves a book of maps (an atlas). Is this an impermissible form of aid? Classifying the atlas would involve a comparison between wall maps and textbooks.

## JUDICIAL DISAGREEMENTS

When justices disagree over the results in a particular case, they often use differing strategies to justify their positions. Take for example the majority and dissenting opinions in *Panhandle Oil Co. v. Truax* (1928). At issue was the constitutionality of a Mississippi law that imposed a tax of one cent per gallon sold on gasoline dealers for the privilege of engaging in business. A gasoline dealer who sold gas to the U.S. Coast Guard and a veterans' hospital refused to pay the tax, claiming it was an unconstitutional tax on the federal government itself. A majority of the Court, in an opinion written by Justice Butler, concluded that the tax was unconstitutional. Justice Butler justified his conclusion using a pure deductive argument. A dissenting opinion by Justice Holmes, which would have upheld the tax, relied on pure balancing. Here is a rough summary of each opinion.

## Justice Butler for the Majority

Precedent establishes that a state may not burden or interfere with the exertion of national power by taxing the means used for the performance of federal functions. This tax falls on the transaction or sale, and its size depends on the quantity purchased. As such, this tax must inevitably retard the amount purchased. Thus the necessary effect of the tax is directly to retard, impede, and burden the exertion of the United States's constitutional power to operate the fleet and hospital. Thus this is an unconstitutional tax: The petitioner is not liable for the taxes.

## Justice Holmes for Justices Brandeis and Stone

The question of state interference with the federal government is one of reasonableness and degree. This is a reasonable tax in that it asks of the federal government only that it help pay for the state services it uses just as every other business or person must. The federal government has itself not complained about the tax. We have never said that sales taxes on the food and clothing the federal government purchases are unconstitutional. And as long as this Court sits it can determine which tax is confiscatory. This tax is reasonable in its purpose; it has only a remote effect on the federal government.

The choice of strategy of justification is not the only way majority, dissenting, and concurring opinions may differ. Even when using the same general strategy (e.g., deduction), the justices may disagree because of reliance on different premises, and, in turn, the reliance on different premises may be rooted in differences in the evidence they chose to emphasize to support their premises (e.g., disagreement regarding the precedent relied upon) or differences in the interpretation of the same precedent. An example of the latter disagreement is to be found in the discussion and analysis of *Parents Involved in Community Schools v. Seattle School District No. 1* (2007) in Chapter 9.

In *Morse v. Frederick* (2007) there was a complex three-way conflict among the justices that had them attacking each other's premises and logical deductions. A five-justice majority in that case concluded that a student's First Amendment right of free speech was not violated when a school official confiscated a large banner a student displayed at an event attended by the whole school that said "BONG HiTS 4 JESUS." The majority said the banner reasonably could be interpreted as advocating drug use. (The student's eight-day suspension was also upheld by the Court.) Justice

Thomas, who joined the majority opinion, wrote a separate concurring opinion that argued, in an originalist argument:

> If it had been the case when the public schools were formed in the nineteenth century that it was understood that students enjoyed free-speech rights, the schools would have respected them and the courts would have enforced them.
>
> 1. The schools did not respect those rights and courts did not enforce them.
> 2. The schools were not places for "freewheeling debates or exploration of competing ideas." "[I]n the earliest schools teacher taught and students listened; teachers commanded and students obeyed."
> 3. Legally, school–student relationship was governed by the *in locis parentis* doctrine which gave school officials control over student speech.
>
> Therefore, the First Amendment does not extend to students the right of free speech in public schools.

A separate concurring opinion by Justice Alito, with whom Justice Kennedy joined (two justices who also joined the majority), attacked premise 3. Justices Alito and Kennedy wrote:

> The public schools are invaluable and beneficent institutions, but they are, after all organs of the state. When public school authorities regulate student speech, they act as agents of the State; they do not stand in the shoes of the students' parents. It is a dangerous fiction to pretend that parents simply delegate their authority . . . to public school authorities.

For their part the dissenters attacked the validity of the majority opinion's logic. The dissent noted two premises relied upon by the majority: (a) The constitutional rights of students in the school setting are not coextensive with those of adults; and (b) deterring drug use is a terribly important interest of the schools. The dissent agreed with these premises, but nevertheless concluded that the majority's ultimate conclusion was a "gross non sequitor."

> But it a gross non sequitor to draw from these two unremarkable propositions the remarkable conclusion that the school may suppress student speech that was never meant to persuade anyone to do anything.

The dissent buttressed this assertion with further claims that the student's uncontradicted explanation for the banner was simply to get on TV and that no one could reasonably interpret the "silly message" as drug advocacy.

## CONCLUSION

There are two important conclusions to come away with from this chapter. First, all Supreme Court opinions either expressly or implicitly involve deduction. And the most fundamental strategy of justification is deduction. Regardless of whether a justice is using an originalist or nonoriginalist approach, relying upon, overruling, or distinguishing precedent, deduction will be involved. And as noted, even when an opinion uses the analogy or balancing, it will be using deduction.

Second, a judicial opinion is like an onion: It contains many layers of argument that all work together to justify each conclusion. A full dissection of any opinion requires that you pull apart the onion one layer at a time, identify the deductive argument within each layer, and then move on to the next layer until you finally reach the overall conclusion at the core. Only when you have identified all the layers—understood the arguments in each, and noted how they fit together—will you understand the opinion as a whole.

## A CLOSER LOOK AT DEDUCTION: AN ADDENDUM

When working with the law the justices must frequently decide whether a particular event, activity, policy, or thing is covered by a phrase that actually appears in the Constitution, or in a rule, test, or standard of review developed in precedent. For example, opinions have wrestled with whether sleeping in a park is, or could be classified as, a form of "speech"; whether a sniff by a dog of the air surrounding luggage should be classified as a "search" of that luggage; whether a job with a public employer is a species of "property"; whether a particular publication can be labeled as "obscene"; whether a particular activity can be characterized as posing a "clear and present danger of imminent lawless action"; whether a government's policy should be deemed to be "legitimate" and/or "compelling."

These questions raise the problem of *labeling* or *classifying*. A persuasive opinion must offer reasons why it does or does not impose a particular label, or does or does not classify something.

Consider the question of whether a Negro slave brought into a free state was a "United States citizen" who was entitled to bring suit in a federal court (*Dred Scott v. Sandford* [1857]). The opinion used an approach to constitutional interpretation that relied heavily upon the "intent of the framers." Hence, the opinion reviewed English and American attitudes toward the Negro before and at the time of the adoption of the Constitution: It also examined the text of the Constitution itself and concluded that the answer was no, Dred Scott was not a citizen. Note the syllogism in this argument:

> *Premise 1:* The Constitution's meaning is determined by the intent of the framers.
>
> *Premise 2:* The intent of the framers was that Negro slaves were not to be considered citizens of the United States and could not be made citizens by the action of an individual state.
>
> *Premise 3:* Dred Scott is a Negro slave who claims to have become a citizen by having traveled in a free state.
>
> *Premise 4:* Scott's claim is inconsistent with the Constitution.
>
> *Conclusion:* Scott is not a citizen of the United States and may not bring this suit.

Here is a more complex example: The dispute in *Munn v. Illinois* (1877) involved a claim by the plaintiff that a state law that set the maximum fee a private warehouse could charge for the storage of grain was unconstitutional because, among other reasons, it violated the Fourteenth Amendment's prohibition that states not *deprive* persons of life, liberty, or property without due process of law. The Court upheld the regulation against this and all the other challenges. A central problem was the meaning of the word *deprive*. The opinion justified this conclusion in the following way:

A. *Premise:* The text of the Constitution prohibits the "deprivation" of property.
   *Proof:* This point was easily established as it required nothing more than a direct quotation of the text of the Fourteenth Amendment.
   The problem the Court faced at this point was that "The Constitution contains no definition of the word 'deprived.'" Hence the Court noted that "it is necessary to ascertain the effect which usage has given it, when employed in the same or like connection." (Note that the Court offered no justification for selecting this approach to determining the meaning of the text.) Thus the Court went on to establish the next premise of its argument.

B. *Premise:* When government regulates the use of property—even the price of that use—this is not necessarily a "deprivation."
   *Proof 1.* When one becomes a member of society, one necessarily parts with some rights and privileges.
   *Proof 2.* The body politic is a social compact through which people agree that they shall be governed by certain laws for the common good. This means people authorize government to pass laws that require citizens to use their property so as not to injure one another unnecessarily.
   *Proof 3.* Regulation of a variety of businesses has been a custom in English law from time immemorial, and in this country from its first colonization. In 1820, only a few decades after the adoption of the Fifth Amendment, which contains the same due process clause as in the Fourteenth, Congress passed a law that regulated the rate of wharfage at private wharves, and an 1848 law regulated the rates of hauling by cartmen and others. (Note: This line of argument presupposes the premise that, in interpreting the Constitution, it is the "original intent of the framers" that is the best evidence of the meaning of the text.)

C. *Premise:* When one devotes property to use in which the public has an interest, one must submit to public regulation.
   *Proof:* The common law, from which the right to property derives, recognized that property "affected with the public interest" may be subject to public regulation. Property devoted to use in which the public has an interest becomes affected with the public interest.

D. *Premise:* Public grain warehouses are "affected with the public interest."
   *Proof:* If cartmen, the wharfinger, and other business regulated in the past are affected with the public interest, so is this warehouse. And we must assume that "if a state of facts could exist that would justify such legislation, it actually did exist when the statute now under consideration was passed. . . . Of the propriety of legislative interference within the scope of legislative power, the legislature is the exclusive judge."

*Conclusion:* Public grain warehouses may without violating the Constitution be regulated.

Toward the end of the opinion, the Court acknowledged that this power to regulate could be abused, but "for protection against abuses by Legislatures the people must resort to the polls, not to the courts" (*Munn v. Illinois* [1877]).

Look back now over the argument of the Court and take note of the materials the Court used in constructing its argument: text, political philosophy, traditional practices, analogy, and a principle of deference to the legislature.

## Practice Pointers

1. There are several ways in which you can attack a syllogism.
   a. Argue that the legal premises were not well grounded, that the legal materials used to support the premises were insufficient or inappropriate, that the conclusion given does not flow naturally from the premises, or that a different conclusion can be deduced from the premises.
   b. Argue that a premise was too narrow or too broad.
   c. Demonstrate that a factual premise is not supported by evidence.
   d. Suggest an additional or alternate legal premise that trumps the premises given in the opposing argument.
2. Opinions that apply a test or principle, previously established in precedent, rely on the syllogism with the established test or principle serving as the first premise. Opinions may also be more complex, with one syllogism used to arrive at a new test or principle, and a second syllogism employing the conclusion from the first syllogism as the premise of a second syllogism.
3. Be aware when reading an opinion that the justices often write in a way that mimics ordinary speech more than the writing out of a formal proof. You will find the opinions filled with "asides," digressions, premises out of order, and linked syllogisms intertwined rather than schematically set forth.
4. If opposing counsel makes an argument based on an analogy, you can counter the argument by pointing out important differences between the two cases that make the analogy inappropriate or misleading.
5. Statistical evidence can be very useful when mounting an argument that relies on balancing.

# PART 3

Chapters 4–7 examined the craft of judicial opinion writing by dividing the practice into separate parts. Chapter 4 took up the topic of the materials used in formulating a constitutional opinion or argument. We thus looked at the use of the text, original intent, tradition, and tacit postulates of the Constitution. Chapter 5 looked at tests or standards of review. Chapter 6 examined the doctrine of *stare decisis* and the problem of developing the *ratio decidendi* of a precedent. Finally, Chapter 7 reviewed the strategies of justification, specifically, the analogy, balancing, deduction, and combinations of balancing and deduction. Having looked at the separate components of an opinion, we must now look at two whole opinions and see all these elements working together. We shall do this in Chapter 8 by looking at the majority, concurring, and dissenting opinions of a single case and then providing an example of a brief of the opinions in the case. Briefing an opinion is unavoidably an act of interpretation, that is, different people will in all likelihood brief the same case differently. And an advocate for a particular point of view would most certainly seek to brief the opinion in a way that supports his or her legal position. Furthermore, understanding an opinion requires more than briefing it but also answering a variety of questions about the opinion. Chapter 9 takes us a step further into the art of opinion briefing and the analysis of an opinion.

# Chapter 8

## Briefing a Supreme Court Opinion

The chapter begins with a synopsis of the facts of *Griswold v. Connecticut* (1965). The next two sections examine in detail first the majority opinion and then the concurring and dissenting opinions. The chapter concludes with an introduction to the craft of briefing an opinion. The chapter focuses on this older decision because it illustrates many of the points made in previous chapters and because *Griswold* represents the headwaters for one of the most important line of cases in modern Supreme Court history—the line of cases that addresses personal lifestyle privacy inclusive of the right to terminate a pregnancy with an abortion and the right to engage in same-sex sexual practices.

### THE FACTS

Connecticut law made it a crime for any person to use any drug, medicinal article, or instrument for the purpose of preventing conception. The appellants in the case, Griswold, executive director of the Planned Parenthood League of Connecticut, and Buxton, a licensed physician, were arrested, charged, convicted, and fined $100 under another Connecticut statute that made it a crime to assist or abet another person in committing any offense. Specifically, they were convicted because they provided information, instruction, and medical advice to married persons regarding the use of contraception. They appealed their convictions to the Connecticut Supreme Court, claiming that the law that prohibited the use of contraception was unconstitutional under the Fourteenth Amendment of the U.S. Constitution. The Connecticut Supreme Court affirmed the convictions, and the appellants appealed to the U.S. Supreme Court.

Justice Douglas wrote the majority opinion in which Chief Justice Warren and Justices Brennan, Clark, and Goldberg concurred. Justice Goldberg filed a concurring opinion, which was joined by Chief Justice Warren and Justice Brennan. Justice Harlan and Justice White concurred in the judgment only and wrote their own separate concurring opinions. Justices Black and Stewart each wrote their own dissenting opinions in which the other joined.

## THE MAJORITY OPINION

The almost complete text of the majority opinion is reprinted below in the left-hand column. The Roman numerals printed in bold type are not in the original opinion but are added to facilitate your relating the commentary—found in the right-hand column—to the appropriate section of the majority opinion.

*Majority Opinion*

[I.] We think that appellants have standing to raise the constitutional rights of the married people with whom they had a professional relationship. . . . The rights of husband and wife pressed here are likely to be diluted or adversely affected unless those rights are considered in a suit involving those who have this kind of confidential relation to them.

*Commentary*

[I.] Federal courts may address only those conflicts over which they have jurisdiction. One of the jurisdictional requirements imposed by Article 3 of the Constitution is that the conflict involve a "case" or "controversy." These are technical terms that have many dimensions to them. One part of the requirement is that the party who brings the suit have a sufficient "stake" in the controversy. Not just anybody can bring a constitutional suit. A citizen who simply decides she thinks some policy is unconstitutional does not have standing[1] (a sufficient stake) to bring a suit challenging the policy. To bring the suit, the person must have suffered some actual or threatened injury, and must be able to trace that injury to what the government did. Thus people may sue only to protect their own constitutional rights and not the rights of some other people. Nevertheless, in this case the Court permitted Griswold and Buxton to seek judicial protection of the constitutional rights of the married couples they were assisting.

---

[1] "Standing" is a complex and technical requirement that cannot be fully explored in this text. It focuses on the question of who may go to court. Other closely related doctrines focus on whether the problem being brought to the court is the kind of problem the Court can resolve (the political question doctrine), and whether this is the right time to bring the case to the Court (ripeness).

[II.] Coming to the merits, we are met with a wide range of questions that implicate the Due Process clause of the Fourteenth Amendment. Overtones of some arguments suggest that *Lochner v. New York*, 198 U.S. 45, should be our guide. But we decline that invitation as we did in . . . *Williamson v. Lee Optical Co.* 348 U.S. 483. . . . We do not sit as a super-legislature to determine the wisdom, need, and propriety of laws that touch economic problems, business affairs, or social conditions. This law, however, operates directly on an intimate relation of husband and wife and their physician's role in one aspect of that relation.

[II.] Having concluded that Griswold and Buxton may raise the question of whether the state has infringed the rights of married couples, the Court now turns to that question. The constitutional amendment implicated by the arguments of the appellants is the due process clause of the Fourteenth Amendment. Specifically, the opinion says the arguments made to it suggest that the Court should approach this case the way it approached the Fourteenth Amendment in *Lochner*. In that case the Court broadly interpreted the concept of liberty to include a right to freedom of contract and then strongly protected that right against governmental regulation. The decision, thus, struck down a law that prohibited bakeries from requiring employees to work more than a ten-hour workday. This decision, representing both judicial activism and nonoriginalism, has come under severe criticism as an example of a conservative Court's reading its own preferred economic philosophy into the Constitution, thereby frustrating an arguably reasonable regulation that a majority in the legislature preferred. Douglas announces here that he is not going to make this mistake—the Court in this case will not simply read its personal policy preferences into the Constitution. He alludes to *Lee Optical*, a more modern case that illustrates the Court's more deferential, less activist approach in dealing with constitutional challenges to the regulation of business. But then he pointedly notes that this case is not about the regulation of a business, thus suggesting that personal rights are more important and deserving of more protection than the right to run one's business.

[III.] The association of people is not mentioned in the Constitution nor in the Bill of Rights. The right to educate a child in a school of the parent's choice—whether public or private or parochial—is also not mentioned. Nor is the right to study any particular subject or any foreign language. Yet the First Amendment has been construed to include certain of those rights.

[III.] Without any transition, the opinion now starts to discuss the fact that the Constitution does not expressly deal with rights of married couples. Douglas starts building the argument that the Constitution may and should be interpreted to embody a right relevant to this case. His first move is, thus, to inform us that the Court has in the past found certain rights to be implicit in the Constitution, rights that today we take for granted, for example, the right of parents to choose the type of school to which they send their child. The message is that the Court is not going to do anything it has not done before when it develops the new right it will announce later in the opinion.

[IV.] By *Pierce v. Society of Sisters,* supra, the right to educate one's children as one chooses is made applicable to the State by the force of the First and Fourteenth Amendments. By *Meyer v. Nebraska,* . . . the same dignity is given the right to study the German language in a private school. In other words, the State

[IV.] In many respects these passages represent what many scholars would call a sloppy piece of judicial writing. First, precedent is interpreted in an extraordinarily broad way. Take, for example, the comment about *Pierce.* That case struck down a law that in effect made attendance at a private school may not consistently with the spirit of the First Amendment, contract the spectrum of available knowledge. The right of freedom of speech and press includes not only the right to utter or to print, but the right to distribute, the right to receive, the right to read (*Martin v. Struthers*, 319 U.S. 141, 143) and freedom of inquiry, freedom of thought, and freedom to teach . . . indeed the freedom of the entire university community [case citations omitted]. Without those peripheral rights the specific rights would be less secure. And so we reaffirm the principle of the *Pierce* and the *Meyer* cases. In *NAACP v. Alabama*, 357 U.S. 449, 462, we protected the "freedom to associate and privacy in one's associations," noting that freedom of association was a peripheral First Amendment right. Disclosure of membership lists of a constitutionally valid association, we held, was invalid "as entailing the likelihood of a substantive restraint upon the exercise of the petitioner's members of their right to freedom of association." *Ibid.*

[V.] In other words, the First Amendment has a penumbra where privacy is protected from governmental intrusion. In like context, we have protected forms of "association" that are not political in the customary sense but pertain to the social, legal, and economic benefit of the members. In *Schware v. Board of Bar Examiners*, 353 U.S. 232, we held it not permissible to bar a lawyer from practice, because he had

illegal. The Court specifically said it was not dealing with whether those private schools could be reasonably regulated. Thus for Justice Douglas to say the case established the principle that parents have a right to educate their children as they choose is inaccurate. Second, *Pierce* and *Meyer* were not decided by the Court as First Amendment free speech cases, though some people, such as Justice Douglas today, would prefer to read the cases that way. Third, some of the rights addressed in these cases, such as the right of association, are truly "peripheral rights" that were recognized to make the specific right of free speech more secure, but other cases such as *Pierce* and *Meyer* dealt with rights whose prime function is not to shore up and secure the right of free speech.

[V.] This passage does two things. First, it introduces the concept or metaphor of the "penumbra." Apparently this is just another way of talking about peripheral rights. Second, Justice Douglas specifically notes that the right of association linked to the First Amendment need not be a right of political association. He thus opens the door to considering the marriage relationship as also protected by this implicit right of once been a member of the Communist party . . .

association. He makes this point explicitly in Section IX of the opinion. If he stopped here it would appear that this was a First Amendment case, not a Fourteenth Amendment case.

[VI.] Those cases involved more than the "right of assembly"—a right that extends to all irrespective of their race or ideology. . . . The right of "association," like the right of belief, . . . is more than the right to attend a meeting; it includes the right to express one's attitudes or philosophies by membership in a group or by affiliation with it or by other lawful means. Association in that context is a form of expression of opinion; and while it is not expressly included in the First Amendment its existence is necessary in making the express guarantees fully meaningful.

[VI.] Sticking with his First Amendment approach for the moment, Justice Douglas makes the point that the implicit right of association is a complex right that entails more than merely a right to physically gather together in a meeting. It is also a form of expression of opinion. But his main point is that implicit rights are recognized by the Court in order to make the expressly listed rights more meaningful. The Court shores up expressly protected rights by recognition of these additional *implicit* rights. We now have Justice Douglas's rationale for going beyond the explicit constitutional text in this case.

[VII.] The foregoing cases suggest that specific guarantees in the Bill of Rights have penumbras, formed by emanations from those guarantees that help give them life and substance. . . . Various guarantees create zones of privacy. The right of association contained in the penumbra of the First Amendment is one, as we have seen. The Third Amendment in its prohibition against the quartering of soldiers "in any house" in time of peace without the consent of the owner is another facet of that privacy. The Fourth Amendment explicitly affirms

[VII.] In the previous sections Justice Douglas spoke both of peripheral rights and penumbras; the implication was that a right formed by a penumbra was the same as a peripheral right. The first sentence of this section seems to support this view. But the remaining portion of the section does not. That is, Justice Douglas goes on to say that the First, Third, Fourth, and Fifth Amendments create zones of privacy. Then these zones seem to merge to become a single zone of privacy that is a unique and the "right of the people to be secure in their persons, houses, papers and effects, against unreasonable searches and seizures." The Fifth Amendment in its Self-Incrimination Clause enables the citizen to create a zone of privacy which government may not force him to surrender to his detriment. The Ninth Amendment provides: "The enumeration in the Constitution, of certain rights, shall not be construed to deny or disparage others retained by the people."

distinct right. This distinct right is not given a definition by Justice Douglas, nor does he make the claim that it operates like a peripheral right to secure, for example, the right not to have soldiers quartered in one's home in times of peace. What really seems to have happened here is that Justice Douglas believes there is a single notion of privacy that animated the writing of each of these amendments, and he has simply uncovered this notion as an underlying purpose of them all. (It is important to note that he has not defined his concept of privacy.) Regarding the Ninth Amendment, Justice Douglas does nothing more with it than to quote it. In doing this he suggests yet a different approach to finding new implicit rights in the Constitution, an approach he turns to in Section IX.[2]

[VIII.]  The Fourth and Fifth Amendments were described in *Boyd v. United States*, 116 U.S. 616, 630, as protection against all governmental invasions "of the sanctity of a man's home and the privacies of his life." We recently referred . . . to the Fourth Amendment as creating a "right to privacy, no less

[VIII.] Having found a right of privacy in the Constitution, Justice Douglas now takes another important step. He informs us that this right is no less important than any other right. This is an important claim in that it elevates this right to the same degree of importance as the right of freedom of speech. It also

---

[2] This new right is based on amendments that comprise part of the Bill of Rights, and but for the doctrine of incorporation would operate only to constrain the federal government. But it is also the fact that the Court has interpreted the Fourteenth Amendment to incorporate significant aspects of the Bill of Rights; thus because the Fourteenth Amendment is applicable to the states, so are the incorporated elements of the Bill of Rights. See, for example, *Duncan v. Louisiana* (1968).

important than any other right carefully and particularly reserved to the people." . . . We have had many controversies over these penumbral rights of "privacy and repose." [Case citations omitted.] These cases bear witness that the right of privacy which presses for recognition here is a legitimate one.

suggests that the right is more important than the freedom of an employer to operate a business as the employer wishes. Furthermore, the cases that Justice Douglas cites carry the implication both that the Court has protected privacy in the past, and that the concept is multifaceted—its applicability ranges from forced sterilization cases to captive audience cases.

[IX.] The present case, then, concerns a relationship lying within the zone of privacy created by several fundamental constitutional guarantees. And it concerns a law which, in forbidding the *use* of contraceptives rather than regulating their manufacture or sale, seeks to achieve its goals by means of having a maximum destructive impact upon that relationship.

[IX.] Justice Douglas now ties his general discussion of the right of privacy to this case. His use of the word *relationship* shows he is not solely out to protect the home, the bedroom, from the intruding eyes of the police. He also sees the case as about protecting the relationship of husband and wife, a point he alluded to in Section II. And he makes the point that Connecticut's law forbidding the use of contraception has "a maximum destructive impact on that relationship." This point, together with the point he made in Section VII, tells us that he believes Connecticut is seeking to achieve its goals by a method that is destructive of a fundamental right.

[X.] Such a law cannot stand in light of the familiar principle, so often applied by this Court, that a "governmental purpose to control or prevent activities constitutionally subject to state regulation may not be achieved by means which sweep unnecessarily broadly and

[X.] The Court gives fundamental rights strong protection by the use of tough tests or standards of review. This is precisely what Justice Douglas does. He announces a version of the strict scrutiny test: This Connecticut law will not survive judicial review unless it pursues its goals by means that do the least thereby invade the area of protected freedoms."

[XI.] Would we allow the police to search the sacred precincts of marital bedrooms for telltale signs of the use of contraceptives? The very idea is repulsive to the notions of privacy surrounding the marriage relationship.

[XII.] We deal with a right of privacy older than the Bill of Rights—older than our political parties, older than our school system. Marriage is a coming together for better or for worse, hopefully enduring, and intimate to the degree of being sacred. It is an association that promotes a way of life, not causes; a harmony in living, not political faiths; a bilateral loyalty, not commercial or social projects. Yet it is an

possible harm to the protected right.

[XI.] Without saying so directly, Justice Douglas tells us that this law seeks to achieve its purposes by means that "sweep too broadly," that is, unnecessarily infringe upon the rights of the married couple. He does this by conjuring up an image of policemen rummaging through bedrooms for condoms, diaphragms, spermaticide, and pills. Note that Justice Douglas reaches this conclusion without discussing what purpose the law is intended to serve. Apparently, the purpose is not significant for Justice Douglas; whether the purpose is to stop the use of contraception per se, or to try to prevent illicit sex, there are other methods, in Justice Douglas's view, that could be used (e.g., banning the manufacturing of contraception) that do not involve destruction of the right of privacy.

[XII.] The concluding section does many things for Justice Douglas. He tells us that the right involved in the case is not merely his invention. He also indirectly invokes the aid of the Ninth Amendment to support his conclusion that the recognition of this right is legitimate. Remember that the Ninth Amendment says the Constitution does not protect just those rights that are enumerated in the text. And association for as noble a purpose as any involved in our prior decisions. Reversed.

he assures his readers once again that the right being protected here is very important and deserving of strong judicial protection.

We now need to step back from the details of the opinion to obtain an overall sense of Justice Douglas's argument. Let us first look at the issues he addressed. In this case, the fundamental issues that the justices had to deal with included the following issues:

1. Did Griswold and Buxton have standing to raise the question of whether this law violated the constitutional rights of married couples?
2. Is there an implicit right in the Constitution that protects the decision of married couples to use contraception? If there is, is this right fundamental, requiring the protection of the strict scrutiny test, or not fundamental and protected only under a rational basis test?
3. Did this Connecticut law satisfy the relevant test?

If you look back at the opinion you will see that Justice Douglas provided an answer to each of these questions. These answers are called the **holdings** of the opinion. One way to formulate these holdings is as follows:

1. An exception to the usual rule that a litigant must assert his or her own legal rights and cannot rest the claim on the legal rights of third parties will be relaxed when rights of the third party will be strongly affected by the judgment of the Court—whatever that judgment turns out to be.
2. The Constitution protects a general and fundamental right of privacy that includes the decision of a married couple regarding the use of contraception.
3. The Connecticut law banning married couples from using contraception does not satisfy the strict scrutiny test because this way of trying to prevent extramarital relations unnecessarily intrudes upon that intimate relationship.

Note that in reaching these holdings the opinion did not rely on a close analysis of the text of the Constitution; discussion of the intent of the framers; discussion of the requirements of tradition or of contemporary morality. Justice Douglas did cite precedent, but clearly his use of precedent did not entail a careful analysis of the facts of each case or the development of a specific *ratio decidendi* for each case. Instead he used precedent to justify his general approach to finding a new right within the Constitution, to support his claim that this right was very important, and to support his selection of a version of the strict scrutiny test.

Justice Douglas used precedent in conjunction with a mixed strategy of justification. The first part of his strategy is a deduction loosely based on precedent that could be formulated as follows:

1. *Premise:* It is permissible for the Court to announce "new" constitutional rights when: (1) the right is a peripheral right needed to shore up an explicit right in the Constitution; or (2) the "new" right is discovered to be a more general right that animated the writing of the specific rights in the Constitution.[3]
2. *Premise:* The Third, Fourth, and Fifth Amendments to the Constitution were animated by a general concern with privacy.
3. *Conclusion:* There is a constitutional right to "privacy."

Without providing a clear definition of the nature and scope of this new general right to privacy, Justice Douglas supports the conclusion that the right is sufficiently important to deserve the protection of the strict scrutiny test. There is an implicit syllogism also operating here:

1. *Premise:* Precedent has said that Fourth Amendment rights are as important as any other right in the Constitution, that is, as important as the right of freedom of speech (see Section 8).
2. *Premise:* If the specific right mentioned in the constitutional text is fundamental, then the underlying right that animates it is also fundamental (implicit unstated premise).
3. *Conclusion:* The broad right to privacy that animates the Third, Fourth, and Fifth Amendments is a fundamental right, with the consequence (based on precedent) that it is to be protected by the strict scrutiny test (see Sections 9 and 10).

Justice Douglas then concludes that the marriage relationship falls within the scope of this fundamental right of privacy; he proceeds to examine the Connecticut law in light of the test noted in Section 10. At this point in his opinion his strategy of justification is that of balancing, because this is what the test or standard of review he used seems to call for. Thus Justice Douglas looks on the one hand at the degree of infringement of the right caused by Connecticut's law, and on the other at the need for Connecticut to achieve its purposes in this way. He finds (see Section 9) that the law has a maximum destructive impact on the marital relationship. He also implies, without saying so explicitly, that whatever the goals Connecticut has in mind, there are other less damaging ways to achieve those goals (see Section 11).

There are other aspects of the majority opinion worth commenting upon, but that discussion will benefit from additional information found in the concurring and dissenting opinions, which we turn to look at now.

---

[3] Remember that Justice Douglas also alluded to the Ninth Amendment and the fact that the right to privacy is older than the Bill of Rights (see Sections 7 and 12). He thus has another not fully developed technique in the opinion for grounding the right of privacy.

## CONCURRING AND DISSENTING OPINIONS

Concurring opinions, it will be recalled, are written by justices who agree with the final judgment of the majority or plurality opinion. Nevertheless, th·y write separate opinions for any of a number of possible reasons. Sometimes the justice offers an entirely different set of reasons for agreeing with the judgment; the justice also might want to add a reason to support the judgment, a reason not relied upon by the majority or plurality opinion. In other cases the justice may wish to clear up an ambiguity in the majority or plurality opinion by emphasizing his or her preferred interpretation of that ambiguity; or, the justice simply may want to emphasize a point made in the majority opinion.

In this case Justice Goldberg filed an opinion that offered a somewhat different set of reasons for the judgment, reasons that were compatible with the majority opinion. His opinion followed the same overall outline of the majority opinion, but at various points of the outline he offered a different argument.

| *Majority* | *Justice Goldberg* |
|---|---|
| Is there a constitutional right at stake? Yes. See Sections III–VII. | Justice Goldberg cites the Ninth Amendment, claiming it justifies the finding of rights not expressly stated in the constitutional text. He goes on to conclude that if we look to the traditions and collective conscience of our people, we will find there a fundamental right of privacy. |
| Are marital relations covered by this right? Yes. See Section IX. | "The Connecticut statutes here involved deal with a particularly important and sensitive area of privacy—that of the marital relation and marital home." |
| Is this right fundamental, so that we should use the strict scrutiny test? Yes. See Section X. | "The entire fabric of the Constitution and the purposes that clearly underlie its specific guarantees demonstrate that the rights to marital privacy and to marry and raise a family are of similar order and magnitude as the fundamental rights specifically protected." He goes on to adopt the strict scrutiny test: Where there is a significant encroachment upon personal liberty, "the state may prevail only upon showing a subordinating interest which is compelling. . . . The |

law must be shown 'necessary, and not merely rationally related, to the accomplishment of a permissible state policy.'"

Applying that test, do we find that this law should be upheld or struck down? Struck down. See Section XI.

After noting that the state said that its statute helps to prevent married couples from engaging in extramarital relations, Justice Goldberg wrote: "The rationality of this justification is dubious, particularly in light of the admitted widespread availability to all persons in the State of Connecticut, unmarried as well as married, of birth-control devices for the prevention of disease, as distinguished from the prevention of contraception. . . . [I]t is clear that the state interest in safeguarding marital fidelity can be served by a more discriminately tailored statute, which does not, like the present one, sweep unnecessarily broadly."

In addition to offering his own somewhat different approach to the case, Justice Goldberg answered the central criticism of the dissenters. You can expect the dissenters to "go for the jugular" and to offer a wholly different perspective on the case. In this case the dissenters objected most vigorously to the willingness of the majority to protect rights not specifically and expressly protected in the constitutional text. We shall get a sense of their argument in a moment. Let us look first at Justice Goldberg's defense of the willingness of the majority not to stick to the literal text and not to stick to a literal and narrow reading of the intent of the framers.

The logic of the dissents would sanction federal or state legislation that seems to me even more plainly unconstitutional than the statute before us. Surely the Government, absent a showing of a compelling subordinating state interest, could not decree that all husbands and wives must be sterilized after two children have been born to them. Yet by their reasoning such an invasion of marital privacy would not be subject to constitutional challenge because, while it might be "silly," no provision of the Constitution specifically prevents the Government from curtailing the marital right to bear children and raise a family . . . [I]f upon a showing of a slender basis of rationality, a law outlawing voluntary birth control by married persons is valid, then, by the same reasoning, a law requiring compulsory birth control also would seem to be valid. (*Griswold v. Connecticut* [1965], p. 497)

You can analyze this passage yourself. It is included here to illustrate the point that in reading Supreme Court opinions you should recognize that these opinions often are part of a cross-Court dialogue, with one justice attacking another who is then answered in turn. A close comparison of these points and counterpoints will carry you a long way in developing a better understanding both of all the opinions and of the fundamental issues with which the justices are wrestling.

To provide an answer to the issue of whether the right of privacy is protected by the Constitution, the justices had to address the question of the appropriate philosophy of constitutional interpretation. For example, should originalism or nonoriginalism be used? It was this underlying question that Justice Goldberg addressed in the last quote. And it was this question of the philosophy of constitutional interpretation that most engaged the attention of the dissenting justices.

Justice Black summed up his position most succinctly when he wrote, "I like my privacy as well as the next one, but I am nevertheless compelled to admit that government has a right to invade it unless prohibited by some specific constitutional provision." Why does he insist that only specifically mentioned rights can be protected by the Court? Justice Black's answer to this question is *scattered* throughout his opinion. He says on page 512 that to do what the majority did allows the justices to read their personal preferences into the Constitution. On page 513 he says that the majority has ended up "making" law, a power not granted to the Court. Later, on page 521, he insists the Court is not a supervisory agency and that for the Court to read new rights into the Constitution would entail a shift of power to the Court, and a breach of the doctrine of separation of powers. And he adds on page 522 that if the Constitution needs to be kept up-to-date, we have a method of doing this—the amendment process. "That method of change was good for our Fathers, and being somewhat old fashioned I must add that it is good enough for me."

The lesson we need to draw from this is that parts of an opinion may in fact be related to other parts that appear earlier and later in the opinion, *and in the footnotes*. Readers of constitutional opinions face the task of having to reconstruct the opinion, disassemble and reassemble it in a new way, so to speak, in order to make complete sense of it.

## THE DYNAMICS OF OPINION WRITING

Usually all that we have available to understand the thinking of the justices are the final published opinions. But in the *Griswold* case we also have available the original draft of the opinion written by Justice Douglas. Professor Bernard Schwartz has published this draft (as well as other draft opinions from the Warren and Burger Courts), along with a commentary based in part on internal letters and memoranda from the justices to each other to which he had access.[4] We learn from this that in the first draft of the opinion Justice Douglas spoke only of a First Amendment right of

4 Bernard Schwartz, *The Unpublished Opinions of the Warren Court* (New York: Oxford University Press, 1985), and *The Unpublished Opinions of the Burger Court* (New York: Oxford University Press, 1988).

association, which protected husband and wife. Justice Brennan, unhappy with this approach, wrote back to Justice Douglas that the "association" of married couples was not akin to the association for purposes of advocacy protected by the First Amendment. Professor Schwartz also noted that "the Douglas draft's broad-gauged approach, Justice Brennan warned, might lead to First Amendment protection for the Communist Party simply because it was a group, an approach that Justice Douglas himself had rejected" in connection with an earlier case a decade before (pp. 237–238). Justice Brennan went on to suggest that Justice Douglas use the Court's development of a right of freedom of association as an analogy to justify development of a right of privacy. This is, of course, what Justice Douglas did, and as a result Justice Brennan voted with him instead of writing a separate concurring opinion.

There are other features of the final opinion that appear to have been added in order to obtain the support of other justices. The original draft opinion made no mention of the Ninth Amendment, but the final opinion tosses in a partially developed argument based on the Ninth. This addition may have helped to garner the vote of Justice Goldberg. The original draft of the opinion did, however, raise the specter of the police rummaging through bedrooms for "telltale signs of the use of contraceptives." Justice Douglas may very well have used this imagery in connection with his "sweeps too broad" conclusion in order to obtain the vote of Justice Harlan. Justice Harlan had invoked similar imagery in a dissent he had filed in an earlier contraception case.

The justices are not above using humor when working with each other. Justice White sent the following memo to Justice Douglas as he was working on the majority opinion:

> Any one of the following dispositions would be wholly justified, wouldn't you [agree]?
>
> 1. The Fourth Amendment—because the Connecticut law would authorize a search for the intra-uterine coil.
> 2. *Escobedo* and the right to counsel—from a doctor.
> 3. *Robinson v. California*—since there is an obvious addiction to sex involved and it is cruel and unusual punishment to deprive one of it or to permit it only at the cost of having children. A grizzly [*sic*] choice.
> 4. *Reynolds v. Sims*—one man, one child.[5]

## BRIEFING *GRISWOLD*

Look back now at the concluding section of Chapter 1, which reviews the basic features of a Supreme Court opinion. You should now be able to identify the facts of *Griswold v. Connecticut*; its procedural history; the legal claims; the issues, rulings,

---

[5] Quoted in Del Dickson, ed. *The Supreme Court in Conference (1940–1985)* (New York: Oxford University Press, 2001), p. 802.

reasoning of the majority opinion; and the holding. As a matter of fact, you should now be able to write a "brief" of this opinion (i.e., a summary of the opinion organized in terms of facts, procedural history, etc.). Here is an example of a brief written in a way that attempts to remain "neutral" (i.e., the brief was written to minimize the expression of a point of view as to the deeper meaning of the case).

1. **Name of case**

   *Griswold v. Connecticut*, 381 U.S. 479 (1965)

2. **Statement of facts**

   A Connecticut law made it a crime to use "any drug, medicinal article or instrument for the purpose of preventing contraception." Mrs. Griswold, director of a birth control clinic, and Dr. C. Lee Buxton, its medical director, were criminally convicted and fined $100 each for assisting and abetting the commission of the offense of using contraception because they had provided their clients with family planning advice and contraceptives. They appealed their conviction to the Supreme Court claiming that not only were their Fourteenth Amendment rights violated but also that they had standing to assert that the Fourteenth Amendment rights of the married couple who were their clients were violated.

3. **Procedural history and decision(s) in lower court(s)**

   Following their conviction the appellants appealed their conviction to the Connecticut Appellate Division of the Circuit Court and then again to the Connecticut Supreme Court of Errors. Both courts affirmed the conviction that was followed by the appeal to the U.S. Supreme Court.

4. **Decision in the Supreme Court**

   The Supreme Court overturned the convictions of Mrs. Griswold and Dr. Buxton, striking down under the Fourteenth Amendment the Connecticut law imposing criminal sanctions on persons using contraception.

5. **Statement of issue(s)**

   (1) Did Mrs. Griswold and Dr. Buxton have standing to argue that the Connecticut law violated the Fourteenth amendment rights of their clients?

   (2) Should the Fourteenth Amendment be interpreted to include a right of privacy that extends to a decision by married couples to use contraception?

   (3) Is a right of privacy under the Fourteenth Amendment a fundamental right requiring the use of the strict scrutiny test?

   (4) Does the Connecticut law banning the use of contraception serve a compelling state purpose, and is banning the use of contraception a necessary means to achieving that purpose?

6. **Rulings and Reasoning**

   (1) Yes. Precedent permits an appellant in certain circumstances to invoke the rights of a third party, in this case the clients of Griswold and Buxton,

in challenging the constitutionality of a law. In this case the rights of the married couple, who were in a confidential relationship with the appellants, "are likely to be diluted or adversely affected unless those rights are considered."

(2) Yes. The Court reviewed a number of prior cases noting that in the past it has found certain rights to be implicit in the Constitution, for example, the right of parents to choose whether or not to send their child to a private school. In some of the cases the implicit right, such as the right of association, was recognized to make the specific right expressly mentioned in the Constitution more secure. Thus the Court noted that explicit rights can have "penumbras" that are formed by "emanations" from those guarantees and they help give them "life and substance." Using this approach the Court concludes that the First, Third, Fourth, and Fifth Amendments create "zones of privacy" inclusive of the home. This case, the Court noted, involves a relationship "lying within the zone of privacy." And the law involved in this case forbidding the use of contraception has a maximum destructive effect upon that relationship.

(3) Yes. The Court's opinion notes that the right involved here is "older than the Bill or Rights" and the association involved here, marriage, is for as "noble a purpose as any other recognized in our prior decisions."

(4) No. The law seeks to achieve its purpose by means that "sweep unnecessarily broadly" in that the law would have the police "search the sacred precincts of marital bedrooms for telltale signs of the use of contraceptives."

## 7. *Ratio Decidendi*

A state violates the right of privacy of married couples, a right protected by the Fourteenth Amendment's due process clause, when it makes it a crime for the couple to use contraception.

## 8. Concurring and Dissenting Opinions

Justice Goldberg concurred in an opinion that relied upon the Ninth Amendment as incorporating the same right of privacy identified in the majority opinion. Justice White's concurring opinion stressed that the state had other, less intrusive, means to achieve the goal of reducing the incidents of adultery. Justice Black dissented by first acknowledging that he liked his privacy as much as anybody, but that the majority erred in reading into the Constitution a right of privacy that was not expressly in the text.

The issues of a case are those factual and/or legal questions regarding which parties to the case would answer differently. That is to say, these are the points of dispute. In this sense the basic legal issue of *Griswold* could be phrased as follows: whether or not the Connecticut law banning the use of contraceptives is constitutional. The problem with this formulation is that it does not convey enough information—it leaves out any reference to the specific section of the Constitution that may be involved in the case. And we know that this was an important problem in the case—was it the First Amendment free speech clause (right of association) or the Fourteenth Amendment that was to be used in deciding the case? The brief illustrates better versions of the issues.

Justice Douglas reached a conclusion on each of the issues set out above. These conclusions are sometimes called "holdings," but to avoid confusing these "holdings" with "the holding" of the opinion I will call them "rulings."

Turning to the justifications for these rulings, you should be aware of the opinion's use of all the materials out of which a constitutional justification is built (e.g., text, intent of framers). Be sensitive to whether precedent was read broadly or narrowly. What analogies were used? Was precedent distinguished? What strategy of justification was used? What tests and standards of review were involved? What rules, principles, doctrines, tests, or standards of review may have precedential value? You may not include all this material in the brief, as the brief is intended to be brief.

Finally, let us turn to the holding or *ratio decidendi* of *Griswold*. A version of the *ratio decidendi* is provided in the brief. Further thought about the *Griswold* decision should lead you to other possible ways in which the case might be interpreted. In a broader reading of the case, we might conclude that the Court held that a state violates the Fourteenth Amendment if it bans the use of contraception by anybody, married or unmarried. More broadly yet, *Griswold* can be interpreted as finding that the Constitution strongly protects from state interference all decisions regarding procreation. Read in this way, the decision provides a precedent that can be used (and was used) to support the Court's decision in *Roe v. Wade*, striking down a law that made it a crime to obtain an abortion. Further, *Griswold* might also be read to say that the right of privacy encompasses a broad range of sexual activities, for example, fornication and sodomy, that the state can regulate only if it has an extraordinarily good justification for doing so. In this connection *Griswold* can be, and has been, used to strike down laws making homosexual sodomy a crime (*Lawrence v. Texas* [2003]). Perhaps a truly broad reading of *Griswold* would open the door to constitutional attacks on helmet and seat-belt laws. In other words, *Griswold* might be interpreted as embracing a right to be left alone as long as what one is doing is not hurting anybody else. Thus laws that prohibit same-sex marriages may be attacked using *Griswold* and *Lawrence*.

## THE LEGAL SIGNIFICANCE OF *GRISWOLD*

The decision in *Griswold* has served as the headwaters of a significant line of Supreme Court decisions recognizing and protecting a variety of noneconomic liberties. Starting with *Griswold* the Court has interpreted the Fourteenth Amendment's due process clause as protecting various fundamental values not expressly mentioned in the text of the Constitution and that arguably were not considered by the framers of the Fourteenth Amendment. Among the significant "privacy" interests protected by this line of decisions are the right of a woman to terminate her pregnancy with an abortion, the right of a minor to obtain an abortion with judicial consent but without parental consent, the right of a minor to have access to contraception, and the right of individuals to be safe from criminal prosecution for engaging in intimate same-sex sexual conduct. These and other lines of cases may in the future support the notion of a dying patient's right to palliative care, the nature of which must be left to be decided by the patient and his or her physician free from 'undue' burdens imposed by governmental regulations.[6]

---

## Practice Pointers

1. Do not rush through the briefing of a case. Briefing takes thought and, consequently, time.
2. In writing the Statement of Facts, concentrate on including the **material facts** of the decision. Sometimes **background facts** should also be included. (See Chapter 1.)
3. Recall that the issues in cases are questions to which the parties to the case sought different answers from the Court. (See Chapter 1.)
4. In writing the Rulings and Reasoning you will often find that you will want to organize the materials differently than that found in the opinion(s) in order to be able to summarize and clarify the opinion(s).

---

[6] Stephen Arons, "Palliative Care in the U.S. Healthcare System: Constitutional Right or Criminal Act?" *Western New England Law Review* 29 (2007): 310, 356.

# Chapter 9

# Analysis of a Supreme Court Case

Although briefing a judicial opinion is a useful way to achieve a concise understanding of the opinion, to obtain a broader and more in-depth understanding you have to do more. You need to raise and answer a series of questions about the opinion—questions regarding the background of the opinion, its legal sufficiency, and its policy and political implications. This chapter illustrates this effort after first briefing the opinions in *Parents Involved in Community Schools v. Seattle School District No. 1* (2007). In this case, a majority of the Supreme Court barred two school districts, one in Seattle and another in Kentucky, from using race as a criterion for admission. The opinions in this case are too lengthy to reprint here. You can find a hard copy in your local library, or you can download the full opinion online at http://www.law.cornell.edu/supct/html/05-908.ZO.html.

## THE BRIEF OF *SEATTLE SCHOOL DISTRICT NO. 1*

### Name of Case

*Parents Involved in Community Schools v. Seattle School District No. 1*, 551 U.S. ____, 127 S. Ct. 2738 (2007).

### Statement of Facts

In 1998, the Seattle School District adopted a school choice student assignment plan. Before entering the ninth grade, students were asked to rank the district's ten high schools in order of preference. If too many students listed a particular school as their first choice, the district would use three "tiebreakers" to determine who would fill the open slots in the oversubscribed school. Justice Roberts described these tiebreakers as follows:

> The first tiebreaker selects for admission students who have a sibling currently enrolled in the chosen school. The next tiebreaker depends upon the racial composition of the particular school and the race of the individual student. In the district's

public schools approximately 41 percent of enrolled students are white; the remaining 59 percent, comprising all other racial groups, are classified by Seattle for assignment purposes as non-white. If an oversubscribed school is not within 10 percentage points of the district's overall white/non-white racial balance, it is what the district calls "integration positive," and the district employs a tiebreaker that selects for assignment students whose race "will serve to bring the school into balance." If it is still necessary to select students for the school after using the racial tiebreaker, the next tiebreaker is the geographic proximity of the school to the student's residence.

The petitioners, who were white, were denied their first choice of school because of the racial tiebreaker. Approximately 300 ninth-grade students out of 3000 were denied admission to their preferred school because their race would upset its "racial balance." According to Seattle's brief to the Court, "More than half of the non-white students who gained access through the integration tiebreaker to north-end schools resided in predominantly non-white neighborhoods in the central area or south Seattle." Furthermore, Chief Justice Roberts noted that the racial composition of the popular schools was little changed by the tiebreaker. For example, Ballard High School moved from 62.3 percent to 56.4 percent white using the racial tiebreaker. According to Seattle's brief, if the racial tiebreaker had not been used, the overall percentage of ninth graders receiving their first choice of schools would have increased by only a tenth of a percentage point, from 80.3 percent to 80.4 percent. No court had ever found the Seattle district guilty of *de jure* discrimination. Accordingly, it had never been subject to a court-ordered desegregation plan.

Jefferson County Public Schools in Kentucky, on the other hand, had operated under a court-ordered desegregation plan until 2000. The district was then declared to have eliminated the last vestiges of its prior segregationist policies and released from judicial supervision. The district thereafter adopted the voluntary student assignment plan challenged in this case—the same plan that had been approved by the courts prior to relinquishing jurisdiction. Stated simply, elementary school students were assigned to particular schools, but were given an option to transfer to another nonmagnet school within a "cluster" of schools of the same type. An application to transfer would be denied if it would upset a school's racial balance. The overall racial profile of Jefferson County Public Schools was 34 percent black and 66 percent white. In its nonmagnet elementary schools, it sought a minimum black enrollment of 15 percent and a maximum black enrollment of 50 percent. Hence a student's request for a transfer would be denied if it would create a school at which less than 15 percent or more than 50 percent of students were black. In this case, the petitioner sought to transfer her son, who was white, to a school near her home, but the transfer was denied because it would have had "an adverse effect on desegregation compliance" at the preferred school.

Both school districts claimed their plans were intended to achieve educational and socialization benefits, to reduce racial isolation with its adverse consequences. Seattle also claimed its admission plan was designed to help assure access for nonwhite students to popular schools located in predominantly white parts of the city. White parents in both districts claimed that the use of a racial criterion in school placement policies was a violation of the Equal Protection Clause of the Fourteenth Amendment.

[*Comment:* Writing the facts of a case unavoidably entails interpretation and takes thought, judgment, and time. Briefing the set of opinions in *Parents Involved in Community Schools v. Seattle School District No. 1* (2007) presented particularly difficult problems. First, the length of the combined set of opinions was nearly 200 pages. Second, both legally and factually, the case was extraordinarily complex. Capturing this complexity in summary form without oversimplifying was difficult. Third, the exact phrasing to be used in writing the brief can "bias" or distort the opinion in favor of a particular interpretation. For example, in this case the racial percentages used by the school districts were characterized as unconstitutional "quotas" by the plurality and constitutionally permissible "useful starting points" by the dissent. Fourth, one should include in the statement of facts the **material facts**, but it is often a judgment call regarding what is properly viewed as a material fact. I have included in this brief as material the fact that some 300 Seattle students were denied their first choice because of that district's racial tiebreaker. Justice Breyer thought the history of how these districts addressed de facto segregation was material to the case, but the majority did not. I chose to omit that history here. It also appeared to be material for the plurality that the "quotas" or "useful starting points" in a particular school were derived from each district's overall racial composition, not any pedagogic theory on the level of diversity needed to obtain certain educational benefits. Had the racial composition desired by each school district been tied to, or derived from, an explicit, fully developed, sound pedagogical theory, the Supreme Court might have decided quite differently. In an effort to write a "neutral" brief, I have avoided the use of the term "quota," and discussion of how the districts arrived at the racial benchmarks they used. I will return to these matters later in the brief.]

## Procedural History and Decision(s) in Lower Court(s)

The Ninth Circuit Court of Appeals, *en banc*, upheld the Seattle assignment policy, and the Sixth Circuit Court in a *per curiam* opinion affirmed the district court that had previously upheld Jefferson County's assignment plan.

[*Comment:* This is a simplified version of the procedural history of the cases in the lower courts. There may be circumstances when a more detailed outline of the procedural history of the case is warranted.]

## Decision in the Supreme Court

The Supreme Court overturned both decisions. Chief Justice Roberts wrote the opinion of the Court, joined in some parts by Justices Scalia, Kennedy, Thomas, and Alito (a majority of 5) and in other parts by Scalia, Thomas, and Alito only. Justices Kennedy and Thomas wrote separate concurring opinions. Justice Stevens wrote a dissent, and Justice Breyer wrote a separate dissenting opinion joined by Justices Stevens, Souter, and Ginsburg.

## Statement of Issues

May a school district that is not racially segregated and that normally permits a student to attend any school of her choosing deny a child admission to her chosen school solely because of her race in an effort to achieve a desired racial balance between whites and nonwhites in particular schools, or does such racial balancing violate the Equal Protection Clause of the Fourteenth Amendment? [This formulation omits the separate issue regarding whether parents had standing to bring the suit in the first place.]

[*Comment:* Formulating the issues when engaged in litigation calls on the arts of the advocate to the maximum. The formulation of the issue reported above was taken from the brief of the Seattle parents who originally sought the policy overturned. Now consider this formulation of the issue taken from the brief of the Seattle school district:

> Did the Seattle School District's limited consideration of race in its high school student assignment plan comply with the Equal Protection Clause of the Fourteenth Amendment because:
>
> (a) the District had compelling government interests in promoting the educational benefits of diverse public high school enrollments, alleviating the potential harms of racial isolation, and ensuring equitable access for minority students to the District's most popular high schools; and
> (b) the limited consideration of race in the District's student assignment plan was narrowly tailored to serve these compelling interests while promoting the race-neutral educational values of parental choice, neighborhood schools, and keeping families together?

The Solicitor General of the United States used the following formulation of the issue in his brief supporting the petitioners:

> The question presented in this case is whether the Seattle School District's race-based student assignment plan violates the Equal Protection Clause of the Constitution.

The Ninth Circuit Court of Appeals, in upholding the Seattle policy, formulated the question before the court in this more neutral way.

> This appeal requires us to consider whether the use of an integration tiebreaker in the open choice, noncompetitive, public high school assignment plan crafted by Seattle School District Number 1 violates the federal Constitution's Equal Protection Clause.]

## Rulings and Reasoning

A majority of five agreed that the case was to be decided using the strict scrutiny equal protection test. (For details on strict scrutiny, see Chapter 5). Citing *Johnson v. California* (2005) and *Grutter v. Bollinger* (2003), *Adarand Constructors, Inc. v. Pena* (1995) Adarand, the Chief Justice wrote: "It is well established that when the government distributes burdens or benefits on the basis of individual racial classifications, that action is reviewed under strict scrutiny." In an attack on Justice Breyer's dissent, Roberts rejected the view that adoption and use of the strict scrutiny test would vary when the state sought to exclude minorities and/or include minorities. Both precedent and considerations of prudence, said the plurality, supported the view that an unadulterated version of the strict scrutiny test must be used in *all* racial classification cases. Thus the plurality also rejected Justice Breyer's argument that both precedent and prudence required deference to local school boards in their efforts to combat de facto racial segregation. In support of its view, the plurality quoted from *Richmond v. J. A. Croson Co.* (1989): "'The history of racial classifications in this country suggests that blind judicial deference to legislative or executive pronouncements of necessity has no place in equal protection analysis.'"

In applying the strict scrutiny test, the plurality rejected the school districts' claims that their policies served a compelling governmental interest. There are only two compelling government interests that the Supreme Court has recognized as a basis for using a racial criterion: (1) remedying the effects of past intentional racial discrimination and (2) in the context of higher education, promoting a diverse student body. Neither was available in this case. Seattle had never been adjudged by a court to have engaged in intentional discrimination, while Jefferson County had already been determined to have eliminated the last vestiges of its discriminatory past. The use of racial ratios by these two districts was nothing more, said the plurality, than an effort to promote racial balance. Despite the claims by the districts that they were seeking educational and social benefits, the plurality concluded the actual goal being pursued was racial balance per se and to permit racial balance as a goal "would justify the imposition of racial proportionality throughout American society. . . ." Citing *Freeman v. Pitts* (1992), the plurality noted that the Constitution is not violated by racial imbalance per se. "We have many times over reaffirmed that 'racial balance is not to be achieved for its own sake.'" The plurality then added, "This working backward to achieve a particular type of racial balance, rather than working forward from some demonstration of the level of diversity that provides the purported benefits, is a fatal flaw under our existing precedent." Neither district had offered "evidence that the level of racial diversity necessary to achieve the asserted educational benefits happened to coincide with the racial demographics of the respective school districts." Although the school districts had "use[d] various verbal formulations to describe the interest they seek to promote—racial diversity, avoidance of racial isolation, racial integration—they offer[ed] no definition of the interest that suggests it differs from racial balance." In saying this, the plurality explicitly refused to address the school districts' claim that racial diversity has a positive impact on student test scores and other intangible socialization benefits.

In any event, even assuming the goals of the districts were to realize educational and social benefits, as opposed to the goal of racial balance per se, the majority/plurality further concluded that the challenged policies were not narrowly tailored. "In fact," noted the Court, "in each case the extreme measure of relying on race in assignments is unnecessary to achieve the stated goals, even as defined by the districts." In support of this conclusion the plurality cited data on the racial diversity of the schools. "When the actual racial breakdown is considered, enrolling students without regard to their race yields a substantially diverse student body under any definition of diversity." Further, according to the plurality, even if the goal were "sufficient diversity so that students see fellow students as individuals rather than solely as members of a racial group, using means that treat students solely as members of a racial group is fundamentally at cross-purposes with that end." Policies that classified students in white/nonwhite terms employed only a limited notion of diversity—an approach .inconsistent with the Court's higher education affirmative action decisions. A majority of the Court also found that the minimal effect the racial criterion actually had on the schools' racial balance suggested that other means would have been equally as effective. That is, the tiebreakers served to shift only small numbers of students between schools, but had the real effect of denying hundreds of students access to schools merely because of their race. The majority quickly added, "While we do not suggest that *greater* use of race would be preferable, the minimal impact of the districts' racial classifications on school enrollment casts doubt on the necessity of using racial classifications." Finally, the majority asserted that the districts had failed, as required by precedent, "to show that they considered methods other than explicit racial classifications to achieve their stated goals."

Responding to the opinion of Justice Breyer, the plurality made several additional points: (a) Strict scrutiny is needed because of the difficulty in distinguishing good from harmful uses of a racial criterion; (b) the societal harms (e.g., racial division and racial politics, associated with the use of racial criteria was "undeniable"); (c) the *Brown* decision required students to be assigned to schools "on a nonracial basis"; (d) the *Grutter* decision could be distinguished as a higher education case; and (e) even if *Grutter* were applicable, the school districts' policies violated the multifactor individualized admissions policy approved by the Court in that case.

[*Comment*: First, briefs can be of various lengths. This section of the brief could have been reduced to a few sentences just as one might reduce a synopsis of Hamlet to one sentence—"This is the story of a man who could not make up his mind." A longer version might have expanded upon, for example, the justices' discussion of the precedent they relied upon and distinguished. Second, I have organized this summary in terms of (a) test selection; and (b) test application. By following this format I somewhat "cleaned up" and reorganized the actual opinion. Third, it should be noted that a brief might also include an analysis of the following kind:

> The majority/plurality parts of the opinion of the Court did not explicitly adopt the doctrine that the Fourteenth Amendment should be interpreted to incorporate a color-blind rule, a position taken by Justice Thomas in his concurrence. Nevertheless, the plurality in practical effect embraced the color-blind position of Justice Thomas.

My own preference is to leave this kind of assessment to a separate commentary outside the brief. By analogy, many newspapers seek to separate their "news" articles from their opinion/analysis articles. I tend to see the brief as a "news" article, reserving my commentary for a separate and explicitly designated section of the analysis.]

## *Ratio Decidendi* (of the plurality opinion)

The promotion of racial balance per se by means of a school choice plan that incorporates a racial criterion by which a student might not gain access to his or her preferred school primarily because of his or her race cannot meet the strict scrutiny test and accordingly violates the Equal Protection Clause of the Fourteenth Amendment.

[*Comment:* There are other possible ways one might formulate the *ratio decidendi.*]

## Concurring Opinion: Justice Thomas

Although concurring in all parts of the opinion written by the chief justice, Justice Thomas concluded his concurrence by asserting, "My view of the Constitution is Justice Harlan's in *Plessy v. Ferguson*: 'Our Constitution is color-blind, and neither knows nor tolerates classes among citizens.'" But he also stated, citing precedent, "The Constitution does not permit race-based government decisionmaking simply because a school district claims a remedial purpose and proceeds in good faith with arguably pure motives. . . . Rather, race-based government decisionmaking is categorically prohibited unless narrowly tailored to serve a compelling interest. . . . Therefore, as a general rule, all race-based government decisionmaking—regardless of context—is unconstitutional." He noted two exceptions to the rule—judicially compelled remedial efforts to address *de jure* segregation, and the voluntary remediation of past illegal discrimination that the governmental entity can establish as having occurred, based on specific findings. He reiterated the position of the chief justice that correcting for mere racial imbalance was not a compelling interest. "Nothing but an interest in classroom aesthetics and a hypersensitivity to elite sensibilities justifies the school districts' racial balancing programs," he wrote. "Moreover, the school boards have no interest in remedying the sundry consequences of prior segregation unrelated to schooling, such as "housing patterns, employment practices, economic conditions, and social attitudes." The opening sentence of his opinion captures his characterization of the plurality opinion: "Today, the Court holds that state entities may not experiment with race-based means to achieve ends they deem socially desirable." His attitude toward the goals of the districts and the goals supported by the dissenting opinion of Justice Breyer became clear when he wrote, "In reality, it is far from apparent that coerced racial mixing has any educational benefits, much less that integration is necessary to black achievement."

[*Comment:* The bulk of Justice Thomas's concurrence consisted of an attack on Justice Breyer's dissenting opinion. What those criticisms were, and the extent to which any or all were warranted I have omitted from the brief, as this material is best dealt with in separate commentaries. I will simply note here that the tone of Justice Thomas's comments was often scathing, even disrespectful: "The segregationists in *Brown* argued that their racial classifications were benign, not invidious. . . . It is the height of arrogance for Members of this Court to assert blindly that their motives are better than others." Then there was this observation: "The dissent appears to pin its interpretation of the Equal Protection Clause to current societal practice and expectations, deference to local officials, likely practical consequences, and reliance on previous statements from this and other courts." He noted that the infamous 'separate but equal' ruling in *Plessy v. Ferguson* (1896) had also been based on contemporary social practices. "The segregationists in *Brown*," he continued, "embraced the arguments the Court endorsed in *Plessy*. Though *Brown* decisively rejected those arguments, today's dissent replicates them to a distressing extent."]

## Concurring Opinion: Justice Kennedy

Justice Kennedy summarized his disagreements with the chief justice by noting that parts of the plurality opinion "imply an all-too-unyielding insistence that race cannot be a factor in instances when, in my view, it may be taken into account. The plurality opinion is too dismissive of the legitimate interest government has in ensuring all people have equal opportunity regardless of their race. . . . The plurality opinion is at least open to the interpretation that the Constitution requires school districts to ignore the problem of *de facto* resegregation in schooling. I cannot endorse that conclusion." But, like the chief justice, Justice Kennedy insisted upon the use of the strict scrutiny test, and disagreed with what he called "permissive strict scrutiny," which "could invite widespread governmental deployment of racial classifications." Nevertheless he concurred in the judgment of the chief justice because the districts in this case had failed to meet the requirements of the test. His quarrel with the position of the districts was not so much with the goals they were pursuing as with the chosen means. His view on permissible goals is captured in this paragraph:

> This Nation has a moral and ethical obligation to fulfill its historic commitment to creating an integrated society that ensures equal opportunity for all of its children. A compelling interest exists in avoiding racial isolation, an interest that a school district, in its discretion and expertise, may choose to pursue. Likewise, a district may consider it a compelling interest to achieve a diverse student population. Race may be one component of that diversity, but other demographic factors, plus special talents and needs, should also be considered. Thus when individual students are assigned to schools districts must use a multi-factor individualized decision process. What the government is not permitted to do, absent a showing of necessity not made here, is to classify every student on the basis of race and to assign each of them to schools based on that classification.

Here neither district adequately explained or justified the means it chose to achieve its goals. With regard to Jefferson County, Justice Kennedy wrote,

> While it acknowledges that racial classifications are used to make certain assignment decisions, it fails to make clear, for example, who makes the decisions; what if any oversight is employed; the precise circumstances in which an assignment decision will or will not be made on the basis of race; or how it is determined which of two similarly situated children will be subjected to a given race-based decision. . . . Jefferson County fails to make clear to this Court—even in the limited respects implicated by Joshua [McDonald]'s initial assignment and transfer denial—whether in fact it relies on racial classifications in a manner narrowly tailored to the interest in question,

rather than in the far-reaching, inconsistent, and *ad hoc* manner that a less forgiving reading of the record would suggest. Turning to Seattle, he wrote that "school district does not explain how, in the context of its diverse student population, a blunt distinction between 'white' and 'non-white' furthers these goals. . . . Far from being narrowly tailored to its purposes, this system threatens to defeat its own ends, and the school district has provided no convincing explanation for its design."

[*Comment:* As the "swing vote" in this case, Justice Kennedy's opinion will be searchingly examined by school districts and legal scholars in order to pin down the kind of multifactored plan that might win his approval and perhaps then also the approval of the four dissenting justices.]

## Dissenting Opinion: Justice Stevens

[I have omitted a summary of Justice Stevens's comparatively short opinion.]

## Dissenting Opinion: Justice Breyer, joined by Justices Stevens, Souter, and Ginsburg

Justice Breyer argued that the plurality's opinion undermined *stare decisis*, distorted precedent, misapplied constitutional principles, and turned its back on a body of law that "has consistently and unequivocally approved both voluntary and compulsory race-conscious measures to combat segregated schools." Further, he said the plurality "announces legal rules that will obstruct efforts by state and local governments to deal effectively with the growing resegregation of public schools, it threatens to substitute for present calm a disruptive round of race-related litigation, and it undermines *Brown*'s promise of integrated primary and secondary education that local communities have sought to make a reality." Nothing in the history of desegregation efforts over the past 50 years gave him any reason to believe that any other less-race-based method than the approach these districts employed could effectively deal with the resegregation of the schools.

Although Justice Breyer wrote that he would uphold both districts' plans under the strict scrutiny test, before he turned to that analysis he argued that, in cases such as this, a less strict test should be used. "I believe that the law requires application here of a standard of review that is not 'strict' in the traditional sense of that word . . ." Reading the purpose of the Fourteenth Amendment to "forbid practices that lead to racial exclusion," he argued that the framers "would have understood the legal and practical difference between the use of race-conscious criteria in defiance of that purpose, namely to keep the races apart, and the use of race-conscious criteria to further that purpose, namely to bring the races together." Furthermore, precedent (and the policies of several Congresses and presidents) supported the principle "that the government may voluntarily adopt race-conscious measures to improve conditions of race even when it is not under a constitutional obligation to do so." This precedent, he insisted, was *not* limited to *de jure* discrimination and *not* limited to situations when the courts ordered integration. ". . . I have found no case," he noted, "that otherwise repudiated this constitutional asymmetry between that which seeks to *exclude* and that which seeks to *include* members of minority races." Furthermore, all students are guaranteed a seat in a public school—therefore, this case does not involve the rationing of a scarce resource. Hence the higher education affirmative action cases in which a strict scrutiny test was used are distinguishable.

Justice Breyer nonetheless proceeded to apply the strict scrutiny test, finding the policies of Seattle and Jefferson County to be constitutionally permissible. Regarding whether the districts were pursuing a compelling interest, Justice Breyer's position had several prongs: First, he rejected the view that "a court finding of *de jure*" segregation was crucial. Second, he said the history of desegregation efforts in the two districts "make[s] clear the futility of looking simply to whether earlier school segregation was *de jure* or *de facto* in order to draw firm lines separating the constitutionally permissible from the constitutionally forbidden use of "race-conscious criteria." Third, he found the districts were pursuing three compelling goals: (a) a remedial goal—"setting right the consequences of prior conditions of segregation"; (b) an educational goal—"overcoming the adverse educational effects produced by and associated with highly segregated school"; and (c) a democratic goal—"producing an educational environment that reflects the 'pluralistic society' in which our children will live." Despite contrary research findings, Justice Breyer accepted the view that "black children from segregated educational environments significantly increase their achievement levels once they are placed in a more integrated setting." Despite conflicting research findings, he also accepted the view that "evidence supporting a democratic interest in racially integrated schools is firmly established and sufficiently strong to permit a school board to determine, as this Court has itself often found, that this interest is compelling."

Applying the "narrowly tailored" requirement of the strict scrutiny test, Justice Breyer then found the race-based policies at issue to be as narrowly tailored as they possibly could be. The ratios used by the districts set only broad ranges. They were useful starting points, not racial quotas. (Quoting *Croson*, Justice Breyer defined a quota as "a program in which a fixed number or proportion of opportunities are 'reserved exclusively for certain minority groups.'") Second, he found these plans were more narrowly tailored than the policy upheld in *Grutter*, the law school affirmative action case. In that case, race affected only a fraction of the students and the consequences of using race were less severe than for students here. Third, he could uncover no race-based plan that would have been less burdensome. As for the use of the white/nonwhite distinction, Justice Breyer said, among other things, that it made sense, as the relevant circumstances for different minority groups were, in his view, "roughly similar." "Regardless," he continued, "the plurality cannot object that the constitutional defect is the individualized use of race and simultaneously object that not enough account of individuals' race has been taken." And he pointedly noted that the Jefferson County plan had been approved by a court. "But if the plan was lawful when it was first adopted and if it was lawful the day before the District Court dissolved its order [relinquishing jurisdiction over desegregation efforts in the district], how can the plurality now suggest that it became *unlawful* the following day?"

[*Comment*: I have omitted from this section of the brief Justice Breyer's lengthy history of the two districts' desegregation efforts. Also omitted are Justice Breyer's riposte to the criticisms made by the plurality of his interpretation of precedent, and his response to Justice Thomas. These are not unimportant parts of Justice Breyer's opinion, but these materials might best be taken up in a separate, more in-depth analysis.]

## QUESTIONS DIRECTED TO 'EXPLAINING' THE CASE

As a preliminary matter, I would like to make clear the distinction between explanations, evaluative judgments, and predictions. Explanations, as that term is used here, are statements about the case that take up and elucidate the factors that influenced the outcome. For example, we may say the Supreme Court at a particular historical moment was comprised of liberal justices and offer this as an *explanation* for a ruling in favor of a criminal defendant. When, however, we criticize that judicial decision saying that, for example, it rested on a misinterpretation of precedent, we are making an *evaluative judgment*. Then when we add that the opinion is going to limit the ability of the government to prosecute crime, we are making a *prediction*. If we add that we think this limit on government is unfortunate we have added another *evaluative judgment*.

With these distinctions in mind, I will turn to three sets of questions you should raise about a case which, when answered, will further your understanding of the case. The first set of questions addresses factors—sociological, legal, and political—that help to explain the case and its outcome:

- What was the historical, legal, social, and political background of the case?
- What were the circumstances that led to the suit in this case?

The social and political background of the Seattle suit, as described by Justice Breyer, was marked by persistent legal and political pressure. A number of suits had been brought against the school board by the NAACP, resulting in a series of plans to achieve greater racial integration in Seattle schools. The most controversial plan involved mandatory busing of both black and white students to schools that were often far from their homes. Statewide opposition to the plan led to a voter-adopted initiative amending state law to require that students be assigned to the schools closest to their homes. Pursuant to a challenge by the Seattle School Board, the Supreme Court ultimately found this law unconstitutional because it placed special burdens on racial minorities, making it more difficult for certain racial minorities than for others to adopt policies that were in their interest (*Washington v. Seattle School District* [1982]). In the wake of the busing controversy, the school board adopted a new approach that relied on student choice. The choice plan went through several modifications; it was ultimately the 1999 plan that was challenged by Parents Involved in Community Schools—a group of parents whose children were not or might not be assigned to the high school of their choice. Thus the Seattle case arose out of the contentious racial politics of Seattle.

The Jefferson County case also arose out of racial politics but with an important twist. The schools in Jefferson County had previously been segregated by law. Almost two decades after the *Brown* decision, civil rights groups and parents obtained a court order requiring the desegregation of local schools. Between 1975 and 1995, the district modified its integration plan under court supervision. In 1996, it adopted the plan ultimately reviewed in the case at hand. In 2000, the federal court absolved itself of jurisdiction, finding that the district had eliminated all vestiges of *de jure* segregation. The district chose, however, to continue operating under the 1996 court-approved integration plan subsequently challenged in court by a white parent whose child was denied admission to a school near their home. Thus, as Justice Breyer pointedly observed, a plan that had had court approval was now under constitutional attack.

What was the larger legal background that made these suits in Seattle and Kentucky possible? Legally, the decision in *Seattle School District No. 1* was the culmination of decades of litigation in the Supreme Court and lower federal courts. Most significant, of course, was the 1954 decision in *Brown v. Board of Education* in which the Court declared that the "separate but equal" doctrine had no place in public schooling. The Court was not faced in *Brown* with an example of de facto segregation but with *de jure* segregation. As a technical matter, the Court did not in fact declare that de facto segregation unconstitutional; nor did it say it was permissible, nor that its voluntary elimination was a compelling interest. In the years following *Brown*, the Court had to revisit the issue of segregation in the schools several times. Most important, the question of remedial powers available to the federal courts in requiring school districts to undo the effects of their unconstitutional segregationist policies needed to be answered. One of these decisions, *Swann v. Charlotte-Mecklenburg* Board of Education (1971), made clear that the lower courts had the authority to promote integration by ordering school busing and other race-based policies. The Court in *Swann* also stated that

> School authorities are traditionally charged with broad power to formulate and implement educational policy and might well conclude, for example, that in order to prepare students to live in a pluralistic society each school should have a prescribed ratio of Negro [sic] to white students reflecting the proportion for the district as a whole. To do this as an educational policy is within the broad discretionary powers of school authorities.

Seattle argued that this statement showed it had constitutional authority to adopt its policy; the petitioners, on the other hand, viewed the statement as mere dictum. (See Chapter 6.)

The use of a race-based policy by educational institutions arose prior to *Seattle School District No. 1* in a series of higher education cases. In both *Grutter v. Bollinger* (2003) and *Regents of University of California v. Bakke* (1978), the Supreme Court upheld the use of racial considerations as part of a multifactor decision. One case, however, found that an undergraduate admissions policy that relied *too* heavily on race was unconstitutional (*Gratz v. Bollinger* [2003]). The decision in *Wygant v. Jackson Board of Education* (1986) held unconstitutional a minority preference in public school teacher layoffs. And there were several cases that relied on strict scrutiny to strike down a racial preference in the handing out of public contracts (*Richmond v. J. A. Croson* [1989] and *Adarand Constructors, Inc., v. Pena* [1995]). By the time *Seattle School District No. 1* reached the Supreme Court, the law was to some degree inconsistent with regard to the use of racial considerations in the alloca- tion of scarce governmental resources (such as a seat in an elite law school) and indi- vidual decisions were open to somewhat conflicting interpretations. Thus when Seattle and Jefferson County incorporated a racial criterion into their school choice plans, both the petitioners and respondents had reason to believe precedent was on their side. Each had an incentive to litigate.

As the litigants moved their case through the lower courts, two unforeseen events further shaped the ultimate outcome of the case. On July 1, 2005, Justice O'Connor announced her retirement from the Supreme Court. Her announcement cast some doubt on the Court's continued willingness to uphold the use of racial criteria in school admissions, as Justice O'Connor held the crucial swing vote that had led to a majority opinion in support of the University of Michigan Law School's admission policy in *Grutter*. Then, in September 2005, Chief Justice Rehnquist passed away. Both vacancies on the Court were to be filled by President George W. Bush, who had publicly vowed to fill the Supreme Court with judicial conservatives. The president initially nominated John Roberts to replace Justice O'Connor, but with the death of Chief Justice Rehnquist, he nominated Samuel Alito for this position and Roberts for Chief Justice. Roberts was sworn in as chief justice in September 2005 and Justice Alito in February 2006. In June 2006 the Supreme Court agreed to review the lower- court decisions in *Seattle School District No. 1*. Thus by the time *Seattle School District No. 1* was argued, the voting balance in the Court had shifted, with Justice Kennedy the likely key swing vote between a four–four liberal–conservative split on the Court. And as it turned out, Justice Kennedy did play a pivotal role in blocking the emergence of a five-justice majority (plurality) behind a color-blind doctrine.

## EVALUATIVE JUDGMENT: THE LEGAL SUFFICIENCY OF THE DECISION

An examination of factors explaining how and why a particular case arose does not of course address the "prescriptive" or "evaluative" questions: Did the majority or the dissent have the better argument from a legal perspective? Here are some more specific questions that probe the legal sufficiency of the opinions in the case:

- Are the legal premises of a particular opinion plausibly backed up by evidence from the constitutional text, the intent of the framers, evidence of tradition, consideration of prudence, and precedent? Is the opinion logically valid and sound? (See Chapter 7.)
- What judicial philosophy does an opinion reflect—some version of original- ism or nonoriginalism? Does the opinion appropriately execute the adopted approach? (See Chapter 4.)

- Has the opinion properly or improperly used the evidence listed in the first bullet? For example, does the opinion rely on fair interpretations of a particular precedent in either relying upon or distinguishing past decisions? (See Chapter 4.)
- Does the majority opinion overrule a significant precedent and send constitutional doctrine off in a new direction? Is the overruling expressly announced, or is it accomplished *sub silentio*? Should precedent have been overruled? (See Chapter 6.)
- Does the majority opinion continue existing doctrine while carving out an "exception," thereby limiting or expanding it? Is this modification a good change? (See Chapter 6.)
- Is the majority opinion simply inconsistent with precedent, leaving constitutional doctrine in a state of confusion and uncertainty? (See Chapter 6.)
- Is the opinion (majority or dissent) a bargained result? Is the opinion internally coherent, or does it reflect an uneasy compromise among justices with different views? (See Chapters 3 and 7.)

I will not address all these questions but will illustrate the evaluation of an opinion by focusing on one centrally important point of dispute between the plurality and the dissent in *Seattle School District No. 1*. The opinions evinced strong disagreement regarding the constitutional test to be applied in this case. The plurality insisted that strict scrutiny be used because a racial criterion was involved—period. Justice Breyer argued for a less stringent test. More specific questions now have to be asked: Did the Court in *Brown v. Board of Education* (1954) and the companion case of *Bolling v. Sharpe* (1954) rule that the Fourteenth Amendment was color-blind and **any** deviation from that principle must be examined using the strict scrutiny test (as the plurality in the Seattle case contended), or was the decision in *Brown* (as Justice Breyer said) more narrowly focused on prohibiting *de jure*, state-mandated segregation and that the promise of *Brown* was racially integrated education? In other words, one needs to determine the correct *ratio decidendi* for the *Brown* decision. My own analysis has led me to conclude that Justice Breyer's interpretation is closer to the mark. In examining the *Brown* decision, I have found no language supporting any color-blind doctrine despite the fact that such had been invoked by the parties involved in the case. In fact, the Supreme Court expressly focused on the problem of "segregating students by race"—on the *separation* of students solely because of their race. "In the field of public education the doctrine of 'separate but equal' has no place," the Court declared. Thus *Brown* did not itself embrace a color-blind rule even if the outcome was consistent with this principle. The majority, as far as the *Brown* decision is concerned, was not correct in asserting that precedent *required* the use of the color-blind principle.

A thorough examination of the use of precedent in the opinions comprising *Seattle School District No. 1* would have to move beyond an examination of *Brown* to the post-*Brown* decisions of the Supreme Court with a view to determining whether these opinions established the color-blind rule as a constitutional doctrine.

A closely related question that should be included in the analysis concerns the framers' intent: What did they mean when they drafted and adopted the Fourteenth Amendment? Assuming, for the sake of discussion, that the plurality's color-blind reading of *Brown* was correct, was *Brown* a correct or fair interpretation of the Fourteenth Amendment from an originalist standpoint? Stated differently, did the framers of the Fourteenth Amendment intend to impose a color-blind principle upon government? This is an interesting question because the members of the plurality are avowedly originalist. Now consider this comment from Professor Jed Rubenfeld: "Strict color blindness would be clearly unsupportable from an originalist viewpoint (segregation was originally considered permissible, and segregation is of course a violation of color blindness), so it is a little embarrassing to see our self-professed 'originalist' judges righteously insisting on a color-blind equal protection clause. Nevertheless, color blindness would certainly be consistent with the Fourteenth Amendment's paradigmatic applications."[1] If Professor Rubenfeld is correct, one could argue that racial segregation was viewed by the framers as constitutionally permissible. Yet Professor Rubenfeld argues that the decision in *Brown* was one the Court could properly reach *without violating* the Fourteenth Amendment.

We have thus reached two conclusions: One is that the plurality misread *Brown*; the other is that this misreading was insupportable from an originalist perspective. These are ironical conclusions, given that the plurality was made up of originalists. Moreover, it would follow that Justice Breyer's reading of *Brown* was correct from an originalist viewpoint.

But you might not want to leave your legal analysis at this point. Here are some additional questions: Even if Justice Breyer is right about the original intent of the framers, does it necessarily follow that the Court should not adopt a color-blind rule? Did the framers prohibit reading the Constitution as embracing a color-blind rule? Perhaps such a rule is a permissible expansion of what the Fourteenth Amendment was meant to prohibit.

Or how about this question: What would be the view of a nonoriginalist? Why or why not might a nonoriginalist interpret the Fourteenth Amendment as embodying a color-blind rule? Justice Thomas asserted that not adopting a color-blind rule opened the door to the misuse of racial criteria and perhaps even a return to the Jim Crow era. We simply cannot trust either government or the courts with the authority to develop race-based policies. Justice Breyer of course saw the color-blind rule as a source of dire consequences for integration and equal educational opportunity. In his view, barring any use of a racial criterion would doom society to segregation and persistent inequality. An extended analysis of the opinions in *Seattle School District No. 1* might explore this profound conflict in depth.

Finally, let's look at the following interesting implication of the plurality's ruling: It may create incoherence in constitutional doctrine. Professor Rubenfeld notes that when black petitioners have complained about the unintended adverse consequence of a policy, the Court has ruled that such unintended consequences are **not** a violation

---

[1] Jed Rubenfeld, *Revolution by Judiciary* (Cambridge, Mass.: Harvard University Press, 2005), pp. 196–197.

of the Fourteenth Amendment [*Washington v. Davis* (1976)].[2] However, as we see in *Seattle School District No. 1*, when white petitioners complain about the unintended consequences of a policy—albeit one with a racial criterion—the Court has found these consequences to be an undue burden, leading to a finding of unconstitutionality.

This analysis is far from complete. It did not take up issues that divided the Court as to whether the districts' goals were compelling (and what constitutionally may or should count as a compelling state interest), whether the means chosen to pursue the goals were narrowly tailored, and whether *Grutter* could be or should be distinguished, or how it should be distinguished. Recall that the plurality and dissent distinguished *Grutter* in different ways. In connection with the analysis of whether the districts' goals were compelling one may plunge into the issues surrounding the use of social science-based evidence: (a) Is the social science literature sufficiently conclusive to support a finding that integration is correlated with improved test scores amongst minority students and supportive of the conclusion that integration is correlated with improvements in racial attitudes and race relations? (b) If the social science is not 100 percent supportive of the districts' policies, does that mean the academic and social goals of the districts are not compelling, or might the goals be compelling despite the absence of conclusive social science findings? (c) Should constitutional doctrine ever be premised on or rooted on the findings of social scientists? This question has been the subject of discussion ever since the Court in *Brown* referenced psychological research.

## POLITICAL AND POLICY IMPLICATIONS OF THE OPINION

A thorough analysis of the *Seattle School District No. 1* case would not be complete without considering the political and policy implications of the plurality opinion. One might begin with questions the case raises about the Supreme Court as an institution:

- Which justices made up the majority and dissenting positions? What does this tell us about who is in control of the Court? And what does the voting pattern of the justices in this case tell us about the "political" alignment among the justices themselves?
- Is the decision a "data point" in support of a particular prognostication of the future direction of the Court?
- With which politically powerful figures and groups does the majority opinion clash or agree?
- What might be the political fallout of the majority opinion?
- How might the opinion affect the Court's institutional relationship with the other branches of the federal government? With state and local governments?

---

[2] Ibid., at p. 197.

Another set of questions goes more directly to the policy implications of the case:

- Does the opinion legitimize existing policy or does it point to a change in governmental policy? What kind of policy changes seem to be required by the decision?
- Will the political forces seeking changes to current policy be effective in obtaining compliance with the opinion? Why or why not?
- Will there be social and economic effects? If so, what will they be? Will the opinion have different effects on different groups and kinds of people?

Again, I won't attempt to address all these questions, but I will say a few words regarding the potential impact of the plurality opinion on the extent of racial segregation and isolation in the public schools. (Recall that Justice Breyer wrote that the plurality opinion "undermines *Brown*'s promise of integrated primary and secondary education that local communities have sought to make a reality.")

Any discussion of these and other such issues would also have to take into account a larger reality not mentioned in any of the opinions in *Seattle School District No. 1*. Racial segregation in urban public schooling is predominantly an inter-district phenomenon, and not an intradistrict phenomenon. That is to say, urban racial segregation has arisen because whites have left cities, leaving large numbers of minorities who cannot (perhaps who also choose not to), for financial and other reasons, move to the suburbs. Since 1978, the percentage of whites in Seattle dropped from 63 percent to 40 percent even as the overall population of the city declined. In 1988, white students comprised 43 percent of the school population. In Chicago, to take another example, the school population was 10.5 percent white, 54 percent black, 32 percent Latino, and 3.2 percent Asian in 1996–1997.[3] Detroit public schools were 90.1 percent black. A federal district court's effort to change the racial makeup of the public schools of Detroit by ordering interdistrict busing as a remedy in a case challenging *de jure* segregation within Detroit was blocked by the Supreme Court in 1974 (*Milliken v. Bradley* [1974]). Thus, arguably, it is this earlier decision of the Court that, far more than the decision in *Seattle School District No. 1*, is the primary judicial contribution to the de facto segregation of the public schools. In other words, in strictly causal terms, the plurality ruling in *Seattle School District No. 1* may be a relatively minor contributor to continuing racial imbalance in urban schools.

Thus data shows that the trend is that black students are increasingly attending schools that are predominantly minority. The percentage of black students in schools with 50 percent or more minority students increased on average across the United States from 63 percent in 1988 to 73 percent in 2005. Between 1988 and 2005 the percentage of black students in 90–100 percent black schools rose from 32 percent to 38 percent.[4]

---

[3] Gary Orfield and John T. Yun, "Resegregation in American Schools" *The Civil Rights Project*, Harvard University, June 1999, Table 4, p. 9.

[4] Gary Orfield and Chungmei Lee, "Historic Reversals, Accelerating Resegregation, and the Need for New Integration Strategies," *Civil Rights Project/Proyecto Derechos Civiles*, UCLA, August 2007, p. 29, 34.

The discussion should also take into account the very high probability that the opinion that may guide policy making in the foreseeable future is that of Justice Kennedy, who staked out a position between the plurality and the dissent. Thus a policy that assigns individual students to schools based on race might be upheld with the support of Justice Kennedy and the four dissenters if it were a multifactor policy, with race one of a number of criteria used to decide whether an individual student could attend a particular school. In addition, other race-based policies that do not involve the assignment of individual students might get the support of Justice Kennedy. Justice Kennedy wrote that school districts may seek to promote diversity in the student bodies by various means,

> including strategic site selection of new schools; drawing attendance zones with general recognition of the demographics of neighborhoods; allocating resources for special programs; recruiting students and faculty in a targeted fashion; and tracking enrollments, performance, and other statistics by race. These mechanisms are race conscious but do not lead to different treatment based on a classification that tells each student he or she is to be defined by race, so it is unlikely any of them would demand strict scrutiny to be found permissible.

As it turns out, the *Seattle School District No. 1* decision may have negligble impact in Seattle itself: The district suspended the challenged policy five years prior to the Supreme Court decision. Now that the Supreme Court has spoken, counsel for the liberal-leaning district said it would like to explore new ways to promote diversity.

> Gary L. Ikeda, the general counsel for the school district, said, 'The heartening thing is that a majority of the court reaffirmed the principle of diversity in public education, and in Justice Kennedy's opinion we now have some clarification in terms of how the heck we're going to do that.'[5]

However, according to that same article, the winning parents "urged the district to move beyond what they said was a preoccupation with social engineering rather than academics."

As to the rest of the country, to avoid costly litigation, districts that have been using race-based policies will now probably opt for nonracial criteria in school assignments—factors such as family income—in promoting diversity. The Jefferson County district may well adopt such an approach as well. Whether these approaches will result in racially integrated schools remains to be seen. Furthermore, to the extent the opinion slows down or blocks efforts to eliminate de facto segregation, assuming the research is correct that integration has beneficial effects for the academic achievement of minority students, the opinion will make it more difficult for districts to improve the academic achievement of minority pupils. This consequence will in turn cause school districts problems in meeting the requirements of the federal statute No Child Left Behind; schools that fail to meet those requirements in turn

[5] William Yardley, "Seattle School Take Stock After Justices Issue Ruling," *New York Times*, July 1, 2007, on-line archives.

face a legally required reorganization and perhaps even face being closed. Yet it should be noted that school districts, even under the plurality opinion, can adopt policies to promote diversity that involve strategically locating new schools to assure a diverse student population.

In sum, there are powerful demographic and structural obstacles (the reality of separate school districts and the *Milliken* case) that push toward maintaining the current degree of racial isolation. Yet the range of permissible tools available to school districts is perhaps somewhat broader than Justice Breyer assumed. Nevertheless, it is far from clear whether these tools will be sufficient to overcome the overarching demographic and structural barriers to integration.

## Practice Pointers

1. In analyzing the positions of the various justices, it is important to remember that neither those in the majority, plurality, or the dissent may be "correct." You as analyst may have yet another view on some or all of the positions the justices have taken.

2. A useful way of coming to a fuller understanding of the opinions in a case is to examine the briefs of both the parties to the case and of the *amici curiae*. [The term "briefs" refers here to the documents filed by the parties with the Court containing their legal arguments in support of the ruling they seek from the Court.] In *Seattle School District No. 1*, the Court received some 60 *amicii* briefs from the United States Solicitor General, various liberal and conservative civic organizations, the National School Boards Association, and even social scientists and political figures. Briefs filed in a Supreme Court case can be found through LexisNexis, Westlaw, and at http://supreme.findlaw.com/supreme_court/briefs/index.html/. In addition, audio recordings of the oral arguments before the Court in *Seattle School District No. 1* are available online at http://www.oyez.org. Transcripts of the arguments can be found at http://www.supremecourtus.gov/oral_arguments/argument_transcripts.html.

3. Law review articles are a valuable resource for examining and understanding court opinions. Many law review articles are written on significant cases. Hard copies of law review articles can be found in many libraries (even non-law libraries) and online through LexisNexis and Westlaw.

# Table of Cases

# Index